AF541803

HISTORY OF THE JAIPUR CITY

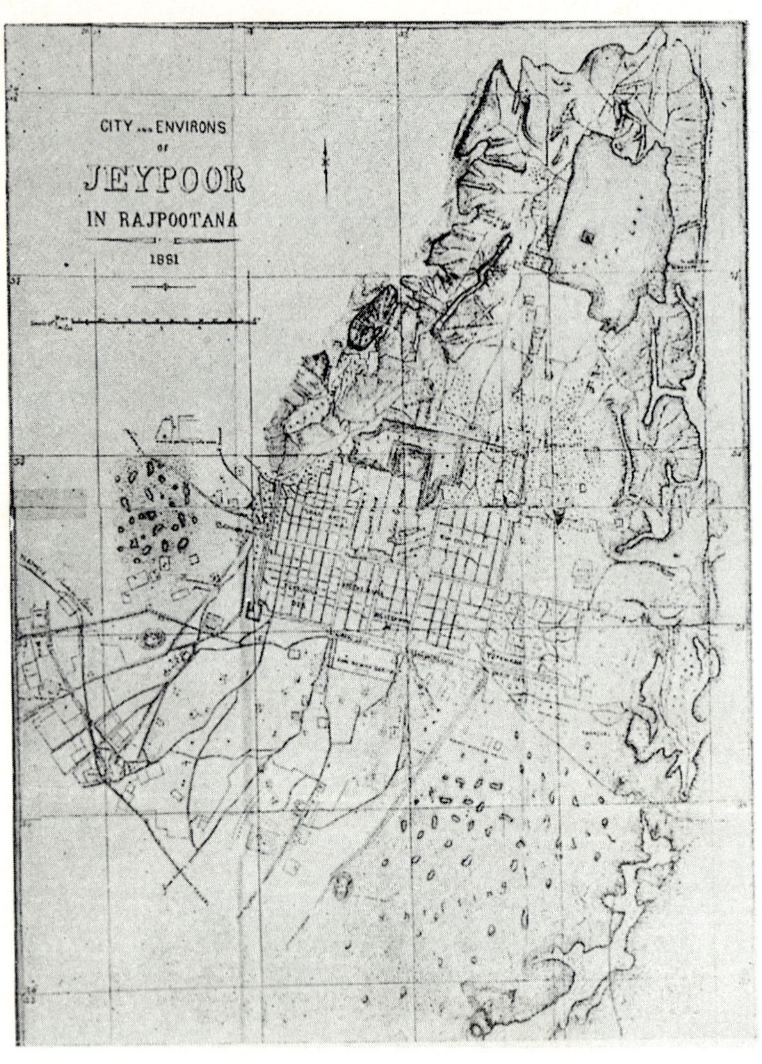
CITY AND ENVIRONS
OF
JEYPOOR
IN RAJPOOTANA
1881

HISTORY OF THE JAIPUR CITY

ASHIM KUMAR ROY

MANOHAR
2006

First published 1978
Reprinted 2006

ISBN 81-7304-697-2

Published by
Ajay Kumar Jain *for*
Manohar Publishers & Distributors
4753/23, Ansari Road, Daryaganj
New Delhi 110 002

Printed at
Lordson Publishers Pvt. Ltd.
New Delhi 110 007

Distributed in South Asia by
FOUNDATION
BOOKS
4381/4, Ansari Road
Daryaganj, New Delhi 110 002
and its branches at Mumbai, Hyderabad,
Bangalore, Chennai, Kolkata

Acknowledgements

Director General of Archaeology for permission to reprint the photographs of Sirkap and Sisupalgarh from *Ancient India*, Nos. 9 and 5 respectively.

Trustees of the Sawai Man Singh II Museum, Jaipur for permission to reprint the photograph of the map No. LS/14.

Professor G.C. Pande for instruction and guidance.

My brother Arun Kumar Roy and my wife Tapati Roy for their constant encouragement.

Contents

Preface

Among the older cities of India, Jaipur is in some respects unique. It is not only the only planned city of northern India, but is also its most beautiful city. A city in order to be beautiful has to be prosperous. And Jaipur gained prosperity quickly after its founding and has remained more or less a prosperous place since then. Few cities in India have had such a record.

Jaipur is an administrative centre and a centre of trade. Besides, it is one of the important centres of Vaishnavism in northern India. Almost all the sects of Vaishnavas, both Ramavats and Krishnavats, are represented here, and some of these sects have their most important temples or monasteries situated in this city. For instance, the most important temple of the Gaudiya Vaishnava sect in India, namely, the temple of Govindadeva is in Jaipur. Again Galta, the headquarters of the Ramanandi sect, is situated on the outskirts of the city. The Balanandis, another important Ramavat sect also have their main monastery here.

The city is also of importance to the Digambar Jainas. The Jainas have for many centuries dominated the administration of the larger states of Rajasthan. In Jodhpur, Mewar and Bikaner the Svetambar Jainas or the Oswals gained prominence. In Jaipur, however, it was the Digambar sect who occupied important administrative posts, especially during the period 1750-1830. There were also a number of famous scholars among the Jainas during this period. Among them Todarmal and Daulatram Kasliwal were well known even during their lifetime. Both of them wrote Hindi prose. Daulatram's contribution to the development of Hindi prose was recognised by no less an authority than Ramchandra Shukla in his famous history of Hindi literature. Todarmal wrote much better Hindi, but his work does not seem to have been appreciated before.

Maharaja Jai Singh who planned and built the city in 1727

as his new capital was a versatile man. A clever politician and statesman, he enlarged his state, and in his lifetime made Jaipur from one of the smaller states of Rajasthan into the most important one. As a builder and town planner he was perhaps second to none in the history of this country. Besides he was a learned man, his academic interests being mainly in religion and astronomy. There have been other Indian rulers like Akbar who have been interested in religion; but interest in astronomy is unusual among princes. What is still more unusual he was an observational astronomer, perhaps the only one of his kind in India till then.

The eighteenth century was a very turbulent period for northern India. After the attack of Nadir Shah there were frequent invasions of the Delhi-Agra-Mathura region by Ahmad Shah Abdali. The Marathas from the south also started their depredations in the north at this time. The Sikhs almost paralysed the imperial trade route through the Punjab. All this made Jaipur a haven for the traders, specially for the money-lenders and jewellers from the neighbouring cities of Delhi and Agra. It thus became in time a centre of jewellery industry and banking. Banking transactions in the city continued to remain important. In the 1869-70 report on Jaipur administration the British resident said that, "Jeypore is as it were a sort of Lombard street of Rajpootana".

From the beginning of this century, Jaipur has been a centre for gem stone cutting; and to-day it is one of the most important centres for emerald cutting in the world.

The walled city of Jaipur as built by Jai Singh has remained almost unchanged up-till now. Ram Singh who was the Maharaja during the third quarter of the nineteenth century tried to renovate the city. He got the streets metalled, and had all the buildings facing the main roads painted pink. He also built many public buildings all of which except for the public library building, were outside the city walls. But the bulk of the population of the city continued to remain within the city walls.

After Ram Singh's death in 1880 there was no perceptible change in the look of the city for nearly sixty years. The population of the city, however, started increasing during the 1930s and by 1940, it tended to spill over. Plans were made for the growth of the city outside the walls. Fortunately for

Jaipur the Diwan of the State at that time was Sir Mirza Ismail who was a town planner with great aesthetic sense. He saw to it that the new city outside the walls would grow into a beautiful place in its own right.

It was Mirza Ismail again who conceived the idea of a university for Rajputana at Jaipur. Perhaps he thought that the university would be a unifying factor for the native states of Rajasthan whose number was more than twenty.

After the integration of the States of Rajasthan in 1949, Jaipur became the capital of the new state. However, this choice was challenged twice. Independent committees were set up by the Central Government to examine the claims of other towns, but Jaipur's position was vindicated in the recommendations of both the committees. Jai Singh had at one time thought of suzerainty over the whole of Rajasthan. The choice of the city built by him as the capital of Rajasthan partly fulfilled his dream.

The history of Jaipur city is thus interesting from many points of view. For historians of the Indian system of town planning and for students of classical astronomy, of Vaishnavism, and of the economic history of urban areas, the history of the city is a fascinating study. It should also be of great interest to the students of the history of the various aspects of urban life such as the educational system and the culture of the city, of the water supply without which no city can live and grow, of its health and medical facilities, of the street lighting, garbage removal etc. On many of these Jai Singh the founder of the city has left his lasting impress.

We thus start with the life of Jai Singh himself. Jai Singh's career as a Mughal general and Governor of various Mughal provinces, the stories of his many battles, and his moves to establish his pre-eminence over other states of Rajasthan, need not detain us here. It only needs to be said that all these contributed to the enlargement of his state and gave Jaipur an importance as the capital of the state. However, Jai Singh's interest in astronomy, religion and town planning deserve close attention as it has left a lasting effect on the character and the look of the city.

As an astronomer Jai Singh has been eulogised by many eminent writers. It has generally been assumed that since he was a Hindu he must have been an exponent of the Hindu system of astronomy. This however is not quite the correct position. Jai Singh's original inspiration to learn the subject might have come from his Hindu teachers, but ultimately in his work he followed the Hellenic-Arab system of astronomy. His actual contribution in this system was in the shape of corrections to certain astronomical constants. The correct values of these constants were found out by him by using instruments some of which were undoubtedly built as per his own innovations.

Even so, except for the five massive observatories that he built, Jai Singh's contributions to the revival of classical astronomy in India was negligible. By adopting the Sayana system for his calculations—and this was necessary to carry on any observational work—Jai Singh departed from the main stream of Hindu astronomy. He thus could not make any change in the methods of even the local almanac makers.

All through his life Jai Singh was devoted to the Vaishnava religion in all its aspects. He brought into the city the votaries of many Vaishnava sects and ensured that they lived in peace with each other. He also introduced many important reforms among them. In matters of rituals he was an orthodox Hindu and gained a reputation almost as a defender of the faith in the whole of northern India. A few documents some of which are in the Kapaddwara (Household department) suggest that he was treated as a arbitrator in matters of religious practices, even in Bengal.

Vaishnavism was the religion of most of the successors of Jai Singh also, but it is generally believed in Jaipur that Maharaja Ram Singh did not like the Vaishnavas. Evidence to the contrary was however most unexpectedly available in one of the administrative reports sent by the Resident of Jaipur. In any case they did not have any narrow sectarian belief, and it was not possible to identify the sect of even Pratap Singh, the most ardent Vaishnava of them all.

The manner in which Jaipur was planned has raised the curiosity of many people. The subject has, therefore, been dealt with in some detail here. Since there are many ancient Indian books on architecture and town planning and since our Dharma Shastras and Arthasastras mention details of town planning, it has always been assumed that some of our ancient towns must have had a planned structure. This, however, as not turned out to be a fact. From the archaeological excavations carried out so far, it appears that none of the older towns of India except the Indus Valley towns such as Mohenjodaro and the second city of Taxila had been built on any plan.[1] Taxila was planned on the Greek model and Mohenjodaro is, of course, protohistoric. Jaipur was therefore the only planned town built by Indians at least in northern India.

Another belief which was found unsubstantiated was that Jaipur city was planned on the design which is known in the Shilpa Shastras as 'Prastara'. Jaipur does not resemble the Prastara design in any manner. The origin of this belief was traced to a stray remark of E.B. Havell. So far as Jaipur was concerned it was planned by Jai Singh himself who perhaps did not follow any of the Shilpashastra designs. His famous minister Vidyadhar is supposed to have helped him in planning the city. No direct evidence of this is available. Records exist, however, to prove that Vidyadhar was in many respects responsible for implementing the plan.

From one of the maps found in the city palace it is seen that the shops on the main streets were constructed by the state itself. This map is a sort of progress report. Since the shops on the main streets were constructed by the State, it was possible to give the main streets a neat and uniform look. A widely quoted line from the Imperial Gazetteer says that the main streets of Jaipur are 111 feet in width and other streets are half or quarter of this in width. On actual measurement this was not found to be true. The main streets are approximately 108 feet wide, but the other streets are rarely any exact fractions of this.

All the contemporary writers state that Jaipur became a prosperous city shortly after its foundation and continued to be so for about seventy years. Jaipur is situated almost on the borders of the Indian desert and far away from any navigable river. The various historical factors which made a city so disadvantageously

1. Professor G.C. Pande suggested to the author that the failure to find any evidence of planning in the ancient towns of India might be due to the fact that there have been no horizontal excavations of the sites of the old towns. Most of the archaeological excavations of the old towns have been done at spots. These would not reveal whether the town was planned or not. Also, the indications of town planning, if any, might have been obliterated by haphazard constructions during their period of decline.

located, a prosperous one have been discussed in some dteail in this book.

The general economic condition in the city for a period of more than two centuries have also been discussed. The economic conditions in a city would to some extent depend on the social and caste structure of the population. Two sets of statistical tables giving information on this subject were available. The first was a table given by Boileau, an officer of the survey of India who passed through Jaipur in 1835. Boileau gives the number of houses occupied by each caste and profession living in the city. He reasonably assumed that each house had five residents, but he said the total number of houses in the city was 80,000, which was four times the probable figure. The number of persons of each caste and profession given by Boileau is therefore wrong but some reliance can be placed on the figures of relative strength of these castes and professions. The second set of tables on this subject are available in the census report of Jaipur for 1901.

An analysis of these two tables is of interest from different angles. First we get an idea of the social structure of an Indian town in the pre-modern age. People of various professions such as horse doctors or elephant drivers or bangle makers were required to meet the needs of the richer sections of the people. The tables also give us an idea of the economic life of people. It appears that a very large number of people were either traders or Brahmans. There is some evidence to show that Brahmans were mostly engaged in priestly duties and many of them had jagirs given to them. In any case they were not employed in any productive work. This added to the fact that there were few industries in the town means that the common people depended mainly on the agricultural production in the surrounding country from year to year. Since rainfall in this part of India is erratic, their economic fortunes fluctuated from year to year. In extreme misery some people would *even* sell or mortgage their children. Two sale deeds of children found in a temple in Jaipur give evidence of this. In some really bad years as in 1899-1900 the people from the neighbouring rural areas would flock into the town in the hope of getting food, and would die in the streets in thousands.

On the other hand the general look of the town was

prosperous. It was not like Delhi of Aurangzeb's time as described by Bernier, a jumble of palaces and hovels. Perhaps two reasons can be ascribed for this. Firstly the Hindus in Jaipur were not afraid to show off their wealth. This was not possible, according to European travellers of that time, in cities ruled over by Mughals or other Muslim rulers. Secondly, unlike the Mughal system the wealth of a Jagirdar was not escheated to the state when he died. Permanent buildings could therefore be built by all types of Jagirdars and their servants for occupation by them and their sons generation after generation.

Jaipur essentially remained a mediaeval city even up to the twenties of this century. Some modernization had no doubt been started by the second half of the nineteenth century by Maharaja Ram Singh. In the field of administration, modernization was confined mainly to the engineering departments and to a small extent to the medical department. The laws and their administration remained as in the olden days. There was therefore no political life in the city. As in the mediaeval days, the only thing that agitated the public was the occasional religious controversy. The state gave importance to College education and Sanskrit learning and primary education was neglected. The result was that in the matter of mass literacy, Jaipur was left behind by other important cities of Rajasthan. One Director of Public Instructions assigned this backwardness to the fact that the language of administration of the State was Urdu. People of the city on the other hand for sentimental reasons wanted their children to learn Hindi, and learning Hindi was of no use for getting a job in the government. Primary education therefore had no attraction for the masses.

It was only in the thirties of this century that Jaipur started becoming a modern city. Education was made more broad-based, administration was modernized at the state level and people's participation was allowed in the Municipal administration. By the time India became free, Jaipur had come on par with other Indian cities of equal size and when time came, it was ready to take over as the capital of Rajasthan.

All large cities require that the supply of drinking water for the people should be assured and plentiful. Since Jaipur is not near any perennial river, this posed a difficult problem for the rulers of the city.

From contemporary records it apears that Jai Singh had given attention to this problem from the very beginning. He obtained water for the city from a nearby stream called Darbhavati. No such river or stream exists to-day, and the city historians have speculated on the problem of identification of the stream for many years. A reference to the ruin of an ancient barrage near Jaipur in one of the older reports of the State Public Works department has helped in identifying the old course of this river.

The later Maharajas built dams on the new course of the same river for ensuring the continuance of the water supply. However, the supply could not keep pace with the growth in population. In the thirties the problem was temporarily solved for about twenty five years by arranging supply from the Ramgarh dam. The attempt to meet the needs of the growing population continues even to-day.

Vital statistics have been recorded in Jaipur since 1874. These have revealed that the city was an extremely unhealthy one. The death rate in the city was higher than the birth rate until 1930. Malaria was the biggest killer, but strangely enough people were not afraid of it so much as they were of cholera which was not very common. Deaths due to small-pox diminished quickly when vaccination started in the last century. People here were not averse to vaccination as they were in other places of India. Or, perhaps they got vaccinated because they thought that it was the command of the Maharaja.

It was only in the nineteen-thirties that the health of the city started improving and the death rate went down significantly. It was also from 1930 that the population of the city started going up. From 144,179 in 1931 it went up to 175,810 in 1941 and to 291,130 in 1951.

We have to-day two distinct cities of Jaipur—the old Jaipur within the city walls with a population of 253,264 in 1961, and the new Jaipur outside the city walls with a population of 150,180 in the same year. The walled city has now almost three times the population it had only 50 years ago. It is thus very much over-crowded and living conditions here are unsatisfactory. As time passes, things can only become worse as the poorer people who come here would not easily find accommodation in the new city. They will only make the old city still more overcrowded.

On the other hand, the new city has no physical limitations. It has already spread towards the south and the north-west and will in course of time also expand towards the west where some constructions have already come up. The obstacle in the expansion of Jaipur is not space, but shortage of water. The underground water is being exploited more and more, but this has its limitations. Perhaps water will have to be piped in from Banas, the nearest perennial river.

There are a few modern industries in the city and their number will grow. But the number of people whose livelihood depends directly or indirectly on government service is growing much faster than those employed in industries Jaipur is therefore likely to remain an administrative city in the foreseeable future.

CHAPTER I

Jai Singh II, The Founder Of The City

Jai Singh, the founder of the Jaipur City, was born on November 3, 1688. His father was Vishan Singh (Visnu Singh), the ruler of Amer and a mansabdar of 3000/3000 in the Mughal army. His mother was Indra Kunvari, daughter of Kashi Singh Jodha of Khairwa.

Vishan Singh died in Kabul Subah on January 1, 1700. Jai Singh thus succeeded his father at the age of eleven years and two months. The young boy had shown precocious intelligence and ready wit, and is said to have been given by Aurangzeb the epithet of Sawai,[1] that is one and quarter, perhaps

1. *Ishvaravilasa Mahakavya* (7.47) gives the reason for conferring this epithet by Aurangzeb as "श्रुत्येव संग्राम जयेककारणम्" What this means is not quite clear. It is, however, popularly believed that Jai Singh was given the epithet of Sawai for his repartee, when he was presented before the Emperor for the first time in April 1696. (*Vir Vinod*, p. 1297). At that time Jai Singh was only seven and half years old. It is quite likely, therefore, that Aurangzeb might have been impressed by the smart young boy, and had affectionately predicated that he would be a quarter more intelligent than Mirza Raja Jai Singh. Official orders confirming this epithet came very much later, and perhaps after a great deal of effort on the part of the Vakil (Agent) of Jai Singh in the court at Delhi. Some of the letters of the Vakils are preserved in the State Archives in Bikaner. On February 8, 1713 the Vakil Pancholi Jag Jivan Das wrote to Jai Singh that he was trying through Tula Ram, Dewan of Nawab Hasan Ali Khan for the grant of the title of 'Sawai' for him (the Maharaja). A few months later on June 16, 1713 the Vakil wrote that the Nawab had promised to try for the grant of the title 'Sawai' for him. On June 19, 1713 the Vakil informed the Maharaja that on the recommendation of the

to signify that he would be a quarter more intelligent than his illustrious ancestor Mirza Raja Jai Singh. (Jai Singh's successors also adopted the title for themselves.)

Amer was a small state of Rajasthan when Jai Singh became its ruler. It consisted only of three parganas—Amer, Dausa and Baswa,[2] the total area being between 5,000 and 7,500 square Kilometres.[3] At the time of his death Amer had become a large state and comprised the areas of the modern districts of Jaipur, Sikar, Jhunjhunu, Sawai Madhopur, Tonk and Alwar and part of Bharatpur. Some of the areas had, at the time of Jai Singh's accession, been under other chiefs of the Kachhwaha clan of Rajputs, the clan to which Jai Singh himself belonged, but they mostly did not acknowledge the ruler of Amer even as first among equals.[4] Other parts of this area which formed Jai Singh's State had been under the Mughal rule. In course of time he incorporated these parts, which he

Nawab, the Emperor had granted the title of 'Mirza Raja Sawai' to him. (A descriptive list of the Vakil Reports (Rajasthan) addressed to the Ruler of Jaipur, Bikaner, 1974, p. 42 and p. 45). However, some of the private letters received before 1713 show that the title 'Sawai' was already being used in such letters. (V.S. Bhatnagar, *Life and Times of Sawai Jai Singh*, Delhi, 1974, p. 16).

2. "At the accession of Jai Singh the Raj of Amer consisted only of the three parganas—Amer, Deosah and Bussao, the western tracts had been sequestered, and added to the royal domain attached to Ajmer. The Shekhawati confederation was superior to and independent of the present State". James Tod, *Annals and Antiquities of Rajasthan*, Vol. II, p. 294.

   However, we do not know the exact extent of these Parganas, and it is likely that the area of each Pargana was much larger than that of the Tahsils of the same name today.

3. Wills, *Report on the Land Tenures and Special Powers of certain Thikanadars of the Jaipur State*, para 14.
4. Tod, *op. cit.*, Vol. II, p. 294. Even in the 1930s this was a matter of dispute. The Wills' *Report*, cited above, sought to prove that these chiefs were subordinate jagirdars of the Jaipur State. The important ones among these chiefs, viz. Khetri, Sikar, Khandela, Udaipurwati, Patan and Uniara, challenged the Report and said that the Jaipur State had always recognized their independence in certain respects. The reply was printed and published in 1935.

had received[5] from the Mughal government as *jagir, inam* or on *ijara*, in his State.

As long as Aurangzeb lived, Jai Singh continued to serve the Mughal army like his forefathers and was even appointed the deputy Governor of Malwa under prince Bedar Bakht who was nominally the Governor. He, however, did not get any increase in his rank during this period and remained a Mansabdar of 2000.

Aurangzeb died near Ahmednagar in the Deccan on the 21st February 1707. Two of his three sons, Shah Alam and Azam Shah soon fought out the succession issue on the battle-field of Jajau near Agra on June 8, 1707. Jai Singh backed Azam Shah who lost the battle while his younger brother Vijay Singh supported Shah Alam. Although Jai Singh had come over to the side of the victor during the battle he was never fully trusted by the new Emperor who on the pretext of penalizing him for having joined Azam Shah decided to take over Amer in *Khalisa*, that is, a territory directly administered by Delhi, though parts of the State[6] (including perhaps the Dausa Pargana) were given in lieu of salary to Jai Singh later. Thus shortly after Aurangzeb's death Jai Singh was deprived of the capital and principal fort of his State viz. Amer. Twenty-eight years before this event, Aurangzeb had done the same thing in the case of Jodhpur. When Maharaja Jaswant Singh of Jodhpur died in Afghanistan in 1679, Jodhpur State was

5. The dates of the various *parwanas* by which some of these jagirs were secured by Jai Singh in the form of *inam, jagir* or on *ijara* have been given by Bhatnagar, *op. cit.*, p. 274. Jai Singh's action in incorporating these areas in his State was resented by the Mughal Court Historians; "In the same year (1733 A.D., the 14th year of the reign of Emperor Muhammad Shah), at the instigation of Raja Jai Singh, the vile enemy (the Marathas) took possession of Malwa and the Raja himself added to his own territory many Parganas which belonged to the Emperor in the vicinity of Amer". *Tarikh-i-Hindi* of Rustam Ali, in Elliot and Dowson, Vol. VIII, p. 38, Hindi edition, Agra, 1973.
6. Kaviraj Shyamaldas quotes a letter from Maharana Amar Singh of Mewar to Nawab Asaf-ud-Daula requesting him that the village Khadmani(?) was not sufficient for Jai Singh and he should be given back Amer. Shyamaldas, *Vir Vinod*, p. 777. Bhatnagar quotes a petition from Jai Singh to the Emperor that only Dausa was insufficient for the maintenance of his family. Bhatnagar, *op. cit.*, p. 49.

made *Khalisa* by Aurangzeb. Jaswant Singh's posthumous son, Ajit Singh, born in February 1679, was not recognised by the Emperor. Ajit Singh's guardian Durga Das continued a guerilla warfare unsuccessfully for 28 years to recover Jodhpur from the Mughals. On hearing of Aurangzeb's death Ajit Singh recovered his ancestral capital, Jodhpur and expelled its Mughal commandant Mihrab Khan. Bahadur Shah wanted to stop this defiance of Mughal power in Rajasthan and marched out for that State in November 1707. He reached Amer in January 1708 and after some time renamed this place as Mominabad. Mihrab Khan meanwhile defeated Ajit Singh and occupied Merta (February 1708).[7] Ajit Singh now made his submission, waited on the Emperor like a penitent rebel, and received a command of 3500 and the title of Maharaja.[8] Bahadur Shah then marched towards the Deccan to deal with his brother Kam Baksh. The two Rajput rulers Jai Singh and Ajit Singh were with him, but on the 30th April 1708, they along with Durga Das fled away with their armies and came to Udaipur. Maharana Amar Singh of Udaipur received them cordially and promised them help in recovering their States. Jai Singh married a daughter of the Maharana. Tod describes these events as follows:

> "From the royal oordoo, or camp, they repaired to Rana Umra at Oodipur where a triple league was formed which once more united them to the head of their nation. This treaty of unity of interests against the common foe was solemnised by nuptial engagements, from which those princes had been excluded since the reigns of Akbar and Partap. To be re-admitted to this honour was the basis of this triple alliance in which they ratified on oath the renunciation of all connection, domestic or political with the empire. It was moreover stipulated that the sons of such marriages should be heirs, or if the issues were females that they should never be dishonoured by being married to a Mogul".[9]

7. *Muntkhab-ul-Lubab*, pp. 604-06.
8. Irvine, *Later Mughals*, Vol. I, p. 48.
9. Tod, *op. cit.*, Vol. I, pp. 317-18.

The marriage of Ajit Singh with a daughter of the Maharana actually never took place and Tod himself mentions that Jodhpur chronicles do not mention this marriage.[10] The important term in the agreement accepted by Jai Singh was that the son born of the Udaipur princess would be his heir. *Vir Vinod* which is a detailed history of Mewar, gives a summary of the memorandum of the agreement where such a clause is mentioned.[11] All the troubles in Rajasthan arising out of the battles of succession to the throne of Jai Singh are said to have been caused due to this term in the marriage contact. There is, however, some doubt whether the term that the son born of this marriage would be the heir of Jai Singh was explicitly mentioned in the memorandum. The original memorandum is preserved in the City Palace (Kapaddwara), Jaipur. A summary of the memorandum is available in the Bikaner Archives. It reads as follows and does not mention this clause regarding the succession:

No. Kapaddwara Register No. 1946	Maharaja Sawai Jai Singh, Jeth Budi 15, 1765 V.S.

Maharaja Jai Singh agrees to the following terms:

1. Whatever Maharani Ranawat would say would be acceptable to him.
2. Maharani Ranawat would enjoy more respect than all others in the Zenana.
3. Maharaja would pass all festival nights with the said Maharani.
4. Maharaja would take rest in the palace of the said Maharani after his coming back from a battle.
5. Ranawatji's palanquin would be foremost in a procesion.

But it is quite likely that the clause regarding heirship was there by implication, i.e., it was assumed that the son of the Udaipur princess who was to be the chief Rani would automatically be the heir.

Immediately after this marriage the armies of the three

10. Tod, *op. cit.*, Vol. II, p. 60, footenote 5.
11. Shyamaldas, *op. cit.*, p. 771.

allies first proceeded towards Jodhpur and occupied the palace on July 4, 1708. Thereafter, Jodhpur was never again conquered by the Mughals. At Jodhpur Jai Singh got engaged to a daughter of Ajit Singh on July 26, 1708 and then proceeded towards Amer. The local *Sardars* drove away the Mughal occupation force as soon as they heard of Jai Singh's approach.

Jai Singh finally became the ruler of Amer in October 1708. What however saved both Jai Singh and Ajit Singh from again being attacked by the Delhi forces was the preoccupation of the Emperor with the Sikhs in the north immediately after his return from Deccan. The Emperor, therefore, accepted the two rajas reluctantly.

As long as Bahadur Shah lived, Jai Singh never felt quite easy. But after his death in February 1712, his successor Jahandar Shah made him the Subahdar of Malwa and a mansabdar of 7000/7000. These posts were confirmed by Jahandar Shah's successor Farrukh Siyar in October 1713. Jai Singh returned from Malwa in 1716 and until 1718 was engaged in warfare with Churaman Jat of Thun and Deeg on behalf of the Mughals. By that time Saiyad brothers had become quite powerful at the Mughal Court. And there was no love lost between the Saiyad brothers and Jai Singh. Later, when Muhammad Shah became the Emperor (18th September, 1719), Jai Singh supported him in his successful attempt to suppress the brothers. Jai Singh's relations with Emperor Muhammad Shah (1719-48) remained cordial till the very end.

In 1722, the Jats under Churaman's son Mohakam Singh again rebelled against the Mughal government. The Emperor Muhammad Shah sent Jai Singh to suppress him. Jai Singh with the help of Mohkam's cousin, Badan Singh, was able to drive the rebel out from Thun and seat Badan Singh as the chief of the Jats. Thereafter, Badan Singh remained ever grateful and royal to Jai Singh, and peace was restored in this region after decades of unrest.

In 1713 Jai Singh had managed to confine his step-brother Vijay Singh by a stratagem. He is said to have been put to death in 1729-30. Vijay Singh was allegedly trying to gain possession of Amer with the help of Maharao Budh Singh of Bundi. The intrigue was detected and he was put to death.

By 1723, Jai Singh was free from duties outside the State

and he could stay on in his own capital during the period 1723 to 1729. He made full use of this opportunity for constructive work. On 29th November 1727—Poush Badi 1, Samvat 1784, he laid the foundation of a new capital in Jaipur. The planning of the new capital and the implementation of the plan showed not only his vision but also his administrative ability. No other king before him, however powerful, had been able to construct a planned city in India. Within six or seven years Jai Singh had completed the main portions of the city.

From 1729 to 1734 he made efforts to seat his nominee and son-in-law Dalel Singh on the throne of Bundi and was successful in his plan.[12] Budh Singh, the deposed ruler of Bundi, made desperate attempts to get back his state but could not do so in his lifetime. Budh Singh's queen called in even the Marathas, both Holkar and Sindhia, to his help but Jai Singh was able to recover Bundi after the departure of the Marathas. This incidentally was the first time that the Marathas had intervened openly in the internal affairs of the Rajput States. Later, for about 85 years, that is until 1818 when all the Rajasthan princes sought and obtained British protection, the frequent invasions of Marathas proved a curse to the people and princes of Rajasthan.

During the period when Jai Singh was engrossed in the politics of Bundi he was twice made governor of Malwa by the Mughal Emperor. Earlier he had served in this capacity in 1713 also. Jai Singh's second governorship of Malwa in 1730 lasted only for seven months. The third time he was sent there was in December 1732.[13] He however could not save the province from increasing Maratha encroachments. In 1736, he invited Peshwa Baji Rao to discuss the possibility of a lasting agreement between the Marathas and the Mughal government but his attempt did not succeed due to the machinations of the "war party" at the Court in Delhi. After 1737 he became increasingly involved in the matters concerning his own State and in the conflict between Bikaner and Jodhpur.

A war between Jodhpur and Bikaner in 1739 gave Jai Singh

12. Suraj Mal Mishran, *Vamsha Bhaskar*, pp. 3542, 3285.

13. Letter from Raja Ajamal to Jai Singh dated Asoj Badi 13 V.S. 1789 (6-9-1732 A.D.), *Kapaddwara* letter No. 916.

an opportunity to intervene on behalf of Bikaner which had sought his help. No fight actually took place for Jodhpur abjectly surrendered to Jai Singh's display of force. Some of the clauses of the treaty[14] between Abhay Singh of Jodhpur and Jai Singh show how complete the surrender was:

1. That Abhay Singh would not obstruct Jai Singh in his possession of the Suba of Ajmer.
2. That the relations of Jodhpur with the Marathas would be determined by Jai Singh.
3. That counsellors of Abhay Singh would be selected by barons who were not hostile towards Jaipur.

By helping Bikaner in its hour of need, Jai Singh had made that state also indebted to him. With Mewar too he had friendly relations.

Thus by 1739, Jai Singh had established himself as the pre-eminent power in Rajasthan.

Death of Jai Singh

The last three years of his life, Jai Singh spent mostly within his palace in Jaipur. According to *Ishvar-Vilas Mahakavya* composed in 1749 by Shri Krishna Bhatta, a court poet of Jaipur, Jai Singh devoted himself to the study and practice of *Vaishnavism* and other religious matters. "He spent his time gazing with adoration at the face (of the image) of Govinda-deva". 10.2

But according to the *Vamsha Bhaskar*, the last years of Jai Singh were spent in drunkenness and lechery. "Jai Singh gave himself up to the sexual excess. He had always been a deep drinker and now the habitual use of aphrodisiacs to stimulate his falling powers entirely ruined his health till at last he died of a loathsome disease on 21st September, 1743".[15]

14. M.L Sharma, *History of the Jaipur State*, p. 153. Bhatnagar quoting Kapaddwara document, *Yaddashta* No. 46k/1094, dated July 25, 1740, gives all the eight clauses of the treaty (*op. cit.*, p. 261).
15. *Vamsha Bhaskar*, pp. 3320-3322, quoted from J.N. Sarkar, *Fall of the Mughal Empire*, Vol. I, p. 150.

The *Vamsha Bhaskar* was written in 1840 by Suraj Mal Mishran the court historian of Bundi. Bundi was recoverd by Ummed Singh, son of Budh Singh in 1748 and he had naturally a bitter memory of Jai Singh who had deprived him of his patrimony. It is therefore quite likely that Suraj Mal derived some malicious pleasure in describing that Jai Singh had died of a horrible disease. The *Vamsha Bhaskar* gives a detailed description of Jai Singh's last illness. The symptoms mentioned in the description suggest cancer rather than a venereal disease. Sarkar was perhaps unnecessarily harsh on Jai Singh. There can be no doubt, however, that Jai Singh liked sensual life. He had altogether 27 wives[16] and perhaps 4 concubines, the largest number ever had by the rulers of Amer and Jaipur. His illustrious ancestor, Man Singh who came next, had only 26 wives (The 27 nakshtras are the 27 wives of Moon. Moon thus also has 27 wives. Did Jai Singh stop at the figure of 27 because of this?).

In some respects the most fruitful years of Jai Singh's life were from 1723 to 1729 and 1740 to 1743 for the greater part of which he lived in Jaipur. It was only after 1722-23 that he could devote more time to the activities for which he is remembered. These activities may be divided into four classes: (1) Planning and construction of his capital, (2) Enlargement of the State of Amer and establishing its leadership over the other States of Rajasthan, (3) Building of five astronomical observatories and study of astronomy, and (4) Reform and revival of Hinduism, particularly of Vaishnavism, in northern India.

Contribution to Astronomy

Jai Singh's interest in astronomy is unusual among rulers. It is said that he was drawn towards the subject at quite an early age. But what inner urge made him spend so much time and money (he built five observatories in India at Jaipur, Delhi, Mathura, Ujjain and Varanasi) on the pursuit of knowledge

16. This number is according to the records in the City Palace. It was obtained through the courtesy of Shri G.N. Bahura. Jai Singh had only 5 surviving children, 3 sons and 2 daughters from these 27 wives. Gahlot, however, mentions that Jai Singh had 28 wives and 4 concubines. (*Jaipur wa Alwar Rajyon ka Itihas*, p. 106).

remains a mystery. He had taken as his ideal Ulugh Beg[17] the ruler of Samarkand in the 15th century. Ulugh Beg, the grandson of Timur, had built an observatory in Samarkand and had also prepared a catalogue of stars giving their latitudes and longitudes, right ascension and declination. In his astronomical work *Zeij Muhammad Shahi* (Astronomical Tables of Muhammad Shah) Jai Singh tried to bring Ulugh Beg's catalogue up to date. Jai Singh's star table contains the particulars of 1018 stars. The following particulars are given for each star: (1) Longitude, (2) Latitude, (3) Polar Longitude, (4) Declination, and (5) Right ascension both in degrees and in time (*ghatis* and *palas*). In other words, the extra information given in Jai Singh's catalogue over and above Ulugh Beg's table is the polar longitudes of stars (The difference between the true longitude and the polar longitude is that portion of the ecliptic which is intercepted between the star s declination and latitude circles. This is the Surya Siddhanta method of indicating the position of the stars). In any case, except for these two types of longitudes, the other particulars of a star, viz. latitude, declination and right ascension of a star do not change in course of time unless the star itself has a proper motion.

There was a Devanagari manuscript of the *Zeij Muhammad Shahi* in Jaipur seen by Kaye. The preface to this began as follows:[18] "Homage to holy Ganesh. Catalogue of 48 constellations. From the time of Ulugh Beg's table A.H. 841 to the present date A.H. 1133 or 297 years the mean motion is 4 degrees and 8 minutes". Jai Singh's catalogue gives practically the same figures for the position of the stars as Ulug Beg's except for this correction of 4 degrees and 8 minutes for the longitude.

Clearly Jai Singh found that the celestial longitude of the stars varied by 4 degrees and 8 minutes in 297 Muslim

17. There is a copy of Sanskrit rendering of *Zeij-Ulughbegi* in the *Pothi Khana* at Jaipur. A note on this copy states that it was acquired from Surat City through Nandarama Joshi. See, *Pothi Khana Catalogue*, pp. 58-59.

18. C.R. Kaye, *The Astronomical Observatories of Jai Singh*, Calcutta, 1918, p. 8. Two Persian manuscripts of the *Zeij Muhammad Shahi* are available in the Pothi Khana. G.N. Bahura, *Catalogue of the manuscripts in the Maharaja of Jaipur Museum*, Jaipur, 1971, pp. 72-73.

(=288.2 Christian) years or by 51.6″ in a year. This appears to be the result of Jai Singh's own observation, since this figure of the annual precession of the equinoxes is not found in the writings of Arab or Greek astronomers. And it is very near to the correct figure of 50.26″ a year. (Ptolemy's figure is 36″ a year).

We have the record of another such result of the observations of Jai Singh. This is given in the preface of the *Samrat Siddhanta*, a translation of the Arabic *Al-megiste* (Ptolemy's syntaxis) by Jagannath, one of the Pandits of Jai Singh. It reads as follows:

> "In the Yavana country, the Yavana masters of astronomy, Abarkhas (Hipparchus), etc. found the maximum declination to be 23 degrees 51 minutes 19 seconds, and that in Yunan 36 degrees north, it was found to be 23 degrees 51 minutes and 15 seconds by the observations of Vitlamayus (Ptolemaeus). Ulugh Beg found it to be 23 degrees 30 minutes and 17 seconds at Samarkand, 39 degrees 17 minutes north. By observation with this instrument (Samrat Yantra) we found it to be 23 degrees and 28 minutes at Indraprastha in 1651 Salivahana". (=1729 A.D.).

Jai Singh's figure of 23° 28′ is very accurate. The correct figure of the obliquity of the ecliptic in 1729 was 23° 28′ 29″ i.e. Jai Singh was thus out in his reckoning by only half a minute.

The *Zeij Muhammad Shahi* also contains tables giving the position of Sun, Moon and the planets for a number of years. The purpose of these tables was to correct the almanacs, because it was found that almanacs prepared on the basis of the existing tables did not give the correct positions of the planets as seen by actual observation. In the preface to the *Zeij Muhammad Shahi* Jai Singh has written that

> "he found that the calculations of the places of the stars as obtained from the tables in common use, such as the new tables of Sa'id Gurgani and Khagani, and the Tashilat-Mulchand Akbar Shahi and the Hindu books and European

tables[19] in very many cases give them widely different from those determined by observations: especially in the appearance of the new moons, the computation of which did not agree with the observation".

Jai Singh's attempt to correct the almanacs did not succeed. No almanac maker, not even the Pandits who prepared almanacs in Jaipur, adopted these tables. Jai Singh's tables were perhaps based on the results of actual observations. The longitudes of the planets given in his tables were thus in the Sayana system. The Hindu almanac makers followed the Mirayana system and they therefore continued to follow the handbooks (called *Panchanga Sadhaka*, *Karana* etc.) based mainly on *Surya Siddhanta*. The almanac makers of Jaipur at present use the tables of *Ram Vinod*, a *karana* book, prepared in 1590.[20]

In order to correct the existing tables Jai Singh constructed astronomical observatories and tried to find out the actual position of the planets. The astronomers in India used at that time metal instruments called astrolabes, but Jai Singh found them wanting in two respects. They were not stable, and they were too small in size for taking accurate readings of the observations.[21]

"Therefore", in his own words in the *Zeij Muhammad Shahi*, "he constructed at Dar Al-Khilafat Shah Jahanabad, which is the seat of empire and prosperity, instruments of his own inventions, such as the *Jai Prakash* and *Ram Yantra* and *Samrat Yantra*, the semi-diameter of which is of eighteen cubits, and one minute on it is a barley corn and a half, of

19. Jai Singh's copy of De La Hire's tables where he is said to have spotted the mistakes has, it appears, been lost. The *Pothi Khana*, however, contains the tables of Flamsteed, the first Astronomer Royal. The tables were printed in 1725. (*Pothikhana Catalogue*, p. 77).
20. As reported by Shri Madan Mohan Sharma, one of the two Almanac makers of Jaipur.
21. There is a small Sanskrit booklet called the *Yantra Raj Rachana*. It gives directions on the method of construction of astrolabes. The booklet is ascribed to Jai Singh though it only mentions that it is "*Jai Singh Karita*" which may mean that it was written under the orders of Jai Singh. The booklet has been printed by the *Rajasthan Puratatva Mandir*, Jaipur, p. 1953.

stone and lime of perfect stability, with attention to rules of geometry and adjustment to the meridian and to the latitude of the place and with care in the measuring and fixing in them....

"And, in order to confirm the truth of these observations, he constructed instruments of the same kind in Sawai Jaipur, Mathura and Varanasi and Ujjaini. When he compared these observatories, after allowing for the difference of longitude between the places where they stood, the observations agreed.

"Hence he determined to erect similar observations in other large cities so that every person who is devoted to these studies, whenever he wished to ascertain the place of star or the relative situation of one star to another might by these instruments observe the phenomenon."

From this it is clear that Jai Singh claimed originality for his instruments and also that the purpose of his constructing five observatories— and his plans for more observatories which never got constructed—was to make his country-men interested in the observational aspect of astronomy. In the latter attempt he never succeeded.

The four observatories outside Jaipur fell into disuse after his death, and the one at Mathura has disappeared altogether. This observatory was built on the top of the old fort at Mathura, known as *Kans Ka Kila*. The fort had been rebuilt by Raja Man Singh of Amer. Growse has mentioned: "A little before the Mutiny, the buildings were sold to a Government contractor, Joti Prasad, who destroyed them for the sake of the materials."[22]

The Jaipur observatory continued to be used for some time. Even a new instrument was added to this place in the time of Jai Singh's son, Madho Singh (1751-1768). This was a brass instrument called "*Yasti Yantra*". Garret says that it bore the Sanskrit inscription, "with this instrument one can easily read the time by the wisdom of Madho Singh." The south-facing dial of the *Nadi Valaya Yantra*, according to Garret, was added subsequently by Maharaja Pratap Singh (1778-1803). But even Pratap Singh did not care much for the preservation of

22. F.S. Growse, *Mathura: a District Memoir*, p. 131.

the observatory. "There appear to have originally been three more instruments situated in the west of the observatory enclosure. They were, however, removed during the reign of Maharaja Pratap Singh to make room for a temple of Anand Vihariji, and have never been rebuilt. Two of them were known as the *Agra Yantra* and *Sara Yantra* respectively."[23]

In one respect, however, Jaipur observatory continued to be used until quite recently. The Jaipur Government for its official purpose used the solar time, which was read on the *Samrat Yantra* in the observatory, and a gun used to be fired from the Nahargarh fort as the time signal. In April 1944[24] this practice of using the local solar time was given up and Jaipur started using the Indian Standard time.

Jai Singh's claim that the instrument in his observatories were invented by him may now be examined. The following masonary instruments are found in the Jaipur observatory:—

1. *The Samrat Yantra*—This is an equal hour Sun dial. It is the largest instrument in the Jaipur observatory. Its gnomon is 90 feet high and 147 feet long. The dials for reading the time are quadrants with radius of 49 feet and 10 inches each. The dials are marked to read time up to one second but this is impossible since the shadow is not so clearly defined.

2. *The Shashtamsa Yantra*—This is a high and narrow room with arcs on its opposite walls parallel to the plan of meridian, each of 28 feet and 4 inches radius. There is a hole in the ceiling at the centre of each arc through which Sun light enters and falls upon the arcs at noon. This gives the declination of the Sun.

3. *The Rasi Valaya Yantra*—This is a set of 12 instruments each of the same type as the *Samrat Yantra*, but the quadrants lie, not in the plane of the equator, but in the plane of the ecliptic when the particular zodiacal sign is on the horizon, and the edge of the gnomon then points to the pole of the ecliptic; consequently at the proper moment the instrument indicates the Sun's latitude.

23. Garret and Chandra Dhar Guleri, *The Jaipur Observatory and its builder.*

24. *Report on the Administration of Jaipur for Samvat 2003* (1946-47), p. 13.

4. *The Jai Prakas*—This is a part of concave hemispherical bowl 17 feet and 10 inches in diameter. Cross wires are stretched north to south and east to west, and the shadow of the intersection of the wires falling on the surface of the hemisphere indicates the position of the Sun in the heavens. Other heavenly bodies can be observed directly by placing the eye at the proper graduated point, and observing the passage of the body across the point of intersection of the wires. For this purpose passages are cut into the hemisphere, and the instrument duplicated.

5. *The Ram Yantra*—The *Ram Yantra* is a cylindrical instrument open at the top and having at its centre a pillar. The floor and the inside of the circular wall are graduated for altitude and azimuth observations. The height of the wall from the graduated floor is equal to the distance from the circumference of the central pillar to the inside of the wall. To facilitate observation the floor is broken up with sectors and, consequently, as in the case of *Jai Prakas*, complementary buildings had to be constructed. The walls are also broken up, and one section of the wall corresponds to one sector. In the *Ram Yantra* at Delhi, there are 30 sectors, each of 6 degrees, in each building, but at Jaipur there are 12 sectors only, and their angle is 12 degrees in one instrument and 13 degrees in the other, the spaces between them being respectively 18 and 12 degrees. It is quite likely that in Jai Singh's time the *Ram Yantra* was built in Delhi only. *Ram Yantra* exists in the Jaipur observatory also but it is a more recent one, having been built in 1891.[25]

Other masonary instruments in Jaipur are the (6) *Nari Valaya Yantra*, (7) the *Dakshinorithi Yantra*, and (8) the *Kapali.*

It is quite possible that Jai Singh had himself invented all these instruments. Prossibly also he obtained some help from the Arab sources for some of these instruments. In the *Zeij Muhammud Shahi* he definitely claimed originality for at least three of these instruments, namely the *Jai Prakash*, *Ram Yantra* and the *Samrot Yantra*. There is nothing very remarkable about the *Jai Prakash* and the *Ram Yantra*. Like the other instruments in Jai Singh's observatories they measured altitude and azimuth

25. G.R. Kaye, *A Guide to the old Observatories at Delhi, Jaipur, Ujjain, Banaras, Mathura*, Calcutta, 1920, Chapter II.

and the declination of the heavenly bodies. The *Samrat Yantra*, however, is important. As mentioned earlier, it is essentially an equal hour Sun dial. But it is a most unusual Sun dial, and such Sun dials are not mentioned in the Greek or Arab books. Ordinarily, it would appear that the *Samrat Yantra* was invented by Jai Singh himself. Kaye, however, says[26] "In the British Museums are many dials of the 17th and early 18th centuries constructed exactly on the same principle as the *Samrat*". It is doubtful whether Jai Singh had any knowledge of the existence of these instruments made in Europe, and it may safely be concluded that the *Samrat Yantra* was an independent invention of Jai Singh. The *Samrat Yantra* was so graduated that it was possible to find out the declination of the Sun directly; and as mentioned before, Jai Singh's Pandits determined obliquity of ecliptic very accurately with the help of this instrument at Delhi.

Jai Singh also tried to get European astronomers and European astronomical tables. For these he sought the help of the Jesuit missionaries in India.[27] He also sent a mission to Portugal for this purpose. Since, however, all his contacts were through the Jesuits who were prevented by the Roman Church from believing in modern astronomy, Jai Singh was unable to find out from them about modern astronomy which had reached almost its final form even before Jai Singh was born. (Newton's *Principia* had come out a year before Jai Singh's birth). He thus remained confined within the limits of classical astronomy and he believed firmly that the earth stands still and the celestial sphere goes round the earth every 24 hours. In fact he has given long arguments in support of this theory in the *Zeij Muhammad Shahi.* One might say that Jai Singh was the last great astronomer of the Greek-Arab System.

Astronomy for Jai Singh was a hobby which he keenly persued for at least 15 to 16 years, that is, from the foundation of the Jaipur observatory near about 1718 to the completion of this observatory in 1734. We do dot know where or from whom Jai Singh learned astronomy. The *Ishwaravilas Mayakavya* mentions[28] by name only one of his teachers. His name was

26. Kaye, *The Astronomical Observatories of Jai Singh,* Calcutta, 1918, p. 87.
27. See Appendix I.
28. *Ishwaravilas Mahakavya, Shloka* 2.12.

Shri Poundarik (Ratnakar). But Poundarik, as stated later, was a master of Hindu rituals and not of astronomy. It is quite likely that Jai Singh learned his astronomy from both Hindu and Muslim teachers. We know for certain that in the field of astronomy, his ideal was Ulugh Beg of Samarkand and though Jai Singh's methods were eclectic, his leanings were towards the Arabic system. Astronomy in Jai Singh's time had lost much of its sectarian colour, for Hindus had for nearly 500 years studied the Arabic system and mastered it. As early as in the Tughluq period, Mahendra Suri was the court astrologer of Firuz Shah Tughlaq (1351-1388). Mahendra Suri had in 1370 written a book named *Yantra Rāj*, a text-book on Astrolabes, the Arabic (*Yavana*, in his own words) instruments for observing the position of celestial bodies. Mahendra Suri's disciple Malayendu Suri wrote a commentary on this book. At the end of the commentry he wrote, "The book was written by Mahendra Suri who was Chief astronomer (astrologer?) of Firoze." *Yantra Raj* is taught even today in the astronomy classes of the Sanskrit Colleges of Jaipur and Varanasi.[29]

As mentioned before Jai Singh himself is said to have written a book on the method of construction of this Arabic instrument. The name *Yantra Raj* given to this instrument by the Hindus shows that it was considered the King of observational instruments.

Again Jai Singh's interest in the Arabic system and conversely the interest of Muslim astronomers in Hindu astronomy will be apparent from the fact that in the Jaipur Pothi Khana there are 18 Arabic and Persian manuscripts on astronomy acquired from the time of Jai Singh or from an earlier period. Among these is *Lavaheul-Qamar* which is an Arabic translation of the *Chandrā Sidhanta.* The translation is dated 1667 but the book was acquired in Jai Singh's time in 1725.[30]

Among Jai Singh's court astronomers the most famous was Samrat Jagannath, a Maharashtrian. As stated earlier, Jagannath had translated *Al-megiste*, the Arabic version of Ptolemy's *Mathematike Syntaxis.* No copy of this translation,

29. *Yantra Raj Rachana*, p. iii.
30. *Catalogue of Manuscripts in the Maharaja of Jaipur Museum*, pp. 72-75.

it appears, exists in the Pothi Khana; but copies were no doubt seen in Jaipur by Kaye and also by Garret and Guleri. These last two make adverse comments,[31] on Jagannath's style of writing. The names of Jai Singh's Muslim astronomers are not known, but one Mohammed Mahdi[32] is said to have accompanied the mission to Portugal in search of astronomical knowledge. Thus the prince's astronomical learning, his appreciation of Arabic system and his keen interest in rational enquiry go to prove that Jai Singh studied astronomy from both Hindu and Muslim teachers.

We may summarize Jai Singh's achievements in astronomy as follows:—

1. He found out the declination of the ecliptic, very accurately. The *Samrat Yantra* which was designed by him was used for this purpose.
2. He found out, again by actual observation, an accurate figure of the annual precession of the equinoxes.
3. He revised the star catalogue of Ulugh Beg. This however was more or less a mechanical work, once the average change in the longitudes of the stars since the time of Ulugh Beg had been determined by observations.
4. He got the tables prepared giving the position of the planets in the various years. The purpose of preparing these tables was to make it possible for the almanac makers to give the correct position of these planets in their almanacs. His efforts did not succeed because the almanac makers of India continued to follow their traditional tables.
5. He constructed five astronomical observatories in India. These observatories had masonary instruments some of which were of his own design. The purpose was to create an interest in his countrymen in observational astronomy. He failed in this purpose also.

31. Garret and Guleri, *op. cit.*, Ch. II.
32. Durga Prasad Dvivedi, *Utpattindu Shekhar*, Jaipur, 1936, p. 65. Dvivedi quotes from the Sanskrit version of *Zeij Muhammad Shahi*.

Religion

As mentioned earlier Jai Singh died a *Vaishnava* and a devotee of Govindadeva whose image he had installed within his palace premises. However, three different aspects of Hinduism are discernible in his life. The first was the Pauranika Hinduism with its *Pujas* and rituals. The second was Vedic religion in which performance of *Yajnas* was an important ritual. Jai Singh tried to revive many of the *Yajnas* of the Vedic times and became famous as a performer of the *Ashvamedha.* The third side of Jai Singh's religion was *Vaishnavism.* He perhaps did not belong to any particular *Vaishnava* sect. But as he was acknowledged as the most important and learned Hindu chief in the country, he was invited to arbiter in matters of religious disputes even up to Bengal. Many temples and places in Jaipur are associated with the religious activities of Jai Singh. This also reveals his respectful attitude towards various sects.

Jai Singh was born in a *Vaishnava* family. The rulers of Amer before him were mostly devout *Vaishnavas.* Prithviraj who was the chief of Amer from 1503 to 1527 was important enough as a *Vaishnava* to have a whole *Chhappaya* (NO. 116) written about him in the *Bhaktamal.* Raja Man Singh (1550-1614), the great grandson of Prithvi Raj and the famous general of Akbar and Jahangir finds mention as a *Vaishnava* in the *Chaurasi Vaishnavon ki Katha*[33] and also in the writings of the Bengali poet Mukandaram. But Jai Singh's father Vishnu Singh or Vishan Singh (1690-1700) perhaps followed the ritualistic type of Hinduism. This is surmised from the fact that his *guru* Sivananda Goswami was a man learned in Hindu rituals. A Telegu Brahman, he had written among other books a treatise on rituals called the *Simha Sidhanta Sindhu.*[34] This big volume containing 35130 *slokas* deals with *Mantra Shastra* and describes such practices, religious sacrifices and magic words by utterances of which one could gain one's ends both spiritual and mundane.

33. *Chaurasi Vaishnavon Ki Katha*, Bombay 1958, pp. 297, 298 and 302.
34. A copy of *Simha Siddhanta Sindhu* by Sivananda Goswami, son of Jagannivas, exists in the Pothikhana. The date of the copy is V.S. 1733, but the book was first written in V.S. 1731 (1744 A.D.), vide G.N. Bahura's article in *Sanskrit Kalpataru.*

The *Ishvarivilas Mahakavya* does not mention Sivananda Goswami by name, but it states[35] (2/7) that Vishnu Singh had given his *guru* four villages.[36]

It is quite likely that Jai Singh in his childhood had come under the influence of his father's *guru*. Also Jai Singh's teacher Jagannath Paundarik was himself the writer of the *Jai Singh Kalpadrum*,[37] a book on rituals.

Pauranika Hinduism

Jai Singh was thus brought up in an atmosphere where the Pauranika or classical form of Hinduism was supreme. It is relevant here to mention that he never got interested in the people's *religions* such as the Nath Pantha or the Dadu Pantha. He was not disrespectful towards the non-*Pauranika* gods such as *Shitala* or *Hanuman* as the Tauji records show,[38] but perhaps was not very keen on them.

The Puranas or the Smritis mention the worship of *Pancha Devatas* or the five gods, viz., *Vishnu*, *Shiva*, *Shakti*, *Ganapati* and *Surya*. Out of these five, *Shiva* and *Shakti* are the two most popular gods today all over northern India. Both these gods, especially *Shakti* seem to have been neglected by Jai Singh at least so far as Jaipur city was concerned. We do not have even today any important temple of *Shakti* in the Jaipur city. This was perhaps because he was essentially a *Vaishnava* and both *Shiva* and *Shakti* are mythologically and from the sectarian point of view antagonistic to *Vaishnavism*.

Girdhari in his *Bhojansar* mentions the following about the temples in Jaipur:—

35. In his article in Sivananda Goswami in *Sanskrit Kalpataru*, Ghanshyam Goswami mentions that Vishnu Singh gave Sivananda five villages which are situated a few kilometres from Jaipur on the Amer Road.
36. The printed edition of the *Ishvaravilas Mahakavya* in the editor's commentary on this sloka (2/7) quotes a copper plate deed of a village to Sivananda by Vishnu Singh.
37. The book was written in 1711. It was printed by the *Lakshmi Venkateshwar Press* in Samvat 1982 (1925 A.D.).
38. *Tauji Records*, V.S. 1792-1797 (1735-1740), Bikaner Archives.

मंदिर अनेक जहा गोव्य देव गोपीनाथ
शिवरु गनेशरु दिनैस के दिवार्लें है
देवी देव घिमत गेह् गेह् झालरिसु घटा
झाभ्झि दुंदभि के नादनी के चाले है ॥१६५॥

Here, Girdhari (writing twelve years after the foundation of the city and four years before the death of Jai Singh) mentions two important *Vaishnava* temples, those of Govinda-deva and Gopinath—both belonging to the Gaudiya Vaishnava sect, and also temples of *Shiva*, *Ganesh* and *Surya.*

Some speculation can be made about the temples of *Surya* and *Ganesh* existing at the time of Jai Singh.

The worship of *Surya* in a temple has by and large disappeared in our country, though the recitation of the famous mantra—*Java Kusuma Shankasan* . . . facing the rising Sun while bathing in a river or tank has continued for all time. Jai Singh, it is said, got a temple of *Surya* constructed on a hill just on the eastern boundary of the city. The temple though very prominently situated, is built in a simple manner. It has small brass image of *Surya* and is visited by few worshippers. The temple was built under the supervision of a Jaina official Rao Kirparam.[39] The stone-paved path up the hill leading to the temple was constructed by two brothers Shamlal and Sunderlal.

It is however not certain that the temple of *Surya* was built mainly as a means of reviving the worship of one of the *Pauranika Pancha Devatas.* In later days, and until the integration of the State of Jaipur in Rajasthan in 1949, a procession used to be taken out in the city on *Bhanu Saptami*, the *Saptami* nearest to the vernal equinox (21st March) with the image of *Surya* from this temple.[40] The Maharaja himself used to join the procession. This raises the possibility that the honour to *Surya* was not mainly because he was one of the five principal gods of Pauranika Hinduism but because he was the mythical ancestor of the rulers of Jaipur.

39. Kirparam was the Jaipur envoy in the court of Delhi (See, Tod, *op. cit.*, Vol. II, p. 292).
40. *Jaipur Album*, Ch. XV, p. 2.

The worship of *Ganesh* on the other hand is quite popular in India specially among families engaged in trade and commerce. But public temples of *Ganesh* are not very common in northern India. One old temple of *Ganesh* exists just north of Jaipur city on the top of the high hill range. This temple was most probably built at the time of Jai Singh.[41] The other one temple of Ganesh near Moti Dungri is a more recent one.[42]

Worship of Vishnu as such had all but vanished in northern India by the time of Jai Singh, though the worship of Rama and Krishna, the incarnations of Vishnu, was very popular. Jai Singh did not try to restore the worship of Vishnu in Jaipur, but for the purpose of the various *Yajnas*, he obtained an image of Vishnu from South India. This image called the "Varadaraja Vishnu", is made of brass and is about half a metre in height. It is installed on the top of a small hill near the place of the *Yajnas* about two kilometres north of the town on the Amer Road. At present the image is worshipped as *Narayana* by a family who are the *sebaits* of the image. The family belongs to the *Nimbarka* sect of *Vaishnavas*.[43]

Vedic Rituals

While *Puja* or worship of gods was a *Pauranika* ritual, the ritual of the Vedic times was the performance of *Yajnas*. Jai Singh performed at least two *Yajnas* mentioned in the Vedic literature namely *Vajapeya* and *Ashvamedha*.[44] According to the *Ishvarvilas Mahakavya* (1749), Jai Singh first performed the *Vajapeya Yajna*.

"He obtained the title of *Samrat* (emperor) by performing *Vajapeya* and put on the white umbrella at the time of coronation."

Thereafter he called an assembly of learned people to find out whether the *Ashvamedha* could be performed in the *Kali* age. It was decided to obtain the opinion of the pandits of

41. *Devasthan records*, Register No. 46, pp. 204, 205, Bikaner Archives.
42. *Dastur Komwar*, Vol. VIII, p. 58, Bikaner Archives.
43. Personal interview with the *sebait* in 1971.
44. The possible reasons for performing the *Ashvamedha* by Jai Singh have been discussed by V.S. Bhatnagar in his essay "*Sawai Jaya Singh's performance of the Asvamedha and its significance*" *in Jijnasa*, Nos. 1-2, Rajasthan University, 1974, pp. 111-119.

Varanasi. These Pandits wrote back that Jai Singh could perform the *Yajna*. Accordingly-*Ashvamedha* was performed in a grand manner. A pillar about ten metres high was erected on the site of the *Yajna* as a memorial. Nothing but the pillar exists today at the site which is north of Brahmapuri about two kilometres north of the city.

The celebrations are described in detail in the *Ishvarvilas Mahakavya*. After a *Yajna*, one is supposed to take a final purification bath. This is called *Avabhritham*.

Jai Singh took this *Avabhritham* bath with four of his wives[45] at the Ghat of the *Mansarovar* lake, adjacent to the site of the *Yajna*. The statue of a horse of white marble in the courtyard of the temple of *Kalki*[46] is said to have been installed at that time.

Bhakti Marg

He was not only devoted to the practices of *Vedic* and *Pauranika* rituals but was also eager to apply himself to the task of eradicating the evils from which the monastic order of Galta had been suffering for a long time. It would be interesting to trace the history of the development of the said order.

Of the two main branches of the *Bhakti Marg*, or the way of devotion, the *Rama Bhakti* or the *Ramavat* school had established itself quite early in Galta near Jaipur. Galta is a valley on the eastern side of a hill situated due east of the Jaipur city. It is a narrow valley surrounded on three sides by hills and is only approachable from the east through a hilly path, four to five kilometres long. It has a perennial stream flowing through it and is said to have been in the occupation of *Jogis* for a long time. Payohari Krishnadas, a great

45. *Isvaravilas Mahakavya*, 5.48 & 5.49.
46. One of the few temples established by Jai Singh in Jaipur is the temple of Kalki. This temple is situated in Sireh Deori Bazar opposite the palace gate. Kalki is the tenth incarnation of Vishnu and is yet to appear. Perhaps there is no other temple of Kalki in India. It is generally believed that the temple was built by Jai Singh, in memory of his grandson Kalki Singh, son of Ishvari Singh. Kalki Singh had died at a young age. There is nothing very remarkable about the temple itself but in the yard of the temple there is the statue of a horse. The statue made of white marble is about a metre high.

Ramanandi sadhu, came to Galta early in the 16th century and drove away the Jogis from here by his "*yogic*" powers. He thereafter established his sect there. Galta later became one of the most important centres of the *Ramanandi* sect and came to be known as *Uttar Totadri* or Totadri of the north. (Totadri is a village near Kanya Kumari and is the seat of the *Ramanuja* sect in South India).

Payohari Krishnadas was the disciple of Anantananda who was a disciple of Ramananda, the founder of the *Rama Bhakti* school in northern India.

In the Galta *Gaddi* Payohariji was succeeded by his disciple Kilhadevaji who in turn was succeeded by Videhi Krishnadasji. Another disciple of Kilhadevaji was Agradas or Agradeva. Agradeva left Galta and founded another monastery at Rewasa near Sikar. Nabhadas, the author of the famous book *Bhaktamal* was a disciple of Agradas.

The succession list of the Galta *Gaddi* from the time of Payohari Krishnadas uptil now is as follows:—

1. Payohari Krishnadas.	
2. Kilha Deva.	
3. Videhi Krishna Das.	
4. Vishnu Das.	
5. Narain Das.	
6. Haridevacharya	—From his time all the *mahants* of the Galta *Gaddi* have the word *Acharya* affixed to their names.
7. Madhuracharya	--He was alive in 1726 i.e. at the time of Jai Singh.
8. Hariacharya (Died Jeth Vadi 4, 1814 V.S. — 1757 A.D.)	—He was the first *mahant* to marry. All the subsequent *mahants* were sons or grandsons of their predecessor.
9. Sriacharya (Died Magh Vadi 1, 1839 V.S. — 1782 A.D.)	—Madho Singh, son of Jai Singh, gave the Galta *gaddi* a jagir in 1760 A.D.

10. Janakisharanacharya (Died Magsir Sudi 12, 1856 V.S.—1799 A.D.)
11. Ramacharya (Died Kartik Sudi 10, 1861 V.S.—1804 A.D.)
12. Sitaramacharya (Died Magh Vadi 9, 1885 V.S.—1828 A.D.)
13. Hariprasadacharya.
14. Hariballabhacharya.
15. Harisharanacharya.
16. Ramodharacharya[47] —Nominated by the Maharaja of Jaipur in 1943.

Madhuracharya who was the *Mahant* of Galta at the time of Jai Singh was the first *Mahant* on the *Gaddi* to write books. He wrote a few books in Sanskrit and supported what is called the *Madhur upasana* of Rama. This form of devotion to Rama had started sometime at the end of the 16th century when Tulsi Das also wrote about the joyful and amorous life of Rama and Sita in the *Uttara Kanda* of his *Geetawali.* The literature on *Madhur upasana* of Rama was an imitation of the literature of the *Krishna Bhakti* branch of *Vaishnavism*, and though it depicted only the love life of Rama with his lawfully married wife Sita, in course of time it had become quite erotic.

The effect that these erotic writings had on the lives of the people, specially on the lives of those who were supposedly living celibate lives in the *Vāishnava* monasteries can well be imagined. One of the important acts of Jai Singh was the reformation of these monasteries and he did it in two ways. First he made the *Vaishnava vairagis* follow the Hindu *Chaturvarna* rule in a strict manner, secondly he permitted marriages among them. In the *Kapaddwara* records (No. 1520) there is a document in

47. The names in the list were obtained from the present Mahant Ramodharcharya. The dates of deaths are those mentioned on their respective *chhatris.*
48. This is the position in Bengal even to-day.

the form of a bond. In this bond which is undated Madhuracharya agreed to follw strictly the *Chaturvarna* rules and to permit marriages for the inmate male members if they so wished after the age of fifteen. The bond reads as follows:—

Bond S. No. 559 K.D. No. 1520
Undated.

श्री

लिखित श्रीमघुराचार जइ (जी) इह समत है

इह अर्थ स्वामी सुखराम को समत

(वैष्णव)

लिखित समस्त रामानंदी महांत वैष्यवन की सर्व शास्त्र प्रमाण करियो निश्चय कियो जो परस्पर तुछिष्ट भोजन को करे नहीं चारि वरण मिलि के भोजन न करे, एक पंक्ति में न्योर रसोया परोसि जो बालक वे वैष्णव होय ताको पंदरा वर्ष लों सेवा पूजा में राखि जे आगे अपनी जाति में विवाह करि दी जे वो वाको दृढ़ निश्चय होय तो परीक्षा करिके ब्रह्मचारी राखि जै और सब महांत वैष्णव आंसज को सिस्य न करे ब्राह्मण क्षत्रिय वैश्य इन तीन वरण को जनेकु बीजे। तो विधिपूर्वक बीजे। शूर्द को न दीजे या समत में जो नर है सो श्रीठाकुर जी को सब महोत गे। यवन को श्रीमहाराजाधिराज जी को गुनहगार अपराधी दंडनीय है सब रामानंदी महोंत वैंष्य व अरुणोदय बेद माने पे नवा कपाल वैंध न माने कपाल विद्या एकादशी सर्वथा न करे। श्रीरामानुजाचार्य जी को यों ही संमत है कपाल वैंध सर्वथा माने जो कपाल वैंधीना ने सों रामानुज संम्प्रदाय वाह्य श्रीठाकुर जी की श्री महाराजाधिराज को अपराधी दण्डनीय है।

This permission to marry was not confined to the *Ramanandi Sadhus* of the Galta only but extended to other *Vaishnavas* also, though it seems that the *Ramanandi Sadhus* who were disciples of *Balananda*, the founder of the militant *Naga* sect of Jaipur, did not allow marriage to their members. By removing the ban on marriage of most of the *Vaishnava Vairagis*, Jai Singh removed one of the most important causes of corruption among these people.

Jai Singh's interest in enforcing the *Chaturvarna* rule was noticed even in Bengal. *Kapaddwara documents* numbers 1506 and 1507 are two letters in Bengali from Raja Krishna Chandra—evidently Raja Krishna Chandra Rai (1710-1783) of Nadia. The first letter is a *sammati patra* intimating the rights of *Shudras*. The second letter is to the effect that *Shudras* are not entitled to worship. Document number 1518 in *Kapaddwara* is a petition in Hindi from Brij Ballabh, promising that he would repent for the *Shudra Mantra Deeksha* and would live according to *Vedic* principles.

It would appear from the above as if Jai Singh was assuming the position of the defender of the Hindu faith. As stated earlier he was not only a learned man but also the most important Hindu chief in northern India in his later years. The position of the defender of Hinduism therefore came to him naturally.

Gaudiya Vaishnavas

Jai Singh died a devotee of *Govindadeva* whose image he had installed in 1735 in his palace in Jaipur. The image was originally found by Roop Goswami, one of the six famous *goswamis* of the Chaitanyite sect, in Vrindaban. Four other important *Gaudiya Vaishnava* images were also brought to Jaipur from Vrindaban. They are:—

	Name	*Location*	*Original Finder*
1.	Gopinath[49]	Purani Basti	Madho Pandit
2.	Radha Damodar	Chaura Rasta	Jeeva Goswami
3.	Gokulananda	Tripolia Bazar	Vishvanath chakravarti
4.	Radhavinode	Tripolia Bazar	Loknath Goswami

We do not have much evidence about the time of shifting of most of these images from Vrindaban to Jaipur. The temple of *Gopinath* is mentioned, as stated earlier, in Girdhari's *Bhojanasar* (1739) but there are no other contemporary documents available about this image. Documents exist only in the case of *Radha Damodar* image. According to these, this image

49. The temple gets an annuity of Rs. 34,438.69 from the Jagir department in lieu of the jagir villages held by it. This is the highest amount of annuity obtained by a temple in Jaipur. The second highest annuity is given to Govindadeva temple. This amounts to Rs. 32,063.13. Information given by the Jagir Commissioner, Rajasthan in May 1974.

was brought to Jaipur at the time of Madho Singh, son of Jai Singh, on Magha Krishna Navami of Samvat 1817, i.e. 1760 A.D. and a daily bhog of Rs. 3/- was ordered by the ruler for this image. In 1796 the image was taken back to Vrindaban but was brought back to Jaipur in 1821 A.D. on Jyestha Shukla Navami.

The *Govindadeva* temple of Jaipur is important enough to be discussed separately.[51] The image that arrived in Amer sometime about 1714, was originally in the famous temple built by Raja Man Singh in Vrindaban. From Vrindaban the image was brought to Jaipur. When the image was installed in the city palace here, its *sebait* was one Jagan Nath. The *sebaits* of Govindadeva were all celibates from the time of Roop Goswami (1490-1563). Jagan Nath was the first *sebait* to marry, perhaps in accordance with the permission of Jai Singh that all *Vaishnava Sadhus* might marry if they so desired. Since that time, the *sebaitship* of this temple has descended from father to son.

There is no doubt that Jai Singh was a great devotee of this image of Govindadeva; but he was perhaps not a *Vaishnava* of the *Gaudiya* school. In fact in matters of religious philosophy he did not have any strong views and preferred to be liberal in outlook. This is mentioned by Shri Venkatacharya of the Ramanuj school of *Vaishnavism* in *Bhedasthapanam*. The author while dedicating the book to Jai Singh described this quality of his in the following words:—

> "As Narasimha, the incarnation of God, eliminated the difference between man and lion by conjoining the head of a lion with the body of a man, in the same way King Jai Singh wiped off the controversies of the different schools of thought by propounding that they voiced one and the same fact."[52]

50. Another image, known as Madan Mohan founded by Sanatan Goswami was originally brought to Jaipur from Vrindaban, but was taken to Karauli, by the Maharaja of Karauli.
51. For details see Chapter VII(i).
52. Quoted in the article "Pothikhana of Jaipur" by Shri Gopal Narain Bahura in *Sanskrit Kalpetara*, Jaipur (1972). The manuscript of *Bhedasthapanam* is in the Pothikhana. In the same article Bahura mentions another manuscript of the *Pothikhana* named *Siddhantaikya*

Jai Singh tried to make his new capital an important Hindu centre and to some extent he succeeded in his aim. Jaipur today has more temples than perhaps any other city in northern India except Varanasi. Most of the temples of Jaipur are dedicated to either Krishna in his *Vrindavan Leela* form, or to Ramchandra. It is thus a sacred city for both the followers of *Rama Bhakti* and the *Krishna Bhakti* branches of *Vaishnavism*.

Prakashika (Light on the unity of all Theologies). This was written by the *Pandits* of the court of Jai Singh and corrected by Jai Singh himself. Jai Singh at the end of the correction mentions Chaitanya and his disciples with reverence:

श्रीचैतन्य पदारविन्द मधुप श्री रूप सनातन
श्रीजीवादि महात्मानां करुणया राजाधिराजैः स्वयम्

....

इति श्री महाराजाधिराज श्री जयसिंह देव चरिता ।
तत्परिशोधिता च सिद्धान्तैक्य प्रकाशिका समाप्ता ॥

CHAPTER II

Planning of the Jaipur City

I

TOWN PLANNING IN INDIA—A BRIEF SURVEY

Town planning means the preparation and implementation of a suitable ground plan to meet the needs of a particular type of town. In other words, it means putting down on paper the plans of roads, residential areas, sewage system, water supply system, playgrounds, education centres, office areas, recreational centres and a host of other things, and then of course implementing this plan. The plan must not only fit the topography of the place and be suitable for its climate but it should also meet the needs of the society according to its habits and customs, festivals, fairs, economic conditions, means of livelihood etc. All these factors are taken into consideration by the modern town planners. Also, the plans will vary depending on the nature of the towns. An administrative town like New Delhi or Chandigarh will have a plan which is different from the plan of an industrial town like Durgapur. Town planning today is a very difficult art, for it requires not only a vast knowledge of the society for whom the town is being planned, but also a political sense to estimate how much planning the people would voluntarily accept, even if there is no political power available to enforce the faithful implementation of the plan.

This last point is important; for, accepting a town plan involves accepting a discipline. Such discipline can be enforced either by a kind of a dictator or can arise from the traditions of a community. Such a discipline has been lacking in this country especially in northern India. In any town in this region, whether it be Mathura or Moradabad, there is a constant attempt by the householders and residents to encroach upon the existing roads and make these narrower and uneven on the sides, or construct some platform overnight on the roadside and to place a crude image and start its puja, etc. There is no sense of keeping to a ground plan of the locality in villages either. One can see evidence of this tendency in some parts of Jaipur also. The roads and lanes in most of the *Chowkries* of Jaipur are straight and intersect each other at right angles. *Chowkri* Top-Khana Hazuri, on the other hand, was populated later when the ruler had lost interest in town planning. This *Chowkri* has grown up in a haphazard manner like a slum with winding lanes having pools of stagnant water on them.

Before the advent of modern ideas of town or village planning, town planning meant mainly two things, a ground plan for roads and perhaps drainage for storm water, and secondly in India, the distribution of the various castes and occupations in different sections of the village or town. Each castes occupied one section of the town or village. As far a street plan it is found that villages in northern India do not observe a plan. The village lanes are not straight and houses are built without keeping the civic needs in view.

In the year 1959-61, the Anthropological Survey of India carried out a survey of the various aspects of village life in India.[1] It was found in this survey that there are mainly two types of villages in India—the cluster type and the linear type. In the first type are villages which are clusters of huts either separated as in Bengal, or attached to each other as sometimes in the Uttar Pradesh or Rajasthan. These clusters of huts are put up in a haphazard manner in the residential area of the village. There is no provision of a public street or of rain water drainage, with the result that it generally becomes difficult to move from one part of the village to another during the rains.

In the linear type, or in the terminology of the *Shilpashastras*, the *Dandaka* type of villages, there is a main street in the village and the houses are arranged on both sides of it. If the population increases, and more houses are required, streets

1. A Bengali translation of the report of this Survey was published as a special number of the *Sahitya Parishad Patrika* in August 1961.

parallel to the first one, and cross streets are added, so that the village takes a rectangular shape. The streets also drain out the storm water.

The survey showed that the linear type of villages which may be considered as villages with ground plans, are found all over South India, but are not found anywhere in northern India except in parts of Gujarat and Orissa. In the rest of northern India and Maharashtra the villages are of the cluster type without any plan whatsoever.

No wonder then that there is no tradition of town planning in northern India, for towns are after all only overgrown villages. To find a planned town in northern India before Jaipur we have to go back almost to the proto-historic times when we have the example of the city of Mohenjo-daro but we have not yet been able to get a continuing link between the Mohenjo-daro civilization and the present civilization of India. However, Mohenjo-daro was indeed a planned town, and from the following quotation, it would appear that though a much smaller town Mohenjo-daro's planning had some similarity with the planning of Jaipur:

> "The mounds which represent the city of Mahenjo-daro today cover a square mile, and surface indications of some of the main streets can be traced and have been confirmed by excavation which has also revealed the details of the smaller streets and lanes in some areas. Combining these pieces of evidence, the published plan suggests that the basic layout was that of a grid iron of main streets running north-south and east-west, dividing the area into blocks of roughly equal size and approximately rectangular, 800 feet east-to-west and 1200 feet north-to-south. The existence of six and probably seven of these blocks has been proved by excavation, as have two main streets at right angles (East street and First street), and part of a third to the east of and parallel with First street. The denudation of the edges of the mounds renders the perimeter of the city uncertain in outline and exact position, but if the layout indicated by the central street-plan was continued symmetrically, we would have a square city a mile across comprising twelve major building blocks in three rows of four, east-to-west. The

central western block, on this reconstructed layout would be the citadel, occupying a position commensurate with the distinction implied by its foundation. The main streets, unpaved, seems to have been up to 30 feet wide, and within the main blocks was an irrregular network of small roads, lanes and alleys roughly following the general lines of the layout and dividing the blocks into individual houses."[2]

In pre-modern times India had comparatively few large towns considering the size and population of the country. People lived in villages mainly. Sometimes a village would grow into a town either because it was a centre of pilgrimage, or because it was situated on the bank of a river and was thus suitable to be a trade centre, and in some rare cases also because it became the capital of a kingdom. We have the examples of Varanasi, Pataliputra, Taxila, Kausambi, Sravasti, Ujjaini, Agra, Lahore, Delhi, Allahabad, etc. Some of these towns are dead and only their ruins have been dug out, but some others including Varanasi, perhaps the oldest living city in the world, are still flourishing. There is no indication of town planning in any of these cities—not even in Dhara Nagari, the capital of Raja Bhoj who was the author of the *Samarangana Sutradhar*—a treatise on architecture and town planning. In fact with two important exceptions there is no evidence that there was even one straight and wide road in any of the towns. The two exceptions are Taxila and Shahjahanabad (Delhi). In this latter town, there were according to Bernier[3] two straight roads "leading into the square (in front of the Red Fort) may be five and twenty, or thirty ordinary paces in width. They run in a straight line nearly as far as the eye can reach; but the one leading to the Lahori Gate is much the larger." It appears that at last these two roads in Shahjahanabad were planned.

The excavations at Taxila have revealed three successive city-sites, Bhir Mound, Sirkap and Sirsukh. Of these Sirkap had a planned layout. "The second city Sirkap, founded by the Bactrian Greeks in the second century B.C. and later built by the Scytho-Parthians' on the typically Greek chess-board pattern,

2. S. Piggot, *Pre-Historic India*, p. 165.
3. Bernier, *Travels in the Mogul Empire*, Oxford, 1914, p. 245.

with streets cutting one another at right angles and regularly aligned blocks of buildings (pl.LIII), provides a contrast in layout. The houses here are built neatly of coarsed rubble-stone (pl. LIV), except in the Parthian levels, where diaper-masonary is introduced. To an earlier mud-rampart a stone defensive wall 3½ miles long, with rectangular bastions at irregular intervals was added in the mid-first century B.C., probably by the Indo-Parthion ruler Azes I." "The total occupation of the town, with six or seven strata, lasted till the arrival of the Kushans, who laid a new city, Sirsukh, within a fortified rectangle. This city has, however, largely remained unexcavated."[4]

The photograph[5] of Sirkap (pl. LIII) shows the main street to be a wide and straight one, with side streets intersecting it at right angles. Thus Sirkap, the second city of Taxila was indeed a planned one; but the founders of the city were Greeks who planned it in their own manner. .

It has been conjectured that Sisupalgarh in Orissa was also a planned town. B.B. Lal published an account of his excavation at Sisupalgarh in 1948 in Ancient India.[6] Sisupalgarh is a place about 2 to 3 kilometres south-east of Bhubaneshwar. During the course of excavation "an excellently laid out fort of the pre-Christian era came to light".

To quote him again,

> "The fort forms a rough square on plan. Oriented approximately along the cardinal directions, each of its sides measures about three quarters of a mile long, thus enclosing an area a little over half-a-square mile. The contours clearly suggest the existence of corner-towers (Pl. XXIX-A)[7] and eight large gateways, two on each side besides about the same number of smaller openings (pl. XXIX-B) distributed all over the perimeter. The gateways are so placed that if the distance between two corner-towers of any side is trisected, a gateway will be found at or near each point of trisection. Such a disposition clearly suggests a

4. *Ancient India*, No. 9, Delhi, 1953, p. 134.
5. Reproduced on p. 49.
6. *Ancient India*, No. 5, Delhi, 1949, p. 64.
7. Reproduced on p. 51.

regular planning not only of the fortification but presumably also of the streets inside, which are likely to have run east-west and north-south, connecting the opposite gateways in a grid-pattern."

However, no indication of the existence of such streets have been found in the actual excavation, and the existence of a grid pattern can only be conjectured. Even aerial photographs do not show that such streets existed. All that we definitely know therefore is that Sisupalgarh had boundary walls which formed about a perfect square with each side three-fourth of a mile long and with a gate placed at a point of trisection of each side. There is no evidence that the town or the fort inside the walls was a planned one.

One peculiarity of the fort or town walls of Sisupalgarh is that these walls are not oriented exactly along the cardinal directions, but are turned about 13 degrees in the clockwise direction. The Jaipur city walls are turned 15 degrees away from the cardinal direction clockwise, i.e. almost by the same angle. This point was noticed by G. Bretzler in his Ph.D. thesis.[8] Bretzler had wondered whether *Shilpashastras* prescribe this slight deviation from the cardinal directions.

It may thus not be unsafe to conclude that there is as yet no definitive evidence of a planned city in India in the nearly two thousand years which passed from the time of Taxila and until the foundation of Jaipur in 1727/1728 A.D.[9] Shahjahanabad had only two planned streets. In any case none of the cities built in India before Jaipur, tried to follow the Indian texts on town planning. Whether the planners of Jaipur actually followed any of these texts is not clear.

Though we have not been able to find any town planned according to *Shilpashastras* prior to Jaipur, there is surprisingly no dearth of literature in India giving directions on town planning. In the earlier texts such as *Manusmriti* (vii. 76) the

8. *Jaipur—Studien Zur Stadt—Und Sozialgeographic einer Indischen Gross Stadt*. Ruhr University, Bochum, 1970, p. 142.
9. It has to be remembered that horizontal excavations of town-sites in India have not been extensive so far and hence the discovery of town plans should not mostly be expected. Nor are such excavations possible where ancient town-sites are still inhabited.

directions are elementary and are only confined to building the King's palace in the centre of a fort. No directions are given about the construction of the fort which was supposed to be almost a town. In fact this fort where the king lived was the capital town.

In Kautilya's *Arthashastra*[10] there are further details about the inside of the fort or the capital town. "Demarcation of the ground inside the fort shall be made first by opening three royal roads from west to east and three from south to west.

The fort shall contain 12 gates, provided with both a land and water way and a secret passage.

Chariot roads, royal roads, and roads leading to *dronamukha*, *Sthaniya*, country parts and pasture grounds shall each be four dandas (24 feet) in width . . . . ". . . In the midst of the houses of the people of all the castes and to the north from the centre of the ground inside the King's palace, facing either north or the east, shall . . . be constructed, occupying one-ninth of the whole site inside the fort."

Royal teachers, priests, sacrificial place, water reservoir and ministers shall occupy sites east by north to the palace."

"On the eastern side, merchants trading in scents, garland, grains, and liquids, together with expert artisans and the people of Kshatriya caste shall have their habitations . . ."

There are further detailed directions about the location of the habitations of other castes and types of artisans.

It will be seen that at this time the main emphasis of the authors of these shastras was location of the habitations of the various castes. Towns were not distinguished by types or shapes. The reason of course, is that these shastras mainly dealt with other subjects and mentioned town planning and architecture only in passing. Books dealing with these two subjects came later.

No book dealing with town planning only was written in India. Chapters on village and town planning were included in the books mainly dealing with architecture. There are many

10. Kautilya's *Arthashastra*, p. 53.

such books dealing with architecture in Sanskrit. Three of the more important of these books are the *Manasara*, the *Mayamata* and the *Samarangana Sutradhara.* The last of these books was said to have been written by Raja Bhoja of Dhara Nagari. In that case its date should be around 1020 A.D. The other two books were written earlier.[11] There are some *Agama* books which sometimes deal with architecture and town planning also. One of them is *Kamikagama.*

The most important of these books which are called *Shilpashastras* is the *Manasara.* The *Manasara* deals with town planning not in the chapter on towns but in the chapter on villages. The chapter on towns begins with the statement that towns are only large villages. The smallest town should have a size 100 *dandas* × 200 *dandas*, and the largest 7200 × 14400 *dandas*.

The *Manasara* describes 8 types of villages. These differ from one another in street planning, folk planning and temple planning. These types are called *Dandaka, Sarvatobhadra, Nandayarta. Padmaka, Svastika, Prastara, Karmuka* and *Chaturmukha.* Mayamuni, the author of *Mayamata,* bases his classification mainly upon the planning of streets and mentions the following types—*Dandaka, Svastika, Prastara, Prakirnaka, Nandayarta, Paraga, Padma* and *Sripratishthita. Kamikagama* adds four more types to the list given by *Manasara* and *Mayamata.* These are *Sampatkara, Kumbhaka, Srivatsa* and *Vaidika.*

For northern India this impressive list of 15 types of villages is of no practical significance since none of the plans has so far been actually applied in any towns past or present known to us. In some of the types described above, the boundary of the village (or- town) should be more or less circular as in the case of *Nandyavarta* or *Padmaka.* Both these are named after flowers. In one case the shape should be a semi-circle. Some plans give the village a square or rectangular shape. These are *Dandaka, Sarvatobhadra, Svastika* and

11. P.K. Acharya who edited and published the Text of *Manasara*, thought that this book was written in the Gupta period and *Mayamata* was a later work. The different opinions on the antiquity of these books have been discussed by D.N. Shukla in his *Vastu Shastra*, Vol. I, pp. 154 et. seq.

Prastara. Of these four, the last has become significant, because it is widely believed that Jaipur was built according to the *Prastara* plan. We may examine how far this classification of Jaipur is justifiable

According to *Manasara*, a village or town built on the *Prastara* plan is square or rectangular in shape. Space is left between the town wall and the buildings by a road which goes all round the town. This space is called *Paishacha.* The town is divided into four, nine or sixteen wards by a network of appropriate number of highways. These highways are variously widened 6, 7, 8, 9, or 11 *dandas.* In the wards again the roads are placed according to the chess board pattern. But all the wards are not divided into equal number of plots by these roads. One is divided into 9 plots, another into 16, the third into 25 and so on. This distribution in the division is accounted for by the degree of rank and wealth of persons that are to occupy the ward.

In the north the village is quartered by the *Vaishya* class and in the borders called the *Paishacha* plot, all the artisans and craftsmen. Accommodation for the royal palace, shrines, courts, hospitals, colleges and other buildings is made in the same way as in the *Sarvatobhadra* plan. The village is enclosed by walls and ditches with four principal gates on the sides and four subsidiary ones in the corners. The number of gates may also be 12 or more.

Jaipur however is neither a square, nor a rectangular in shape. It has an irregular shape. No road goes round the town. The number of wards into which the town is divided is seven, or eight if the palace is also counted as a ward, not 4 or 9 or 16. The number of highways are five. It is altogether strange therefore that the plan of Jaipur should have been described as *Prastara.*[12]

12. B.B. Dutt in his *Town Planning in Ancient India* (1925) has mentioned that Jaipur was built according to the *Prastara* plan. This statement is repeated by Shukla in his *Vastu Shastra* (Vol. I, p. 271). Shukla states that the plan of Jaipur is "known technically as Prastara".

It might be worthwhile finding out how this theory that Jaipur was built as per the *Prastara* plan started. I believe that the first mention of this theory is in Havell's *Indian Architecture* (1913). Havell in his book simply said, "the plan given by Ram Raz called

II

PLANNING OF THE JAIPUR CITY

It is thus quite obvious that the plan of the Jaipur city does not correspond in any manner to the description of the *Prastara* plan. Jaipur is actually divided into two portions by one long road running east to west from the Surajpole gate to the Chandpole gate. On the south of these roads there are 5 rectangular blocks of unequal shapes and sizes. On the north of this road, there is one square, a block containing the city palace, and another block, *Puranibasti*, whose southern and eastern sides are straight roads but northern and north-western boundaries are irregular. A glance at the map of the present walled city of Jaipur will show that its shape is not that of any regular geometrical figure.

A few plans of the Jaipur city at the time of its construction are preserved in the city palace. Most of these are land allotment plans for particular areas of the city but map No. LS/14[13] is important. This map appears to be a progress report of the construction of the city. It is not according to scale since the palace is shown to be much smaller in area than it actually is. Some of the very important points worth-noting in this map are the following:

1. As originally planned, Jaipur was to have only four rectangular blocks, namely those occupied today by the (1) palace, (2) Purani Basti, (3) Topkhana Desh and (4) a block combining Modikhana and Visheshvarji. No road was originally

Prastara is very similar to that of Jaipur". Havell makes a reference to plate XLV of Ram Raz's "*Essay on the Architecture of the Hindus*" (1834), but he also says, "The orientation marked on the plate does not seem to correspond with the quotations from the Shastras given in the text." In Ram Raz's book we do not find any orientation marked on plate XLV. This plate gives a sketch of the Prastara type as understood by Ram Raz. In the text also there is no quotation from Shastras about the Prastara type. All that is mentioned is "6. Prastara (that which has the shape of a conch)"; (p. 42). A copy of the sketch is given on page 58.

It appears that a stray and unsubstantiated remark of Havell has been taken as authoritative by later writers.

13. A photograph of the map which shows the progress report written on it is given on p. 60.

planned to divide these two last named blocks. It is not quite clear when the present Chaura Rasta and the Tripolia gate were planned and built. But clearly Chaura Rasta was never built like a bazar, just as the Johri Bazar was. The shops on this road appear to be more modern. There are today about 10 important temples facing Chaura Rasta.

2. The area now occupied by Chowkris, Ghat Darwaja Topkhana Hazuri and Ramchandarji was left completely undeveloped in the beginning. The map shows that the area was full of depressions, sand dunes etc. These parts were included within the city limits by completing the city wall at a subsequent date.

3. Originally only four bazars were planned for the city. These were later named as Johri Bazar, Sireh Deori Bazar, Kishanpole Bazar and Gangori Bazar. According to the progress report given on the map, 162 shops were constructed by the State on each side of each of these bazars, except that there were only 144 shops on the western side of the Kishanpole bazar. The area occupied by the 162 shops was 18 bighas in all cases. Only the 144 shops on one side of Kishanpole Bazar occupied 16 bighas. All these shops were therefore of uniform size and shape and gave the new city a planned look.[14]

4. A bazar was also contemplated but not constructed at that time in what is now called Chandpole Bazar. Tripolia bazar was however not thought of at all. There was also no provision for Ramganj and other bazars on the eastern side of the city in the original plan.

5. Eighty-eight shops were under construction in the corner of the Kishanpole Bazar and what is now known as the Chandpole Bazar. These shops must have been pulled down later.

6. Two Katlas were contemplated in the squares now built for the Sanganeri gate and the Ajmeri Gate. Perhaps these were never built.

The date of this map is not clear. The V.S. year corresponding to A.D. 1725 is mentioned on it. If this date has been correctly put, it would appear that Jai Singh started the construction of his city in that year but the official foundation ceremony was performed later.

14. One is reminded of the Connaught Circus in New Delhi.

Both from this map and the map of the walled city of Jaipur today, it is clear that originally the city had four blocks which have now grown to seven blocks. As the population grew people occupied the undeveloped land and were thus called "*Koocha Upar*" settlers.

Vidhyadhar: The Chief Assistant of Jai Singh

The original plan of the city of Jaipur was probably prepared by Jai Singh himself with the assistance of his ministers and other officers. The name of the Officer mentioned most often in this case is that of Vidhyadhar. Tod writing nearly eighty years later observes: "The merit of the design and execution (of the city) is assigned to Vidhyadhar, a native of Bengal, one of the most eminent coadjutors of the prince in all his scientific pursuits, both astronomical and historical."[15]

How much hand Vidhyadhar had in designing the city is not clear from the official records. In fact Vidhyadhar was promoted[16] as a Minister, 'Desh Diwan'—only in 1729, more than a year after the founding of the city. Official records however show that Vidhyadhar had been rewarded a number of times for his good work as an engineer. He was thus perhaps the chief architect and engineer for the buildings, both State and private. Apparently the construction of even private buildings was strictly controlled, and their plans had to be approved by Vidhyadhar. When the city was founded, many rich merchants were invited to settle down and construct their houses in the city. One such invitation,[17] to Ghasiram Murlidhar Purohit mentions that the building should be constructed according to the direction of Vidhyadhar: 'Tune Vidhyadhar Kahe tin maphik kijo."

The land allotment plans available in the City Palace show that areas in rectangular plots were allotted to private citizens and temples etc. Some plots were kept reserved for prominent persons. Where the buildings were likely to be constructed

15. Tod, *op. cit.*, Vol. II, p. 289.
16. Vidhyadhar's service record as given in the *Dastur Komwar* is quoted in Appendix IX.
17. The invitation letter is quoted in Chapter II(iii).

soon, directions, regarding the buildings were given. One example,[18] is quoted:

पायाली सामराटजी कैलानी—बीघा 63-3/4; हवेली का दासा बराबरी नीव चौड़ी गज— 1-1/2, ऊंची गज—2-1/2, दूसरी भीत चौड़ी गज—1, ऊंची गज—2-1/2, अरजो बाड़ गज—1, नीव ऊपर चौड़ी गज—1, ऊंची गज—7; नीव सुद्धा=9-1/2.

In other words, the building line, the height of the ground floor and the height of the buildings were controlled. Also, flimsy buildings were not allowed to be constructed.

So far as the State buildings were concerned Vidhyadhar was personally in charge of their construction also. The records[19] of the Building Department show that the building materials were to be delivered to Vidhyadhar and Rai Sheonath, another minister of Jai Singh.

Though the official records do not mention Vidhyadhar's contribution in the planning of the city, it was believed by his contemporaries that it was he who had prepared its detailed design. Girdhari writing in his *Bhojanasar* twelve years after the foundation of the city said, "He (Jai Singh) said to Vidhyadhar that a city should be founded here. Jainiwas should come within the city, this is my wish. There should be many cross-roads with shops on them. The backyards of the houses should meet together."[20]

Vidhyadhar, in course of time, became the most favourite minister of Jai Singh. He was held in great regard even at the time of Ishvari Singh, the son and successor of Jai Singh.

We have contemporary evidence in the writing of Shri Krishna Bhatta six years after the death of Jai Singh. In his *Ishvarvilas Mahakavya* there is a panegyric in honour of Vidhyadhar, in five slokas[21]:—

10.38 "The King's (Jai Singh's) minister was Vidhyadhar—a Bengali of Vedic Gaura Caste. He was good looking and easily accessible. He was well versed in Arts. The Rajadhiraj held him in high regard for his pure wisdom."

18. On Map No. LS/17 in the City Palace Museum.
19. *Siyaha Imarat*, Bhadva Sudi 3, 1793 V.S.,, Rajasthan State Archives, Bikaner.
20. Quoted in Appendix VII.
21. Translated kindly by Shri G.N. Bahura, M.A.

10.39 "The famous Rajadhiraj Sawai Jai Singh founded the beautiful city of Jaipur by dint of his (Vidhyadhar's) wisdom and knowledge. The beautiful city of Jaipur gives pleasure to the inhabitants of all the three worlds."

10.40 "The King Sawai Jai Singh of his own accord handed over his son Ishvari Singh by name and who deserved the glory of Kingship, to Vidhyadhar who was the chief in the Ministry headed by Rajmal."

10.41 "The wealth acquired by the possession of all lands, the province, the cities, and the forts and the whole population are on one side, and Vidhyadhar like an ocean of all virtues is on the other. (Vidhyadhar's virtues are more valuable than all the assets of the kingdom)."

10.42 "The Rajadhiraj Sawai Jai Singh, who had seen all manner of ups and downs during his life was unmoved even at the time of his end, when he placed the Kumar (his son Ishvari Singh) in the lap of Arya Vidhyadhar in the presence of all the ministers headed by Rajmal."

It might be of interest to know how a Bengali became a Minister in the court of Sawai Jai Singh. The descendants of Vidhyadhar were living in Jaipur up to the early years of this century. Babu Meghnath Bhatacharya, Vice-Principal of the Maharaja's College, Jaipur collected the family history of Vidhyadhar from these people and published an article[22] on Vidhyadhar in the Bangiya Sahitya Parishad Patrika Vol. XI in 1905.

It appears from this article that Vidhyadhar was a descendant to the priest who was brought from Bengal along with the image called Siladevi by Raja Man Singh. This priest Ratnagarbha Sarvabhauma Bhattacharya was a Paschatya Vaidika Brahman.

Ratnagarbha had seven daughters whom he married to his class of Brahmans brought from Bengal. Two of these daughters were married to two brothers—Rajendra Chakravarty and Ramnarain Chakravarty. Rajendra had a son Santendra, also

22. The article was translated by Bimalacharan Deb and published in the *Annals of the Bhandarkar Oriental Research Institute*, Baroda, Vol, 28, 1947, pp. 212-218.

known as Santoshram. Vidhyadhar was the son of this Santoshram. Vidhyadhar according to this article was introduced to Jai Singh by his maternal uncle, Kishanram, who was a minister of Jai Singh. Jai Singh was said to have been greatly impressed by the intelligence and knowledge of Vidhyadhar.

If the information given in this article is correct, Vidhyadhar was a Chakravarti and not a Bhattacharya as is widely believed.[23]

The Date of the Foundation Ceremony

Jai Singh and his ministers planned the city keeping in view the topography of the area, and the existing Jai Niwas garden.[24] The foundation laying ceremony of the city was performed on Pausha Badi 1, 1784 V.S. (29th November, (New Style) 1727).[25]

We know the exact date of the foundation laying ceremony of the city. These are given in two documents both quoted in full on pages 8 and 9 of the introduction to the printed edition of *Buddhi Vilas*. The first document mentions that the priest incharge of the ceremony, Jagannath Samrat, was awarded some land near Hathroi on the outskirts of Jaipur city. The second document mentions that in all Rs. 1083/5/- were spent in the ceremony. The first few lines of the latter document read as follows:

डोल करार मिती फाल्गुन बदी १, सम्वत १७८४ पुन्य जो सवाई जयपुर नवो बसायो तीठँ मिती पोस बदी १, १७८४ विन्दायक सांती, वा वासुत सांती, नौगिरह सांती करवाई त्यानें लागया सो रुपया १०८३-५-० के वास्ते स्वाभरास्ट नाथजी की मिती माह बदि ११, सम्वत १७८४ अ्रर्ज पहुंची हुक्म हुआ.........

23. For instance, M.L. Sharma in his history of- Jaipur State says, "The City was planned by a Bengali Brahman, named Vidyadhar Bhattacharya. . . . . ." M.L. Sharma, *op. cit.*, p. 153.
24. *Jai Niwas* garden was constructed in 1725 (See Appendix VI) Girdhari in his *Bhojanasar* says that Jai Singh ordered that the new city should be so constructed that Jai Niwas should come within the city (*Doha* No. 183, Appendix VII).
25. According to the Girdhari's *Bhojanasara*, the date of foundation of the city was Pausha Sudi 1, 1784 V.S. (*Doha* Nos. 190 and 191, Appendix VII).

Official Recognition as the Capital of the State

The new city was officially recognised by the emperor Muhammad Shah to be the capital of the State in the 15th year (1733) of his reign. The Parwana preserved in the Kapaddwara reads as follows[26]:

परवाना अज जाफर कुली खां खाने जाद मोहम्मद शाह बादशाह बनाम चौधरी कानूगोयान मुतसिद्यान व रियाया प्रगना सरकार आमेर सूबे अजमेर तारीख १५ जिल्दकाद सन् १५ जलूसी—

महाराजाधिराज सवाई जयसिंहजी ने लिखा है कि अहद मुबारिक में एक नया शहर बइस्म सवाई जयपुर मुत्तस्सिल आमेर आबाद किया है इसलिये आमेर की येवज मोअल्ला में सवाई जयपुर लिखते रहे सो मंजूर हुआ सरिशेत में सवाई जयपुर लिखते रहें ।

Site and the Topographical Restraints

According to the Jaipur Tehsil records the site of the city covered parts of six villages namely—(1) Nahargarh, (2) Talkatora, (3) Santosh Sagar, (4) Moti Katla, (5) Galtaji and (6) Kishanpole.[27]

It is quite possible that some dwelling houses belonging to courtiers and government servants had been constructed at this site even before the official foundation of the city. This is because one royal garden, the Jai Niwas garden, had already been laid there and it is said that the construction of the observatory also had started some years earlier there in 1718.[28]

26. Copy obtained through the courtesy of Shri G.N. Bahura.
27. At present the Jaipur Municipal area includes 39 more villages.
28. The date is not mentioned clearly. It has been indirectly derived. There are seven *slokas* inscribed on the southern side of the *Nadi-valaya Yantra*. The *sloka* "Yasminnahri Chaturshu. . . ." constitutes a problem in algebra. If this problem is solved we get the date Saka 1640, Vaishakh Shukla 9, Friday, Krittika Nakshatra. Saka 1640 corresponds to 1718 A.D. The problem was solved by Late Shri Madhav Purohit Siddhantavagish—a teacher of the then Parikh Pathshala. (Quoted in *Yantra Raj Parichaya*, p. 'tha'). The full *sloka* is given in *Utpattindu Shekhar* by Durga Prasad Dvivedi (Jaipur 1936), pp. 65-66.

The last is a conjecture based on some *slokas* inserted on an instrument in the observatory.

The city therefore had to be planned keeping certain fixed features already in existence. Immediately to the north of the palace area there was a lake now called Talkatora. Another lake just east of this lake was later called Rajamal-ka-Talab. This latter has now been filled up. To the north-east of the palace about two kilometres away there was a marshy land which was later converted into a lake. Formerly there used to flow a stream[29] into this marshy area. The outline of the city was also determined by the hills on the north of the city.

The width of some of the important roads and lanes[30] are as follows :

A

1.	Johari Bazar—Wall to wall	108 ft.
	Johari Bazar—Veranda to Veranda	92 ft.
2.	Haldion ka Rasta	41 ft.
	After some distance from the Johari Bazar crossing this becomes	29 ft.
3.	Gopalji ka Rasta	41 ft.
4.	Moti Singh Bhomia ka Rasta	21 ft.
5.	Sonthliwalon ka Rasta	15 ft.
6.	Chandpole Bazar wall to wall	107 ft.
	Chandpole Bazar Veranda to Veranda	91 ft.
7.	Mishar Rajaji ka Rasta	27 ft.

29. *Dastur Komwar* (Vol. 23 V.S. 1792—as quoted by G.N. Sharma in his '*A Bibliography of Medieval Rajasthan*', Agra 1965) records that a rivulet named Darbhavati was dammed in V.S. 1792 (1735 A.D.) and opened out into a lake called Mansagar. The dam was built under the supervision of an architect Ganga Ram. Mansagar is the name of the lake north of the city in which Jai Mahal is situated. Curiously enough even the old residents of the city do not know the name of the lake as Mansagar; and the map given along with the 1881 census report of Jaipur mentions it merely as the outer lake. I first noticed the name in Rudyard Kipling's book "From Sea to Sea", London, 1900. Later, I found that a reference to Mansagar also occurs in the *Ishvaravilas Mahakavya* where the poet describes that the site of Jai Singh's Ashvamedha was on the bank of the Mansagar lake).

30. Found by actual measurement in March, 1973.

8.	Dinanath ki Gali	20 ft.
9.	Khajanewalon ka Rasta	54 ft.
10.	Jailal Munshi ka Rasta	30½ ft.
11.	Kishanpole Bazar wall to wall	105½ ft.
	Kishanpole Bazar Veranda to Veranda	94½ ft.
12.	Tripolia bazar wall to wall	107 ft.
13.	Road in front of the Hawamahal (Sireh Deori Bazar).	108 ft.

It appears therefore that the width of the main roads was kept at approximately 108 ft. or 72 *hastas* (cubits). Khajanewalon ka Rasta has half this width and Mishar Rajaji ka Rasta is one-fourth of the main roads in width. Other roads do not appear to have been built to any standard width.

Jaipur as a Beautiful City

The city of Jaipur was planned not only to have straight and wide roads but also to achieve an effect of beauty. What impresses an outsider most on seeing Jaipur for the first time is the almost uniform height and similarity of architecture of the houses built on the main roads. This uniformity has been spoilt to some extent by buildings constructed in recent years on the Chaura Rasta, but otherwise most of the other roads have maintained this regularity. This is specially striking on both sides of the Johari Bazar. In some parts of the city the tops of these buildings have been decorated with domes and arches. Most such buildings house some important temples. The beautiful effect of these external decorations are seen on the buildings situated on the east of the Sireh Deori Bazar, northwards from Bari Chopar. This bazar has perhaps one of the most beautiful skylines in the country.

The Final Shape

The plan of Jaipur City as it finally emerged was very simple. There was a main road slightly more than two miles long running west to east from the Chandpole Gate to the Surajpole Gate. South of this main road are four almost equal rectangles. The rectangle opposite the palace has again been broken up into two equal and smaller rectangles by the Chaura Rasta. Thus altogether there are now five rectangles on the south of the main road. The names of these rectangles, all called Chowkris, from west to east are: (1) Topkhana Desh, (2) Modi Khana, (3) Visheshwarji, (4) Ghat Darwaja and (5) Topkhana Hazuri.

On the north of the main road from west to east are the (6) Purani Basti, (7) the Palace and (8) Ramchandraji.

If we consider the two smaller Chowkris—Modi Khana and Visheshwarji—as one, then Jaipur consists of altogether seven blocks of which six are occupied by the citizens and the seventh by the palace. Of these six residential blocks, the development and planning of Chowkri Top Khana Hazuri on the extreme east of the city on the Agra road seems to have been neglected. This Chowkri did not have, and even now does not have the straight roads dividing the blocks in a grid iron pattern. It appears likely that Chowkri Top Khana Hazuri was more or less unpopulated in the beginning and then grew into a large slum as poorer people from outside came and settled down there. That it was the least populated block will be evident from the figures obtained in the census of Jaipur in 1881 and 1891. These are as follows:

		Population in 1881.		Population in 1891.
Purani Basti		18263		18860
Topkhana Desh		20182		20575
Modi Khana	8822		9658	
Visheshwarji	13435	22257	11928	21586
Ghat Darwaja		22121		21015
Topkhana Hazuri		12297		12512
Ramchandraji		18729		18049

The eastern part of Chowkri Ramchandraji is also not well planned. This Chowkri and Chowkri Topkhana Hazuri have at present a high Muslim population, Muslims forming nearly 50% and 40% of the total population in the respective Chowkris. "Chowkri Ramchandraji predominantly occupied by Muslims engaged in 'varque saji' (silver leaves making) and other manual work."[31] "Chowkri Topkhana Hazuri, which was primarily

31. *City Survey Report of Jaipur*, Rajasthan University, 1969, p. 52.

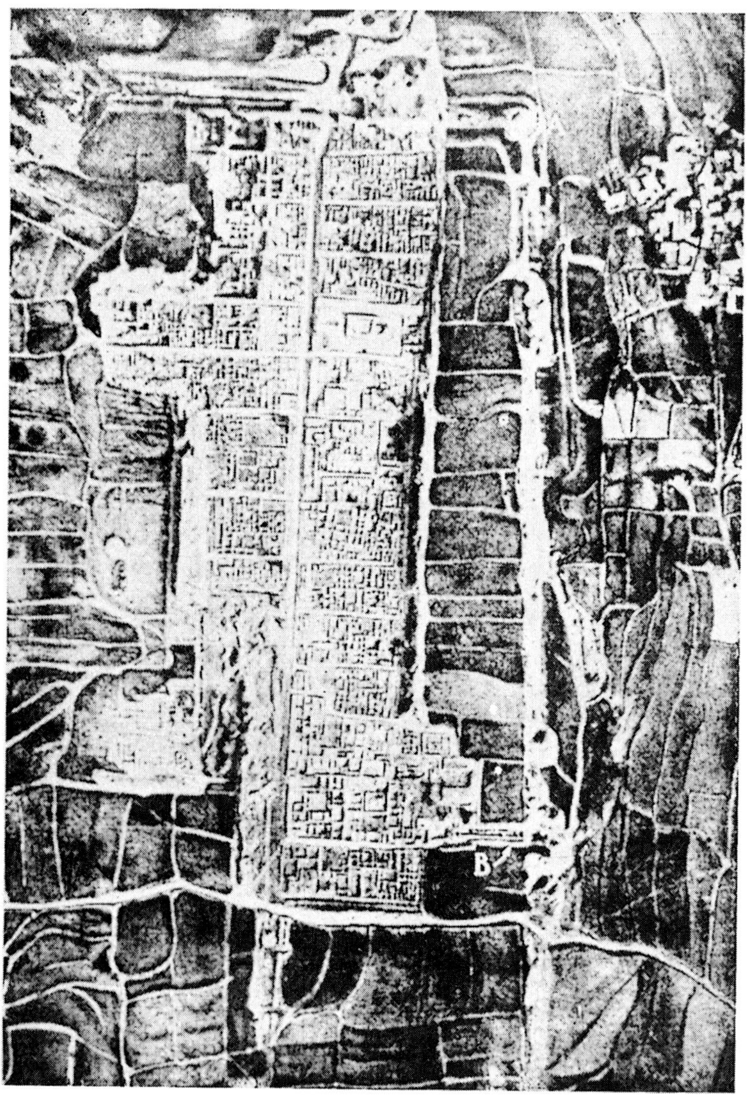

SIRKAP, The Second City of TAXILA.
Plate LIII in *Ancient India*, No. 9

meant for keeping the artillery for the king, was later on occupied by artisans engaged in 'Gota' (silver border) making. They are at present engaged in *Nagina* polishing (cutting of precious stones) work. They have *kachha* houses."[32]

Name of the City

The official name of the city when it was founded was Sawai Jaipur. The name is mentioned in all the documents of the period. For instance, the deed (1728 A.D.) granting land to Jagannath Samrat, who performed the ceremonies connected with the laying of the foundation stone of the city, the invitation letter (1729 A.D.) to Ghasiram Murlidhar to come and settle down in the city, and the emperor's letter (1733 A.D.) recognizing the city as the new capital—all mention the name Sawai Jaipur.[33]

It is not quite clear when and how the title 'Sawai' fell into disuse in the case of the Jaipur City. This title, however, is still used for Sawai Madhopur founded by Sawai Jai Singh's son Sawai Madho Singh in 1759-60. In his *History of the reign of Shah Alum* (1798 A.D.), Francklin calls the town just "Jypore". In fact foreign writers have never used the title 'Sawai' for the town. Tod (1829) also never uses the title while referring to "Jeipoor".

Uptil the end of the eighteenth century and in the early decades of the nineteenth century, Jaipur was also called Jainagar. One of the earliest mentions of Jainagar is in a Bengal document[34] dated 1731 A.D. Bakhtram Shah, who generally calls the city Sawai Jaipur in *Buddhi Vilas* (1770), also mentions Jainagar now and then, e.g.:—

छते राज जयनगर मधि बैठे सहु सावंत

One Ramnarain, also called Rasarasi, a poet in the court of Sawai Pratap Singh, dedicated his book *Sansar-Sara-Vachanika* to the ruler in the following words:[35]

32. *Ibid.*, p. 33.
33. All the documents have been quoted on pp. 70 and 81.
34. *Types of Early Bengali Prose*, Calcutta, 1922, p. 136.
35. Umesh Shastri, *Mahakavi Rasarasi*, Jaipur, 1972, p. 147.

श्री हूजूर के निजिर करी संवत अठारह सौ इकावना फागुन सुदि तीज सूर्यवार को मुकाम सवाई जे नगर

This name finds corroboration in Francklin's book: "Towards the close of the last century, Jysing, a prince no less celebrated for his warlike talents than for his reputation as a philosopher and a cultivator of arts founded the modern city of Jypore, which he called Jynagghar."[36] Francklin's idea about the time of the foundation of the town is of course wrong, but it appears that both the names of the town were fairly commonly known up to the end of the eighteenth century. In his letter of July 27, 1803, to General Lake, Commander-in-chief, Lord Wellesley, the Governor-General of India mentioned Jaipur as "Jyenagur."[37] One might say that the name Jainagar was not quite forgotten even up to the beginning of the present century. In the Imperial Gazetteer (1908) the account of this city is given under the heading "Jaipur City (or Jainagar)".

Roman Spelling of the Name

The spelling of the name of the city in Roman letters as 'Jeypore' was first standardized in the 1818 treaty with the British government.[38] Thereafter, and until the last few years of the nineteenth century the name is spelled as 'Jeypore' in all official documents, administration and census reports, maps, etc. The only prominent exception seems to be the 1876 Gazetteer compiled by Major C.A. Baylay, where it is spelled as Jaipur. In books published later such as the census report for 1891, and in Dr. Hendley's Medico-Topographical Account, 1895, the spelling continued to be Jeypore.

In the last two or three years of the nineteenth century, the official publications suddenly adopted the spelling 'Jaypur'. It is not clear how and when this new spelling was adopted. The Residency Report for 1897-98 uses the spelling 'Jaypur', whereas

36. W. Francklin, *History of the Reign of Shah Alum*, p. 85.
37. Möntgomery Martin, Ed.: *The Despatches, Minutes and Correspondence of the Marques Wellesley*, Vol. III, London, 1836, pp. 211 & 215. See also, C.U. Aitchison, Compl.: *A Collection of Treaties, Engagements and Sanads*, Vol. III, Calcutta, 1932, pp. 66.
38. Aitchison, *op. cit.*, p. 68.

SISUPALGARH, 1948
(Plate XXIX-A in *Ancient India*, No. 5)

in the next year, the Rajputana Administration Report for 1898-99 has the modern spelling 'Jaipur'. In the case of the State government publications, the reports on Public Instruction for both the years 1898 and 1899 write 'Jaypur', whereas the annual reports of the Medical and Meteorological institution never mention this spelling: The report for the year 1898 continued to have 'Jeypore' as before, whereas the one for the year 1899 has the modern spelling 'Jaipur'. It seems likely that the spelling 'Jaypur' lasted officially for only one calendar year viz. 1897. Some government departments adopted it early, and continued to do so for one or two years more. Others probably found that the spelling had changed to 'Jaipur', before they could adopt 'Jaypur'.

From 1898 or 1899 the modern spelling 'Jaipur' was adopted for all purposes official and unofficial.

III

GROWTH OF THE CITY 1727-1800

The population and prosperity of Jaipur appear to have grown at a rapid pace since its foundation. Many rich merchants settled down here in the early years of its growth. The first recorded description of the city is given in Girdhari's *Bhojana-sara* (1739) composed twelve years after the founding of the city. The poet has described that Jaipur with thousands of shops on the *chopars* had become a place of extensive business for traders from many different places:

चौपर केरु बाजार है हाटेक ई हजार ।
देस देस के करत है ब्योपारी ब्योहार ॥१६६॥

Another description of Jaipur written within twenty years of its foundation is given in the *Ishvaravilasa Mahakavya.* This work describes Jaipur as a prosperous city with many tall and palatial buildings. With hyperbole common to the poets of these times, the author says that the flag staffs on the roofs of these buildings were so high that they were a hindrance to the movement of the sun.[39] Many of these large dwelling houses had been built by

39. *Ishvaravilasa Mahakavya*, 3.30.

the businessmen whom Jai Singh had invited to settle down in the newly built town. Quoted below is an invitation given by Jai Singh to Ghasiram Murlidhar, the ancestor of Shri Swarup Narain Purohit, a prominent citizen today:—

सिद्ध श्री महाराजाधिराज महाराजा श्रीसवाई जयसिंह जी देश्रो वचनात घासीराम मुरलीधर दिसेसू परसाद वांच्या। अपरंच तु अपनी खातिर जमा राख सवाई जयपुर में आय-हाट हवेली वद्याय विणज-व्योपार कीज्यो। हासिल राहधारी तथा मापा को सरकार की हद में तू कनां सैंथानी सो अधिकारी लीजेलौ वा निकासु सदा मन्दी माफ और परवानों विद्याधर ने इनायत हुयो छं सौ थारो गौर राखैलौ तूनें विद्याधर कहै तिण माफक कीज्यो। मिति मादवा सुदी ६, संवत १७८६ (१७२६ ए० डी०)

A few important things are to be noted in this document. Businessmen like Ghasiram Murlidhar were offered free land for building residential houses as an inducement to settle down. They were given concessions for carrying on business and some remission on the tax levied on goods carried from one place to another. They were also told that Vidhyadhar had been asked to take care of their interests. It is not quite clear as to what is meant by the final instruction "*tune Vidyadhar Kahe tin Mafik Kijo*"—"You act as per the instructions of Vidhyadhar". Quite possibly these instructions related to the manner of construction of the residential buildings (the height of the plinth, total height etc.). Some old maps of the city preserved in the City Palace contain such instructions for each building site.

As stated earlier the shops on the main market were constructed by the State. This gave the main roads the uniform look they still have.

The main markets of the town were already complete by 1734. The Bikaner archives contain the *Sivaha Hazuri* or the register of the daily deeds of the Maharaja. These are like the other *Sivahas* kept in slips of paper about 10 cm. by 15 cm. The slip for Chaitra Vadi 4 of 1790 V.S. (February 1734) reads as follows:

"Shriji went in a palki to thakurdwara to play Holi and then had darshan (of the deity). Thereafter, the Maharaja and the thakurs came to Manik Chowk via Chandani

Chowk, had darshan of the thakur of Natanis Dehura and came to Chand Pole playing Holi all the way. From Chand Pole they came to Shiv Pole and then passed through Ramganj, playing Holi all along the route. From there, they returned to the Palace via Raja Mal ki Haveli."[40]

All these places mentioned above can still be identified since they retain their original names. The main wards of the city were thus ready by early 1734.

Ishvari Singh

Jai Singh died on 21 September 1743[41] and was succeeded by his son Ishvari Singh. Ishvari Singh ruled only for seven years. For most of this period he was engaged in defending his throne from his step-brother, Madho Singh. A number of battles were fought between these two brothers, and one of the most important battles was fought at Rajmahal (in Tonk district) in March 1747. Madho Singh's allies in this battle were the princes of Kota, Bundi and the Marathas (Khande Rao Holkar). Sarkar described[42] this battle as follows:—

> "He (Ishwari Singh) transferred the command of his advance division to Hargovind Natani, a tradesman by caste but an exceptionally brave and able general, and himself arrived with the reserves one day's march behind the fighting front.
>
> "The battle began at noon on Sunday the 1st of March and ended at sunset the next day. The allies were completely defeated, though both sides suffered heavily. Each contingent of this ill-knit army had been attacked and routed in succession through the skilful planning and personal leadership of Hargovind."

40. Quoted in *Jaipur through the Ages*, p. 37. One might wonder why Jai Singh was still playing Holi on Chaitra Vadi 4, when the day for playing Holi is generally Phalgun Sudi 15.
41. *Ishvaravilas Mahakavya* (X. 11)—Ashvin Shukla Chaturdasi, 1800 V.S.
42. *Selections from the Peshwa Daftar*, ii, 3, 4; xxi, 24. Quoted in Sarkar, *op cit.*, Vol. I, pp. 178-79.

Isar Lat

It is said that the tower called the Isar Lat or *Svarga Shuli* in Tripolia Bazar was constructed by Ishvari Singh to commemorate his victory in this battle.

जय नगरहि जाके जई, विजय स्तंभ बनवाय।
इसर लट्ठडि नाम हल, दीधो अरि यश ढाय॥

"He went back to Jainagar and built a victory tower. He called it Isar Lat (stick and rod) to smash the reputation of his enemies."[43]

The tower is seven storeys high. It is one of the conspicuous landmarks in the city.

Curiously, however, the tower is not known as victory tower by the people in the city. There is a romantic story current about it. It is said that the ruler Ishvari Singh was in love with the daughter of Hargovind Natani, his minister and general. Hargovind's house was in a large building on the Chhoti Chopar. (Part of this house is now a girls' School and in the other part is the Kotwali.) This tower, Isar Lat, is situated about 400 metres away from Hargovind Natani's house. It is commonly believed in the city that Ishvari Singh had built this tower so that he could see from the top of this tower his lady-love without going to her house. The story is obviously absurd. No ruler would climb up a tower situated almost in the centre of the market to look at a girl from such a distance and make himself a laughing stock of the city. The story gained currency for two reasons perhaps. Ishvari Singh was succeeded by his step-brother Madho Singh. Since the tower had been built to commemorate Ishvari Singh's victory over Madho Singh, it was in the latter's interest that people should forget about that victory. The story regarding Ishvari Singh's scandalous love affair with Hargovind Natani's daughter was perhaps first given in *Vamsa Bhaskar*[44] written more than 100 years after the construction of the tower. *Vamsa Bhaskar* is the history of the Bundi ruling family. Since the Bundi ruler was one of the allies

43. Quoted in *Maharaja Shri Ishvari Singh ka Jivan Charitra* by Thakur Narendra Singh (Jaipur, 1917), p. 58.
44. Suryamal Mishran, *op. cit.*, p. 3454.

defeated in the battle, the author of *Vamsa Bhaskar* was not interested in calling *Isar Lat* a victory tower. It is very reasonable to suppose that he should be interested in connecting both the victors—the ruler and the general—in a scandal. The story was also adopted in the *Kachchhavamsa Mahakavya*,[45] a history of the Jaipur ruling family written at the end of the nineteenth century. The tower was completed in 1749.[46]

Jaipur in course of time became also famous as a city of temples. There are today more than one thousand temples of various sizes in Jaipur city.[47] But the number of temples in the beginning were not many. In fact Jai Singh himself had, beside the Govind Devaji's temple, built only one important temple, viz. the temple of Kalkaji. Though as stated elsewhere Jai Singh (whose main interest in later days was in Vaishnavism) had been able to attract to his city practically all sects of Vaishnavas, the main attraction of this place for an ordinary man was not religion. The main reason why the city prospered within a very short time of its establishment was the fact that it became a big trade centre for this part of the country.

Jaipur as a Centre of Trade

Girdhari in his *Bhojanasara* (1739) describes its business as follows: (For the Hindi text see Appendix VII).

45. *Kachchhavamsa Mahakavya* (in Sanskrit) by Krishnaram has not been printed. The relevant stanzas have been published in the introduction to *Ishvaravilas Mahakavya* on page 65.
46. The list of buildings constructed by the rulers and the members of their families (Appendix VI).
47. It is not possible to give the exact number of temples in the city. Many temples are situated in the residential buildings, and sometimes one building contains temples dedicated to various gods. 606 temples, most of them within the city walls, were registered for grants etc. with the *Devasthan Department* in 1973. The break up is as follows:—

Departmentally managed		*Temples obtaining grants-in-aid*	
1. Direct charge	37	Above Rs. 1,000/- per year	8
2. Supurdagi	15	Rs. 500/- to Rs. 1,000/-	15
3. Self reliant	6	Below Rs. 500/-	525
	58		548

Grand Total—606.

(Figures obtained from the Devasthan Department)

"Elephants, Arab horses, camels from Kutch, bullocks and buffaloes are being bought and sold. In this beautiful town built by the Rajadhiraj, embroidered cloth from many countries, plain cloth and jewellery are being transacted. Hundies of lacs and crores of rupees are current here. Thirty two kinds of weights are all used correctly here." (197, 199, 201).

Prevalence of 32 kinds of weights in one town is, of course, not particularly conducive to trade, but this is not an important point. What is noteworthy is the mention of the transactions of *Hundis* of very large amounts in the city. Jaipur, from the very beginning, it appears, became a centre of banking and exchange and continued to be so for 200 years.

In 1751, less than 25 years after its foundation the city had become famous in India. On 10th January 1751 "some four thousand Marathas (who were camping outside) had entered the city of Jaipur to see the temples and other sights of this newly built town, unique in India for the regularity and artistic beauty of its construction and to buy horses, camels and saddlery for which Jaipur was famous."[48]

There is a circular invitation letter[49] for a Jaina festival dated February 1764 issued by the prominent Jainas of Jaipur. This letter though not directly referring to the prosperity of Jaipur shows with what smug satisfaction Jaina businessmen used to find the conditions here. The letter was issued to the Jainas of Delhi, Agra etc. with requests to send copies of the invitation to Jainas in other towns. The purpose of the invitation was to request them to attend a religious celebration called the *Indradhvaja Puja*. The Puja was held on a huge platform constructed near Moti Dungari. The letter stated that the Raja of Jaipur and two of his *Dewans*, Ratanchand and Balchand (of

48. Sarkar, *op. cit.*, Vol. III, Ch. VII. This was the first of two occasions when an invading army had camped near Jaipur, but had not actually attacked it. The second occasion was when Amir Khan with his Pindari freebooters made a siege of Jaipur in 1817. "The Maji-ka-Bagh (The Residency) formed the left of the enemy's line, his right touching the hills to the eastward while Motidoongri formed the centre." (*Notes on Jaipur*, p. 66).
49. The letter has been quoted in full in *Veer Vani*, March 1967.

the *Terapanthi* sect) were helping in the celebrations by financial and other contributions. About Jaipur this letter says:

> "About this city, it lacks seven things. That is to say, in this city you would not find wine sellers, butchers and prostitutes. Also killing of animals is prohibited. The Raja's name is Madhav Singh. In this kingdom you would not find sinful activities which are prohibited by the Raja. And there are many Jainas resident here. All important courtiers are Jainas. And all the merchants are Jainas. Though there are others too, but they are in a minority, not in a majority. Six, seven or eight or ten thousand Jaina merchants have their residences here. In no other town you would find so many Jainas."

With the administration of the State firmly in the grip of their own community, the Jaina merchants no doubt found the conditions in Jaipur very satisfactory. But the important point to note is that Jaipur city had business enough to engage a very large number of merchants.

Buddhi Vilas, a poetical work written in mixed Braja and Jaipuri language in 1770 A.D., gives one of the earliest description of the foundation of Jaipur city and of its condition. It was written by one Bakht Ram Shah of Chaksu; and though it deals mainly with Jaina religious beliefs and rituals, it also contains description of the rulers of Amer and Jaipur, and what is more important describes the Jaipur city of his time:

नगर बसाये यक नयो जय स्यंध सवाई
जाकि सोभा जगत् में दसहों दिसि छाई
ताकौ वरनत करन को हुलसी मति मेरी
इंद्रपूरी हे जानियो ताकी हे चेरी ॥६७॥

If the word *Cheri* here means maid servant, then it would appear from the above that the author considered that the town of Indra, the King of the gods, may be called the maid servant of Jaipur.

Bakht Ram also mentions the fact that tax concession was one of the main incentives to many artisans and traders who were invited to come to the new city:

बहु विधि के कारीगर अनूप
परिवार सहित बुलवाय भूप
तिनको पुर में दीन्हे बसाय
हासिल सबकौं माफी कराय ॥११२॥

It is quite clear from *Buddhi Vilas* that Jaipur was not only a flourishing market place, it had also many industries and handicrafts. The book also mentions that there were 36 *Karkhanas*[50] in the city. Many of these *Karkhanas* or departments were government factories which met the demand for arms, weapons, jewellery, clothes, etc., of the palace. Others were stables for elephants, camels, horses, cows etc. Some of the *Karkhanas* were for the supply of the daily victuals like food, pan etc., or for the supply of medicines, perfumes etc.

Reason Why Jaipur Prospered so Quickly

The reasons for this quick prosperity of Jaipur may now be considered. One of the main reasons of course was that Jaipur was the capital of a much larger State than Amer was. The larger administrative staff and the standing army therefore formed a substantial part of the population. Besides inviting many businessmen to the city Jai Singh, it seems, made it almost obligatory for all the important *Jagirdars* of his State to build their houses in the city. Hanuman Sharma mentions[51] that he had seen the copy of an order which was sent to all the *jagirdars* in the State. The order dated *Chaitra Vadi* 6, 1785 V.S (1728 A.D.) informed them that houses would be built for them in Jaipur city and they should pay for the buildings in instalments by sending 10% of their annual income to Vidhyadhar in Jaipur regularly. In other words, the houses were built by the State and later their costs were realised from the *jagirdars*

50. It had been adopted from the Mughal pattern.
51. Hanuman Sharma, *Nathawaton ka Itihas*, p. 163. One indirect confirmation of this is the fact that through the houses belonging to the jagirdars of various clans of the Kachhawa-Rajputs exist within the city walls, there is no house of any of the important Shekhawat Jagirdars such as Sikar, Khetri, Bisau, Mandawa, Nawalgarh etc. *within* the city walls. Shekhawats never clearly accepted the overlordship of Jai Singh or his successors (Wills' Report).

The PRASTARA Plan

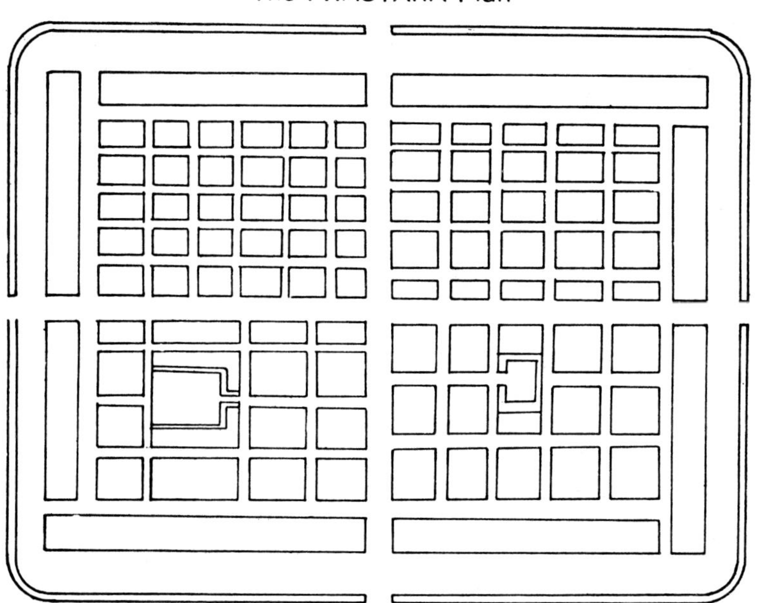

From Ram Raz, *Essay on the Architecture of the Hindus*, London, 1834, Pl. XLV.

in instalments. There are a large number of such houses in all the *Chowkris* of the city except *Chowkri* Topkhana Hazuri.[52]

All these government officials, business people and *jagirdars* formed a large population and there was thus a market in Jaipur for costlier luxuries. *Buddhi Vilas* mentions:

कहुं वस्त्र पाटके बहुरी स्वेत
मेहमूदी षासा तनुसुषेत ॥११४
कहुँपसमीना फुनि विकत पान
कहु विकत किराने वहुरी धान

Gold ornaments and jewellery, costly clothes such as *Khasa* and *Tannsukh*, *Pan* and various kinds of spices were all sold in this city. This shows that the number of people prosperous enough to buy these articles was sufficiently large in Jaipur at that time.

One reason why Jaipur looked so prosperous was that the rich Hindu merchants could display their wealth and build large residential buildings in this city without any fear. This they could not do so easily in cities under the Muslim rule at that time. For instance John Fryer, who was in India between 1673 and 1681, wrote about Surat as follows:

> "The Muhammadan merchants at Surat lived in lofty houses, flat at the top, and terraced with plasters . . .The Mughals wore rich attire, with a poniard at their girdle. . . ."
>
> "The Banias or Hindu merchants lived in a different fashion. They affected no stately houses, but dwelt in sheds. Even the richest crowded together, three or four families in a hovel, with goats, cows and calves, until they were almost poisoned with vermins and nastiness. But they had reason for what they did. Any Banian suspected of being rich was certain to be deprived of his wealth by the Nawab of Surat, unless he had secured the protection of some powerful grandee."[53]

52. On a rough count it was found that there were 19 large residential buildings belonging to the *jagirdars* in *Chowkri* Topkhana Desh alone.
53. *European Travellers in India*, Wheeler and Macmillan, Calcutta, 1956, p. 58.

In Jaipur the rich Hindu merchants had no such fear. Their number in the town must have been quite large for apart from those who came here on invitation, quite a good number must have run away from Delhi and Agra and sought refuge here. Nadir Shah sacked Delhi in 1739, only 12 years after the foundation of Jaipur. And from 1748 to 1757, Ahmed Shah Abdali invaded northern India a number of times, and in fact in 1757 he looted the city of Delhi and sacked the holy city of Mathura. After the battle of Panipat in 1761 he again plundered Delhi.[54]

Jaipur not very far from this area was an ideal refuge for rich Hindu merchants from Delhi, Mathura and Agra. It was a Hindu kingdom and at the same time not situated like Bikaner and Jodhpur in the arid region of Rajasthan. Quite a number of merchant families of Jaipur, especially the Oswals, claim that their forefathers had come from Delhi and had settled down here.

Trade Routes Through Jaipur

Trade in Jaipur flourished not only because the city itself was a big consuming centre, but also for the reason that due to circumstances developing in the neighbouring areas, important trade routes of western and north-western India shifted so that they passed through Jaipur in the eighteenth century.

Before the shifting of these trade routes there was only one route which passed through Jaipur and connected the town to places outside Rajasthan.[55] From Agra this route reached Jaipur. At Jaipur the route was bifurcated so that one of these passed through Malpura, Bhilwara and Chittor. Both Malpura[56] and Bhilwara were important trading centres. The other route

54. *Cambridge History of India,* Vol. IV, pp. 416-26.

55. Boileau in 1835 mentioned the following routes connecting Jaipur to various places in and near Rajasthan: Jaipur-Bikaner (184 miles); Jaipur-Rewari (127 miles), Pilani, Bhiwani (116 miles), Merta (125 miles) and Jaipur-Malwa. . . See, A.H.E. Boileau, *Personal Narrative of a tour through the Western States of Rajasthan in 1835*, pp. 213, 220, 221 and 222.

56. Malpura was also famous for its manufactures of Namda blankets and other woolen goods. See, *Imperial Gazetteer*, Vol. XVII, p. 95.

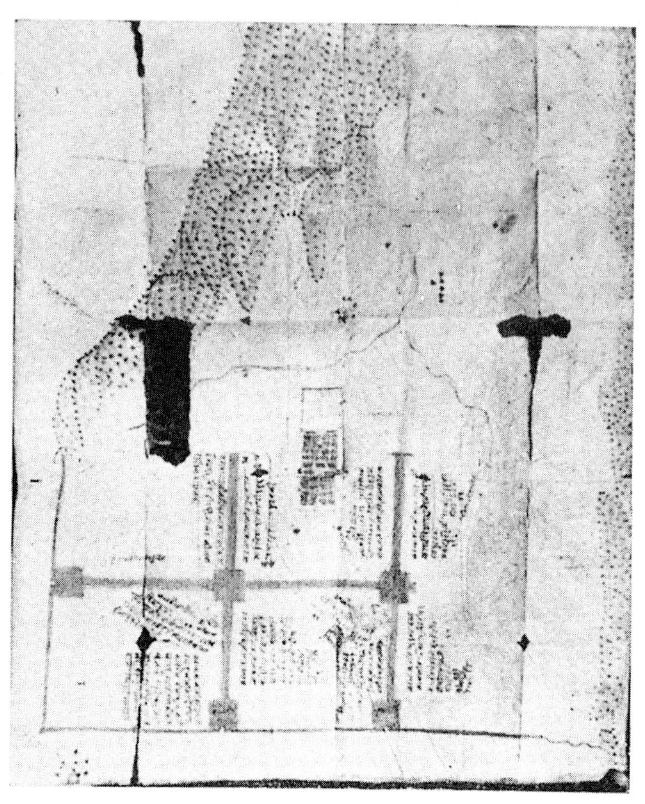

Map No. L.S./14 in the City Palace, Jaipur.

passed through Ajmer, the great centre of pilgrimage for both Hindus and Muslims From Ajmer again there were two routes. One went south to Bhilwara, Chittor, Ujjain and Burhanpur. From Burhanpur the route followed the Tapti river to Surat. This was the route which Sir Thomas Roe the English ambassador to the court of Jahangir had followed in 1615 to reach Ajmer from Surat.

The other route from Ajmer went south-west to Sojat, Pail and ultimately to Surat.

However, the main Mughal route towards the South passed from Agra to Burhanpur through Gwalior and Malwa. "All the great military roads from the northern capitals of the Mughal empire to the Deccan passed through Malwa."[57] This was closed when the Maratha raids on the Mughal empire commenced through Malwa. These first started in 1699.[58] In 1703-04, the Maratha invasion had seriously affected communication and trade between northern and southern India for three months by holding up the official letters and trade caravans on the banks of the Narbada.[59] Maratha raids continued in Malwa until 1741 when the government of the Suba virtually came in their hands.

Meanwhile the alternate route between Gujrat and Agra, which passed via Pali, Sojat, Ajmer and Jaipur, gained in importance. Pali, it seems, gained most and it continued to be an important trade centre until the beginning of the nineteenth century.[60] Tod mentions that Pali "from remote times has been the connecting link between the sea coast and northern India"[61] and perhaps the most important trading centre in Rajasthan in his time. In the list of various articles traded in Pali, Tod mentions, "From Jaipur, various clothes and sugars."[62]

The route from Agra to Pali passing through Jaipur and further on to the sea coast became one of the most important trade routes in the country and remained so until the advent of the railways. In fact one of the first great roads constructed

57. *Cambridge History of India*, Vol. IV, p. 312.
58. *Ibid.*, p. 313.
59. *Cambridge History of India*, Vol. IV, p. 313
60. Tod, *op. cit.*, Vol. II, p. 128.
61. *Ibid.*, Vol. I. p. 553.
62. *Ibid.*, Vol. I, p. 554.

in India during the British period "was that between Agra and Deesa running for 360 miles" through Jaipur, Ajmer and Pali. It was constructed during the years 1865-75.[63]

The factor which had a marked effect in bringing Jaipur on the main trade route of north-west India was the rise of the Sikhs. The Sikhs in the Punjab regarded "highway robbery as a hereditary and honourable profession." Indeed, the Sikh leaders of the area between Ludhiana and Karnal "developed into territorial magnates—the Rajahs of Patiala, Kapurthala, Nabha and Jhind, besides similar chiefs, by first passing through the stage of robbers of the imperial highway from Delhi to Lahore which ran through their homes."[64] The increase of this lawlessness on the main highway from the early years of the eighteenth century and specially after the invasion of Nadir Shah (1739 A.D.) shifted the trade route southwards through Jaipur. In fact, W. Francklin writing in 1798 considered this to be the main reason for the prosperity of Jaipur.

> "This city has of late years increased in commerce and opulence; for since the communication through the provinces of Lahore has been stopped by the Sikhs, the merchants from the north have been accustomed to enter Hindostaun by the route of Jypore."[65]

63. *Imperial Gazetteer*, Vol. XXI, p. 135.
64. Sarkar, *op. cit.*, Vol. I, p. 265.
65. Francklin, *op. cit.*, p. 86.

CHAPTER III

The Period of Decay—1800-1835

Jaipur's prosperity continued almost up to the end of the eighteenth century in spite of the frequent warfare with the Marathas. All the battles with the Marathas were fought well outside the State capital, and the countryside also escaped general devastation up to the end of the century. The Hawa Mahal at Jaipur built in 1799 marks the end of the prosperity of the city.

Hawa Mahal

The date of construction of the Hawa Mahal is given in the official list[1] of buildings constructed by the Jaipur rulers and the members of their families; but the purpose for which this curious structure was built is not clear. It has no conceivable utility. The builder of the Hawa Mahal, Pratap Singh, the ruler of Jaipur was a devotee of Radha and Krishna, and also poet of some repute. He wrote about the Hawa Mahal as follows:—

हवा महल याते कियो सब समझो यह भाव ।
राधे कृष्ण सिधारसी दरस परस को भाव ।।

It appears from this that the building was dedicated to Radha and Krishna.[2]

A court poet of Pratap Singh, Rasarasi Ram Narain also composed a poem about the Hawa Mahal. Some lines[3] from this poem confirm the same surmise:

1. See Appendix VI.
2. *Brajnidhi Granthavali*, Allahabad, 1933, p. 184.
3. From the MSS in the City Palace Museum, Jaipur, obtained through the courtesy of Shri G.N. Bahura.

चहल पहल हवा महल फैला हुं आज
राधे गिरधारी प्यारे पाहुने पधारे हैं
अतुलित सोभा भरयो प्रफुलित प्रभा जामे
छहरित रीझ भीजे विहरत श्यामाश्याम ।

Maratha and Pindari Raids

With the beginning of the nineteenth century things became pretty bad in Jaipur. Large bands of Marathas and Pindaris had started roaming over Rajasthan, plundering the country-side.

> "From the siege camp the parties of Maratha brigades used to issue for plundering the surrounding districts, seizing whatever they found, money, ornaments, utensils, clothes, grains, goats, fowl and anything else including ropes and shoes. Holkar also roamed about in Jaipur, Jodhpur and Udaipur in similar manner. The entire country was laid waste and rendered desolate as a result of these visitations."[4]

The Rajputs were powerless to stop this ruin of their states. In fact, sometimes they took the help of these very Marathas and Pindaris and joined in this oppression of the people of each other's territory. In the famous Krishna Kumari episode (1805-1810 A.D.) it was not greed but a vain idea of prestige that made the Jodhpur and Jaipur Maharajas bring ruin upon the people of each other's states. Shyamaldas writing in *Vir Vinod* says:[5]

> "The Maharaja of Jodhpur and his loyal Rathores plundered and devastated the territory of Dhundhar (Jaipur). The Nawab and Indraraj got together a large army and attacked Jaipur a second time. When the forces of Maharaja Jagat Singh (of Jaipur) retreated, the Marwaris started the lootings. They would cut off the ears and noses of anybody they could get hold of. Many cruelties were perpetrated on the

4. M.L. Sharma, *op. cit.*, p. 237.
5. Shyamaldas, *op. cit.*, p. 866.

poorer people of the territories of both Jodhpur and Jaipur in the war. At first the soldiers of Jaipur started abducting the Marwari women and sold them for two paisas each. Then the soldiers of Nawab Amir Khan and Indraraj Singhvi retaliated and started selling the Jaipur women for one paisa each."

The effect of this devastation of the countryside by the Marathas, Pindaris and the local princes themselves had its effect on the prosperity of the capital towns also; and Jaipur which depended so much on trade and commerce and the income of the absentee landlords, received a setback in its growth. In 1818 the then Maharaja Jagat Singh signed a treaty of subsidiary alliance with the British Government, as a result of which the latter in lieu of annual tribute took Jaipur and other States in Rajasthan under its protection. All the raids and the internecine warfare now stopped. However, soon after the treaty Maharaja Jagat Singh died in December 1818 and Jaipur passed for a long time under the rule of the queen mother who as regent ruled on behalf of her posthumous son.

The Period of Regency

This son, Jai Singh III, born on 25 April 1819, lived only up to 1835. During the first part of his reign the Chief Minister of the State was Rawal Bairisal of Samod. He was liked by the British Resident but was disliked by the Regent Rani who got rid of him after some years and tried to rule herself directly. This, according to the British report[6] dated 10-4-1825 was a period of great anarchy.

"The Regent Ranee, finding herself uncontrolled gave bridle to her base and vicious desires. Her female slave 'Roopa' was invested with a Khillat, and received the title of "Raj Bundharin",[7] by which was understood that the entire and

6. J.C. Brooke, *Political History of the State of Jaypore*, Calcutta, 1868, p. 26.
7. Bundharin is obviously Badaran. There is in "Jaipur Trials" (p. 64) the draft of a petition to the Governor-General in the name of Roopa Badaran, the first few lines of which read as follows:

uncontrolled management of affairs was vested in her, as in a Mookhtiar. To secure her power, she openly murdered those who opposed it, and did not even regard the sanctity of the palace, so that she might strike terror in the minds of all inhabiting it. The revenue of the country was squandered by her, and her associates, with rockless profligacy. To meet the current necessary expenditure, the next year's income was forestalled; while the tribute to the British Government was altogether neglected, and the arrears soon rose to eight lakhs of rupees".[8]

After a few years of chaos, Jhootaram was made the Mukhtiar or the Chief Minister. Jhootaram was a Saraogi Jain trader from Agra.

The countryside around Jaipur also suffered at this time due to famine and drought conditions. "In 1819 the country immediately around Jeypoor exhibited the extreme of poverty and desolation, but it has since greatly recovered from the devastation it had so long experienced."[9]

Description of Jaipur by Bishop Heber and Boileau

We have two important records of travellers through Jaipur during this period. The first was Bishop Heber who was in Jaipur in January 1825. He wrote in his journal: "The town is tolerably clean, but a great part of the houses are in a state

"The petition of Roopa Budarun. Throughout Rajasthan there are Budaruns and in our Raj, generations past they have been inmates of the Palace. The Princes in addressing the Budaruns designate them "Jee Jee" (sister), and all the Thakoors of rank and Moosahibs (Minister) treat them with respect and courtesy. Such has been the observance with reference to females of this description here, and until the present period no Budarun has ever suffered degradation or dishonour. . . Three months ago I was made a prisoner at the Ghat and up to the time have not obtained my liberty, whereas the former Budaruns of Maharaja Prutap Singhjee and Jugut Singhjee, reside in the royal female apartments, in the enjoyment of the allowances fixed for them and are more honoured and respected than ever. We Budaruns partake of the royal food that is prepared in the palace; night and day we remain present. . . ."

8. Brooke, *op. cit.*, p. 26.
9. *East India Gazetteer*, London, 1828, p. 42.

of decay. Still, however, it has a population of 60,000 souls." The decay noticed by Heber continued, and his observation was confirmed by A.H.E. Boileau who passed through Jaipur in August 1835. Boileau was an officer of the Survey of India posted in Shekhawati. He was ordered to travel through some states of Rajasthan and to report back to the Government at Calcutta. Boileau has commented both on the population of the city at that time and on the effect of maladministration on the economic condition there.

He wrote in August 1835:

> "We are greatly pleased with our view of the city of Jaipoor, the exceeding regularity and beauty of which is a just source of the pride to the inhabitants of this part of Rajwara. It is about 2 miles in length and a mile in width, containing by native estimation nearly 80,000 houses which would give a population little short of 400,000 persons; these numbers may be generally exaggerated. . ."[10]

Boileau was correct in saying that the figure of 80,000 houses in 1835 was an exaggeration, but his estimate of 5 persons per house would not have been far from truth. In the first official census of Jaipur city in July 1870 the houses were actually counted. It was found that the number of houses within the city wall was 22,356 with a population of 116,563, approximately 5 persons per house. In 1870 Jaipur wass teadily on its way back to prosperity whereas in 1835 it was perhaps passing through the worst period of its history, though there might have also been a slight setback in 1868-69 due to the famine. Famines generally tend to decrease the population of the countryside and temporarily increase the city population due to the influx of famine stricken villagers. We may assume therefore that the actual number of houses in Boileau's time would have been less than 20,000 and if we accept his average of 5 persons per house, the population of Jaipur in the twenties and thirties of the nineteenth century was approximately eighty thousand to one lakh.

About the condition of the town Boileau reported:

10. Boileau, *op. cit.*, p. 158.

"... the appearance of the (main streets) is very much disfigured by the mud platforms, stalls and hovels that have been erected along their centres.

"Under a good government Jaipur would be a splendid place but at present the exhausted state of Dhoondhar of which it is the capital is strongly typified by the appearance of the metropolis itself. An empty treasury, desolate palaces, stagnating commerce, ferocious populace and a rabble army speak volumes against the late minister or rather autocrat Jhootaram, under whose misrule this miserable country has so long grinded."

The blame for this sad condition cannot, of course, all be put on Jhootaram. It was the commulative effect of all the 35 years of misery that Jaipur had passed through. One point in Boileau's description of the conditions of the town is worth noticing. Boileau mentions the mud platforms, stalls and hovels erected along the centre of the main streets. The people who erected the stalls and hovels were the most probably refugees from the countryside and who perhaps thought that they would escape both hunger and chaos if they could live within the city.[12]

Boileau's Table of Population

At the end of his book Boileau gives a few tables showing the castes, professions and religions of the population of some important towns in Rajasthan. The list gives the number of houses occupied by each caste and its population on the basis of 5 persons to each house.

Boileau's table for Jaipur is worth examining. Brahmans according to this table made up nearly one-fifth of the population. The bulk of them were Gaur Brahmans whose profession is not mentioned. The other Brahmans were priests, family

11. Report on the Political Administration of the Rajpootana States for 1870-71.
12. One is reminded of the large number of stalls erected all along the main streets of Jaipur shortly after the partition of the country in 1947, when numerous refugees from Sind came and took shelter in this city.

priests, chaplains of State, private chaplains, undertakers, etc. Puleewal (Paliwal) Brahmans or Boras were the only exception. They numbered only about 2,500 and were all merchants by occupation.

About one-fifth of the population of Jaipur consisted of various trader castes such as Muhesree (Maheshwari), Siraogee (Saraogi), etc. In other words, very nearly half of the population of Jaipur according to Boileau consisted of Brahmans and Mahajans. His figures of the actual population of these castes were wrong, but there is no doubt that these two castes always dominated all the others in number in Jaipur. Even in the 1901 census, Brahmans were 15% of the total population and Mahajans 14%, together making up nearly one-third of the population of Jaipur. It is reasonable to think that proportionately their number was much higher than 30% in Boileau's time. Boileau's table shows that only 17% of the population in his time were Muslim. This went up to nearly 25% in 1901. There was therefore a relative decline in the population of Brahmans and Mahajans in course of these 60 to 70 years. But as stated above Jaipur's population was dominated by these two castes.[13]

One can only guess the economic consequences of such a large population of Brahmans in the city. Brahmans as a rule are a non-producing class. At best they 'produce' services and that too mainly of a religious nature. It may be presumed that Brahmans of Jaipur mainly subsisted on the religious services. This is also supported by Boileau's table. (But Jaipur even with its numerous temples never became an important centre of pilgrimage.) Brahmans mainly rendered religious services either to the local residents or to the ruler, and were thus a burden either on the residents or on the government, mainly it seems on the latter. Tod compiled[14] a set of figures of the revenue of the Jaipur State for V.S. 1858 (1802-3 A.D.), the year of Raja Jagat Singh's accession. According to this schedule the total revenues of the State including the tributes received from Shekhawati and other important feudatories was eighty-two lakh rupees: Out of this, sixteen lakhs (nearly 20%) were given

13. We can perhaps use the population figure of each caste given in Boileau's table to find its relative numerical strength, though not its absolute number in 1835.

14. Tod, *op. cit.*, Vol. II, pp. 350-51.

away as "Ooduk or charity lands, chiefly to Brahmins". As against this, the Silleposh, or men at arms had jagirs worth one and half lakh rupees only and the Army, consisting of ten battalions of infantry with cavalry had jagirs with an annual revenue of seven lakhs fourteen thousand rupees only. Commenting on this Tod remarks:

> "The observant reader will not fail to be struck with vast inequality between the estates of the defenders of the country, and these drones the Brahmins, nor can anything more powerfully mark the utter prostration of intellect of the Cuchwaha princes, than their thus maintaining an indolent and baneful hierarchy to fatten on the revenue which would support four thousand Cuchwaha cavaliers."[15]

The total number of such religious jagirs and grants to the temple in the early part of the nineteenth century is not known. As stated earlier, at the time of independence there were about 600 temples maintained by the State in the Jaipur city. In addition there were 5534 religious jagirs in the Jaipur district out of a total of 56,981 religious jagirs in the whole of Rajasthan.[16] Thus almost 10 per cent of these were in the Jaipur district.

Jaipur's wealth then was mainly generated by the large population of the merchant class. The city as stated earlier specialised in banking and commerce. The merchants dealt mainly in the goods produced outside the city, for Boileau's table shows that there were not many artisans in this place. The one exception was the cheepas (calico printers—all Hindus) who numbered 15,000. The presence of such a large number of calico printers proves that the main industry of Jaipur at that time was cloth printing and there must have been a very large import of plain cloth and export of the printed cloth. We do not have the figures of cloth trade of 1835, but the figures[17] given in the administration report for 1869-70 for the Rajputana Agency show that the import and export of cloth was indeed

15. Tod, *op. cit.*, Vol. II, p. 351.
16. Figure obtained from the office of the Jagir Commissioner.
17. The import and export figures of the city as given in this report have been reproduced in Appendix XI.

the most important trade of Jaipur in 1868. In 1868, 4227 maunds of cloth were imported into Jaipur mostly from the Delhi and Bhiwanee side. Jaipur exported 4,150 maunds of cloth in that year mostly towards Marwar (3150 maunds) where printed cloth is in great vogue even today. Some cloth was also produced in the city itself, for Boileau mentions that there were 700 families of Jolahas (weavers—all Muslims) here.

Other types of artisans were fewer in number and were sufficient only to meet the needs of the local population. These people were Chooreegur dant-Ka (Bracelet makers of ivory-500, all Muslims), Chamars (cobblers-2500, all Hindus), Jureea (Lapidaries-625, all Hindus), Lohar (Blacksmiths-1000, all Hindus). There were certain occupations peculiar to the needs of those times, such as Topchees (game killers-1,000, all Hindus), Salotrees (Horse doctors-1750, all Muslims), Kahars (Bearers of Baghees (Sedan chairs?)-2750 all Hindus), etc. Jaipur had Kusbees (Prostitutes-6500) and Burwas (pimps-1250) in quite a large number and they were all Hindus.[18]

Sale of Children by Destitutes

We have very little record of the suffering of the people during this period of thirty-five years (1800-1835) of decay available with us. Two sale deeds[19] preserved in the Lunkaranji Pandya's Jaina Temple in Daribapan are perhaps worth mentioning. Both these deeds refer to sale of children by the parents to Pandit Sarupchand and Sadasukh who were possibly the priests of this temple. The first sale deed dated Magsir Sudi 13, 1860 V.S. (November 1803 A.D.) mentions the sale of a six-year old boy by the mother to the priests for seventy-one rupees. The mother said that she wanted twenty-one rupees out of that amount at once. With thirteen rupees she would get her elder son, who was mortgaged with another person, released. The balance of Rs. 50/- she would take for her food and other needs when her husband came back. The second sale deed is by a father who sold his son to the same persons in 1868 V.S. (1811 A.D.) for thirty-seven rupees.

18. The list has been reproduced in Appendix XI. It should be noted, however, that these figures should all be divided by 5 to get a realistic estimate.

19. Reproduced in Appendix VIII.

It is difficult to conclude anything from these two sale deeds. It has remained a common practice for the poorer people of our country to sell their children during years of famine both for saving their own lives and the lives of their children who would be given food by their buyers.

Both 1803 and 1811 appear to have been years of famine. In 1803 there was famine in Uttar Pradesh, and the Jaipur records mention that in the autumn of 1803 Bajra was selling in the town at 15 seers a rupee against 37½ seers in the autumn of the previous year. The 1811 price record of Jaipur was not available, but crops were indifferent near about Agra. It was perhaps a year of scarcity in Jaipur also. The sale of the children is thus explainable.

The children were not perhaps purchased as slaves. In the first sale deed the mother also mentions that the purchaser was free to bring up and educate the child. If the purchasers were the celibate priests of the temple, it is quite possible that they purchased the child as their possible successor in the priesthood of the temple.

Economic Condition of the People

The prices of foodgrains in the Jaipur market from 1761 A.D. are given in Appendix IV. One can only make some rough guess about the economic condition of the people of the city in the various years of this period.

As stated earlier, Jaipur did not have much income from industries. The main income of the richer merchants was from trade and commerce. Most other well-to-do people derived their income from jagirs, whether religious or others. In fact Tod says in the schedule mentioned earlier that servants of the rulers and of the government also got their salaries in the shape of jagirs. He mentions that they had the following jagir income:

Sagird Pesha, servants of the household	—	Rs. 3 lakhs
Minister and civil officers	—	Rs. 2 lakhs

Many other people in the city therefore depended for their living on these jagirdars small or big, either directly as their servants, or by producing goods for them.

In other words the economic condition of most of the people of the city mainly depended on the annual income from the jagirs which in turn depended on the crop conditions. A fairly accurate estimate of the economic condition of the poorer people can therefore be made from the price of Bajra, the grain they ate. If rains were good, Bajra crop would be good, and the people would be happy. Bajra prices varied from year to year enormously during the period. It was the highest—7½ seers per rupee in Rabi 1782, the year of the great famine in Northern India. The famine was known as Chalisi.[20] It was the lowest in 1798 when Bajra was selling at 63½ seers per rupee. For purposes of discussion we might accept that for poorer people the years in which Bajra was selling at 20 seers or less per rupee were bad years. Such years were—

1761 (18¼ seers in Rabi and 19¼ in Kharif)
1763 (18¾ in Kharif)
1764 (14¾ in Rabi and 18 in Kharif)
1779 (18 seers in Kharif)
1782 (7¼ seers in Rabi)
1783 (15¼ seers in Kharif)
1784 (12 seers in Rabi and 16¼ in Kharif)
1792 (19¾ seers in Rabi and 15¼ in Kharif)
1803 (15 seers in Kharif)

Bad years between 1804 and 1840 were the following:—

1808 (Bajra 18 seers in Rabi and 12 in Kharif)
1813 (Bajra 8 seers per rupee in Kharif)
This year famine was reported in Agra and Haryana.
1817 (Bajra 19¼ seers in Rabi and 16 in Kharif)
1818 (Bajra 14¾ seers in Rabi)
These two years (1817 & 1818) were bad for the countryside around Jaipur, from which it did not recover even in 1819 when Bajra was selling in Jaipur at 21¼ seers per rupee.
1820 18¼ seers in Rabi.
1833 14 seers in Kharif.

20. *Imperial Gazetteer* (1908), Vol. XXIV, p. 217.

1834 15 seers in Rabi.
1838 18 seers in Rabi.
1840 $17\frac{3}{4}$ seers in Rabi.

Maintenance of Law and Order in the City

The law and order in the city was maintained by the Faujdar. It appears that it was not possible to leave the city with any kind of property without a permit from the office of this functionary. This would appear from the evidence given by the Deputy Faujdar of Jaipur in the trial of Jhoota Ram and others:—

"Saturday 2nd July 1836.

The court assemble, pursuant to adjournment of yesterday, at 8 O'clock A.M.

The prisoners are present.

Deposition of Tara Chand Sravagee, Naib Faujdar of the city of Jeypoor.

Q. What is your name and what office do you hold in Jeypoor?

A. My name is Tara Chand, and I have been Naib Faujdar of Jeypoor for about eleven years.

Q. What orders were given, and what new forms were directed to be observed after the events of the 4th June 1835, with reference to either quitting or entering the city?

A. No fresh orders were issued after the 4th June, 1835, people came and went as they pleased. The form which has been many years in force is, that such persons as wish to go with carriages and property; or to send off property of any kind; apply to me, or some one in my department for a chit or pass to exhibit to the chowkee at the gateway by which they quit the city."[21]

The same reply was given also by Jeewan Singh. Jamadar of Faujdaree, Jeypoor.

21. *Jaypoor Trials*, Calcutta, 1836, p. 10.

"No fresh orders prohibiting people from quitting the city were issued, and the constant regulation is that notice be given and a pass for the gateway received, on account of carts, baggage, etc."[22]

The city police continued to remain under the Faujdar until the twenties of this century when it were reorganised. In 1908, the Faujdar had under him 855 constables and Chowkidars.[23]

Jaipur and Delhi Compared

It might be worthwhile comparing the Jaipur city in the eighteenth century with Delhi (Shahjahanabad), a hundred years earlier. Bernier in July 1663[24] in a letter gave a vivid description of Delhi.

Among the most quoted lines from Bernier are: "In Delhi there is no middle state. A man must either be of the highest rank or live miserably"[25] This, however, was not the position in Jaipur. Apart from the large number of businessmen and merchants there were in Jaipur a large number of jagir holders, big and small. Mention has also been made of the large number of religious jagirs. All these people constituted a substantial middle class. Apart from these, the Jainas who were three to five per cent of the population of the city were practically all members of the middle and upper middle classes.[26]

There was an important difference between the jagirdars of the Mughals and those of Jaipur. In the case of the jagirdars under the Mughals, their total property was escheated to the state on the death of the jagirdar. This rule applied to servants of the jagirdars also who had been given smaller jagirs in lieu of salary. Banarsidas Jain, who lived during the first half of the seventeenth century, wrote in his autobiography *Ardhakathanaka* that when his grandfather Mooldas, who was servant of a jagirdar, died, the Mughals came and confiscated all the property of Mooldas:[27]

22. *Ibid.*
23. *Imperial Gazetteer*, Vol. XIII, p. 397.
24. Bernier, *Travels*, *op. cit.*, p. 252.
25. *Ibid.*
26. Vide Chapter VII(iii) on Jainas.
27. *Ardhakathanak*, 2nd edition, Bombay 1957, p. 4.

आयो मुगल उतावलो, सुनि मूलाकौ काल ।
मुहर छाप घर खाल से, कीनो लीनो माल ।।

This did not happen in Jaipur. Here one could save and invest and retain properties generation after generation. It was possible therefore for the jagirdars to build large residential buildings which they could hold on because the jagirs passed from father to son. Under the Mughals, as Bernier states, "no subject can hold landed property in his own right."[28] The Mughal jagirdars got temporary jagirs in lieu of salary, which they held until they died or were transferred or replaced.

The physical appearance of *Shahjahanabad* corresponded with the material condition of the people. In a place where there were only very rich or very poor people, mansions and hovels would be found side by side. Bernier wrote:

> "Amid these streets are dispersed the habitations of Mansebdars, or pretty Omrahs, officers of justice, rich merchants and others; many of which have tolerable appearance. Very few are built entirely in brick or stone and several are made only of clay and straw. . . . Intermixed with these different houses is an immense number of small ones, built of mud and thatched with straw, in which lodge the common troopers, and all that vast multitude of servants and camp-followers who follow the court and the army."[29]

Delhi in the middle of the seventeenth century had only two principal streets. Both the streets started from the front of the square near the gate of the Red Fort, one going towards the Chandni Chowk and the other towards the Lahori Gate. Describing them Bernier wrote:

> "The two principal streets of the city leading into the square, may be five-and-twenty or thirty ordinary paces in width. They run in a straight line nearly as far as the eye can reach; but the one leading to the Lahori gate is much the longer. In regard to houses the two streets are exactly alike. As in our Palace Royale, there are arcades on both sides;

28. Bernier, *op. cit.*, p. 284.
29. Bernier, *op. cit.*, p. 246.

with this difference however that they are only of brick, and the top serves for a terrace and has no additional building."[30]

It appears that these two streets of Delhi looked very much like the main bazars of Jaipur except that whereas the Delhi streets were 70 to 80 feet wide, the Jaipur bazars were about 108 feet wide. In fact this wideness of the streets gave Jaipur a grandeur appearance. We have a short description of Jaipur written in 1820:

> "During the campaign in 1817, this city was approached by the army under Sir David Ochterlony, but no European was allowed to enter the gate, through which, however, they were permitted to look as far as they could. From these points of vision the streets appeared wide and the houses of stone, the whole presenting an appearance of grandeur surpassing the generality of Indian Cities."[31]

30. *Ibid.*, p. 245.
31. Walter Hamilton, *Description of Hindustan*, Vol. I, London, 1820, p. 541.

CHAPTER IV

Growth of the City—1835-80

For nearly twelve years, from 1839 to 1851, Jaipur State was ruled by a Regency Council. This was the period when the ruler Ram Singh II was still a minor. The Council was presided over by the British Political Agent. After the near anarchy of the previous forty years, the conditions in the city started returning to normal.[1]

One of the wise acts of the Regency Council was to educate the young prince in as good a manner as was possible in those days. Pandit Sheodeen, who had received his education in the Government College at Agra, was appointed as tutor to the young Maharaja.[2] The result was that Ram Singh after getting full powers proved to be one of the more enlightened rulers among the native princes of India.

Ram Singh attempted to modernize the city both outwardly and culturally. In both these matters he wanted to be a worthy successor of his great ancestor Jai Singh. In so far as the material improvement of Jaipur was concerned, Ram Singh succeeded to a great extent. He got a modern water works constructed. He established a gas works for lighting the city roads. The roads were paved in his time. He also built hospitals, schools, colleges, museums, etc. And it was he who gave the city its pink look.

Ram Singh started his work of improvement of the city earnestly in 1860. In that year "the Maharaja applied for

1. For details, see H.C. Batra, *The Relations of Jaipur State with the East India Company (1803-1858)*, S. Chand & Co., Delhi, 1958, pp. 147-170.
2. *Report on the Political Administration of Rajputana for 1865-66 and 1866-67*, p. 164.

and obtained the services of a European Officer to superintend the public works operation in the State. The final work of any importance undertaken was the trunk road connecting Agra and Ajmer, an imperial work towards which for the length in his territory the Maharaja contributed 80 per cent of the outlay. Many improvements in and about the city were also successfully carried out, notably the paving and draining of the streets, the great ghat road etc."[3]

Among the public works constructed during Ram Singh's period were the Public Library building (started in 1866 and completed in 1881), the Ram Niwas Garden (1868), the museum building in this garden (1876-1887),[4] and the Mayo Hospital building (1870-1875) on the eastern side of the garden. It is worth noticing that except for the Public Library all the other three were outside the city wall. The Ram Niwas Garden was actually started by the Maharaja as a famine work[5] for the poorer people of the city during the great Rajputana famine of 1868-69.

Architecturally the Public Library building was constructed so as to blend with the other buildings near about, in the old Jaipur style. The Mayo Hospital building was purely functional and built architecturally in the style of the then British Indian public buildings. The Museum building was something quite

3. *Rajpootana Agency Report for the year 1878-79*, p. 62.
4. The name of the architect and the dates are inscribed on stone slab attached to the building.
5. *Notes on Jaipur*, p. 83. It appears that the effect of the famine was very seriously felt in the city also. The prices of food-grains in 1869 were among the highest ever recorded in about one and a half centuries. These as per Hendley's tables in seers per rupee were as follows:

	RABI			KHARIF		
	Wheat.	Barley.	Bajra.	Wheat.	Barley.	Bajra.
1867.	16½	24	21½	14	23½	24
1868.	15	20	18½	9¼	11	9½
1869.	6	8	6	7½	14	16
1870.	11	17	17	14½	20½	20½

"In August 1869 the distribution of cooked food commenced at the capital, and more than 131,000 persons were fed up to March 1870." (*Imperial Gazetteer*, Vol. XIII, p. 393).

novel. It does not resemble any existing building in India. The architect was Sir Swinton Jacob who was the Chief Engineer of the State. He built it in what he conceived was the Indo-Saracenic style.[6] It looks beautiful specially when occasionally it is floodlit at night.

The idea of colouring all the houses facing the main streets pink was that of Ram Singh. "Originally the colour was white. Then the late Chief Maharaja Ram Singh tried colouring all the streets differently, green, yellow, pink, etc. Finally pink was adopted for the whole city."[7]

The main features of the city within the walls remain the same today as they were when Ram Singh died in 1880. Substantial changes have occurred only in the Chaura Rasta which did not have many buildings in those days. The open spaces have been filled up by new buildings often not in keeping with the architectural style of the city and a gate was opened towards the south facing the Ram Niwas garden in the forties of this century.

One might think that Jaipur must have looked very beautiful in those days. But this was not so, at least to some people. H.B.W. Garrick who was touring Rajasthan in 1883-84, on behalf of the *Archaeological Survey of India* came to Jaipur and reported.

> "I made a very short stay at the modern Jaipur, which city is uninteresting archaeologically, and in the rigid angularity of its plan excessively ugly. The roads are pretentiously paved along the centre with slabs of stone, and this is very bad for carriages. Matters are not by any means improved by the universal coat of pink-colour wash (often rendered more hideous and paltry by floral ornamentation in white-wash) which the building enmass appear to have received. Everything inside this city, then smacks of brand-newness, bad taste and a hankering after European characteristics."[8]

6. *Notes on Jaipur*, p. 25.
7. *Ibid.*, p. 16.
8. H.B.W. Garrick—Report of a Tour in the Punjab and Rajputana in 1883-84 (*Archaeological Survey of India*, Vol. XXIII, Calcutta, 1887, p. 33).

Obviously, what irritated the archaeologist was the fact that the city looked new.

Ram Singh's attempts to modernize the city outwardly were successful to some extent. On the other hand, in spite of his best efforts to make the city culturally also modern, Ram Singh did not succeed. The Sanskrit College of Jaipur, no doubt in course of time became an important centre of Sanskrit learning in India, but most of the improvement in the College took place after Ram Singh's death.[9] Jaipur essentially had the character of a town of small shopkeepers throughout the time of Ram Singh. There was practically no activity here either in the sphere of creative arts, or in social movements.[10] Swami Dayanand came to Jaipur thrice—in 1865, 1866 and 1878—during Ram Singh's period, but did not leave much impression on the local population.[11] Ram Singh himself tried to goad the population towards some new thinking. In March 1869 he established in Jaipur a Society for Social Advancement, called the "Jeypore Social Science Congress".[12] One important object of this Congress was to create consciousness among the people, specially the Jagirdars that they should not depend for everything on the ruler, but do something themselves for roads, schools, sanitation etc., in their areas. It was thought that with the growth of education many social improvements would automatically follow. The Congress was opened with great fanfare when the Political Agent was on his visit to Jaipur. Nothing however is known about this Congress after its first session. In this session was adopted a resolution recommending to "His Highness the Maharaja the establishment of a separate school to be entitled the Jeypore Nobles' School." This recommendation of the Congress was redundant since a Nobles'

9. See Chapter VI, Section (iii) on education.
10. Jaipur remained educationally one of the backward places even among the cities of Rajasthan up to the twenties of this century. The figures are given in the *Chapter on Education.*
11. For details see H.B. Sarda, *Life of Dayanand Saraswati*, pp. 45-46, 50, 214.
12. *Report on the Political Administration of the Rajpootana States for 1868-69*, pp. 100-104. The full details of the opening ceremony of the Jaipur "Social Science Congress" was published in the Delhi Gazette.

School for the education of their children already existed in Jaipur, albeit in a very poor condition.

Another important attempt of Ram Singh to spread modern ideas among his people was to build a theatre hall in the city. This hall, named Ram Prakash, exists even today; but it did not bring out any latent histrionic talent in the city, and was generally used by itinerant troupes from metropolitan cities.

We may briefly consider why in spite of the enlightened attitude of the ruler the people of Jaipur did not respond to his attempt to bring about a cultural revival.

Pandit Shivadeen, who started as a tutor to the Maharaja and later became his Secretary and eventually on the death of Thakur Lachhman Singh the Prime Minister in May 1862, died two years later on June 13, 1864.

> "To the Moosahibat or ministerial department were appointed Buxshee Fyez Ally Khan, who was also the commander in chief of the Army, and Bishamberdeen, son of late Shivadeen. To the Dewanee or Financial Departments were appointed Moonshee Kishan Suroop and Purohit Ramprashad.
>
> "The only man who may be said to be fully competent and who endeavours to carry out the duties of the administration entrusted to him is the Nawab Fyez Ally Khan. The Pandit's son as well as Kishen Suroop have both worked very unsatisfactorily and lost all confidence of the Maharaja by their lukewarmness in their duties. Pandit Ramprashad, the fourth member is a men of no education and can hardly sign his name."[13]

In other words the whole administration was carried on by Nawab Faiz Ali Khan. It appears that during this period he quietly replaced Hindi by Urdu as the official language of Jaipur. People of Jaipur who did not know Urdu, thus lost touch with administration.[14] The Director of Public Institution in his report[15] for the year 1905 considered this as the foremost reason for educational backwardness of Jaipur.

13. *Report of the Political Administration of Rajpootana State for 1865-66 & 1866-67*, p. 164.
14. Munshi Devi Prasad, *Swapna Rajasthan*, Vidya Bhawan Press, Muradabad, 1892, pp. 89-90.

Nawab Faiz Ali Khan resigned and left Jaipur in 1873 but Urdu remained the official language of the Jaipur State until the end. In 1943, an agitation was started for making Hindi the official language in the Jaipur State.[16] As a result both Hindi and Urdu were declared official languages, but for all practical purposes Urdu continued to be used in official correspondence.

The economic prosperity of Jaipur was notable during this period (1835-1880). The most obvious sign of this was the increase in the population of the city. Bishop Heber had estimated the population of Jaipur at 60,000 in 1824-25. By 1840, the population of the city could not have in any case exceeded one lakh. In an earlier chapter the reason for this estimate has been given. The period between 1825 to 1840 was marked by bad government in the state, and even the estimate of one lakh would seem to be inflated. The first census of the city, one of the earliest in India, was taken in July 1870. In fact, the only city in India where a population count was taken earlier was Bombay in 1864. In Madras city census was taken for the first time in 1871 and in Calcutta in 1876.[17]

The population of Jaipur was found to be 1,37,887 of whom 116,563 lived within the city walls and 21,324 outside.[18] Thus there must have been a large increase in the population of the city by 1870.

The official decennial census started all over India from 1881. If we compare the figures obtained in these countings we get the following information:

Year	Population within the city walls	Population outside the city walls	Total	Increase
1870	116,563	21,324	1,37,887	
1881	125,785	16,793	1,42,578	3.6%
1891	132,421	26,366	1,58,787	11.4%

15. Quoted in the Chapter VI, Section (iii) on Education.
16. Gehlot, *Jaipur wa Alwar Rajyon ka Itihas*, p. 174.
17. *Imperial Gazetteer*, (1908), Respective Volumes.
18. *Report on the Political Administration of the Rajpootana States for the year 1870-71*, pp. 84-85. The relevant portion is as follows:

In all these years the death rate in the city was higher than the birth rate.[19] This indicates that the increase in population was mainly due to a large and steady immigration from outside throughout these years.

"50. In the month of July last a census of the City and its suburbs was taken, and I believe with greater success than previously.

The 30th of July was the day appointed for the work, but for months before preparations were instituted, and on the 15th July each occupant of a house was furnished with an appropriate form to be filled in. The city within the walls was divided into 9 districts and outside portion into 4.

To each district were appointed two officials to superintend the registrations, the whole staff working under Moonshee Ramnarain, an able and responsible hand.

The work occupied 12 hours, and showed the following results:

Inside the wall

Total number of houses		22,356
Men	45,316	
Women	44,031	
Boys under 7 years	16,397	
Girls under 7 years	10,819	
	116,565	

Outside the wall

Total number of houses		5,330
Men	9,400	
Women	6,589	
Boys under 7 years	3,055	
Girls under 7 years	2,280	
	21,314	

Or a total of 27,686 houses and 1,37,877 souls. If these figures are correct, as I believe them to be as far as possible, the statement which have represented the population at one-half to two lakhs must have been either over-estimated, or the city has depopulated in a corresponding degree. It is certainly not impossible that the late famine may have exerted its share in producing this result, but I can scarcely imagine that the difference between the census, said to have been taken between 1858 and 1861 alluded to in Col. Brooke's *Political History of Jeypoor*, p. 8, which gives the number of houses at 50,000 and the total population at 200,000, is to be accounted for in this way, more especially as this starting difference is not so much in the population as in the number of houses which would not be effected to such degree. (The report is dt. 10-5-1871 by Capt. E R.C.B. Officiating Political Agent, Jeypoor).

19. The figures are given in the Chapter on Public Health.

What was it that lured so many people to the city? No definite evidence is available in this regard, and one can only speculate about the new openings for livelihood that were made available during this period in Jaipur. One of them was, of course, administration. The ruler Ram Singh tried to superimpose on the old medieval structure some development departments though keeping the basic departments of revenue and police in the same old forms.[20] Thus a number of departments were established such as the Public Works, Medical and Meteorological, Public Instruction, etc., and since the work of these departments was of technical nature they were placed under British Officers. With the establishment of the Water Works, an assured water supply also became available to a large number of people. All these brought in some direct and indirect employment opportunities. Even so this is not sufficient to explain the large influx of population. This could have come from the growth of trade, industry and banking in the city. Unfortunately detailed figures on these are not available. The 1868-69 report of the Political Agent of the Jaipur contains lists of exports and imports of the city for the year 1924 V.S. or 1868 A.D.[21] These are perhaps the only such lists available giving the statistics of the external trade of the city, and might have been compiled from the figures available in the Custom Office.

The main imports were food articles and clothing. Among the former those which might be considered luxury items were sugar (32,000 maunds worth Rs. 5,60,000 which gives the price of Rs. 17.50 per maund), Pan (757 maunds for Rs. 19,950) and tobacco (6,130 maunds). The quantities imported show that a large number of people in the city could afford these articles. Similarly there was a large import worth Rs. 34,600 of silk, pashmina, gold, cloth etc., but the export worth Rs. 21,450, of these articles was also substantial. Perhaps Jaipur was a central market for these luxury goods. Also the export quantity-wise was only about 5½ maunds against an import of 94 maunds though there was not that much difference in the total prices of

20. *Review of the Administration of the Native States of Rajpootana, 1906-1907*, p. 10.

21. The lists are reproduced in the Appendix X.

the exports and imports. These show that all the imported silk, gold, cloth etc., were converted into articles of higher value within the city, by tailoring or embroidery or by adding sequins etc., on them.

However, the important thing to note in these two lists is the total value of exports and imports of all the articles. The exports were worth only Rs. 2.96 lakhs against the import worth Rs. 23.19 lakhs. Indeed, so far as the city itself was concerned, the imports would be even higher, because these trade figures compiled presumably from the statistics available at the Custom Offices, would not include the city's trade within the territory of the Jaipur State. The city must have been getting the bulk of its requirements of food grain from the areas within the Jaipur State.

Since exports are so much lower than the imports, how was the city paying for its imports? One possibility is that the capital was living on the rent obtained by the Jagirdars residing in it from their tenant farmers. This was, however, not the main balancing factor of its external trade. In the next year's report, i.e. that for the year 1869-70, the Political Agent compiled "a return giving a tolerably accurate estimate of the Jeypore territory of the past year, exclusive of salt, constructed in accordance with the information gained from every source at my disposal." In this return also it was found that for the Jaipur territory as a whole the imports were worth Rs. 57,75,000 against an export of only Rs. 26,50,000." In other words, the imbalance in trade was for the territory as a whole vis-a-vis places outside the territory. It was not merely an imbalance between the city and the rest of the Jaipur State.

It may be noticed however that the trade figures given above do not include the trade in precious metals and gem stones. Commenting on this, the 1869-70 report continues:

> "Jeypore supplies nearly the whole of Rajpootana with gold, silver and precious stones, but during the last two years of scarcity the trade in these articles has very much diminished.
>
> "Business is certainly not so active as to account for the enormous banking transactions which are continuously going on. The only possible explanation is that Jeypore is

as it were a sort of Lombard street of Rajpootana and the amount of legitimate trade actually done within its walls has little influence on its banking interests.

"There are as many as seven Banking Firms, doing an aggregate business estimated at two crores and a half rupees per annum, and possessing a capital of upwards of 6 million sterling. In addition to the above there are many Seths with means under a lakh of rupees whose collective business is not less than half a crore of rupees.

"The import of gold before 1868 could not have been less than 75 lakhs of rupees, the greater portion of which buried by the many rich merchants who have their houses in these States. If it has ever reached, it has never exceeded 25 lakhs of rupees during the last two years, but a large amount of gold produced by its possessors in consequence of the high prices lately prevailing has found its way into Jeypore. The circumstances, combined with that of the influx of grain, has caused a great fall in the value of the precious metal."[22]

"The following table shows the present prices of gold and silver:[23]

		Rs.	As.	P.
Gold —	China leaf per tola	15	7	11
	Bar gold	15	4	3
		Jeypore rupees		
S lver —	Silver hoops per 100 tolas	98	0	0
	Silver bricks	99	8	0
Government rupees per 100		103	0	0"

All this of course does not explain how the balance was achieved. In fact, if so much of gold and precious stones were imported within the city, that would only aggravate the imbalance. This point did not escape the notice of the British Government in Calcutta and they duly asked for an explanation. The Political Agent tried to give a satisfactory reply in

22. *Report on the Political Administration of the Rajpootana States*, 1869-70, Paras 108-111.
23. *Ibid.*, Para 112.

his next annual report, i.e. the one for the year 1870-71. He wrote:

> "With my administration report of 1869-70 as complete a Return as possible for the trade of Jeypore territory was furnished: it showed such an excess in the amount of imports over exports as to form a subject of reference from Government in December last for an explanation of the cause of discrepancy. Amongst other reasons I attributed the excess to the export of precious stones and metals which has been omitted from the Returns, much of which while imported in the raw state were sent out manufactured, and to a large extent found their way to the houses of wealthy Marwaries which lie in Shekhawatee, Bikaner etc., and to the increase of imports and decrease of exports in a corresponding ratio, consequent on the seasons of scarcity in the past years, and to the fact that while it is very probable that a correct and minute register of the imports is kept, it is very doubtful whether the same exactness is observed in respect to the numerous articles particularly precious stones, and metals which by various means find their way into foreign territory. But there is still another cause, which I ought to have added, which appears to account for this discrepancy in a greater degree than perhaps any other, namely that owing to the fact of the Jeypore bankers and traders having branch firms as well in Bombay, Calcutta and other places, with which the trade is carried on by the State, a large portion of the imports is paid for by drafts on these places, a circumstance which though not affecting the 'actuals' as shown by the "Returns" must of course have considerable bearing in counteracting the discrepancy and in preserving the equilibrium of trade."[24]

In other words, Jaipur in those days had two principal avenues of business: banking and manufacture of jewellery and cutting of precious stones. Of these, the first perhaps yielded more money to the city but did not provide many

24. *Report on the Political Administration of the Rajpootana States,* 1870-71, p. 74.

employment opportunities. The manufacture of jewellery and gem cutting on the other hand are the industries which today provide the largest employment in the city.

It will be recalled that Girdhari in his *Bhojanasara* (A. D. 1739) had also mentioned about the existence of jewellery industry and had referred to the extensive banking business in the city. This was within 12 years of the foundation of the city.[25] With the establishment of peace and stable Government after A.D. 1840 both these industries began to flourish in the period under discussion. However, the census figures of the year 1901 reveal that even up to that year, the number of persons employed in the jewellery industry was not large. No definite conclusion can therefore be drawn about the reason why Jaipur's population had increased during this period.

Jewellery Industry

In the making of jewellery and ornaments, Jaipur enjoys a world-wide fame, particularly for two of its specialities. Jaipur is one of the few places in India where enamelling on gold is done. Also Jaipur is an important centre of cutting and polishing of gem-stones, particulary emeralds.

Enamelling is done on silver and copper also, but the best enamelling is done on gold and the colour of the enamel for which Jaipur is famous is red. This work is the speciality of certain Sikh families of Jaipur. It is said that the ancestors of these families were originally brought to Amer by Man Singh I during the reign of Akbar or Jahangir. There were altogether five enamellers who were brought here. The names of four of these were Zorawar Singh, Jawar Singh, Sukh Singh and Bhairon Singh.[26] On the shifting of the capital, the families also moved from Amer to Jaipur.

The report of the Political Agent quoted above mentions about the import of precious stones in the raw state and their cutting and finishing in Jaipur. It is not known how and when

25. According to the famous jeweller Shri Bhuramal Rajmal Surana, his ancestors and the ancestors of a number of important jeweller families of Jaipur moved to Jaipur from Delhi at the time of Jai Singh, the founder of the city.

26. *Jaipur Album* (1935), p. 9.

this industry started here. No large mines of precious stones are found in the vicinity of the Jaipur State.[27] There is, however, quite a good source of garnet, a semi-precious stone in Sarwar in Kishangarh and near Rajmahal.[28] The raw garnets were finished by the gem-stone cutters of Jaipur. The larger pieces were used for jewellery, and towards the end of the nineteenth century smaller pieces began to be exported to Switzerland and other European countries for the manufacture of watches and musical boxes.[29] It is quite possible that the gem-stone cutters of Jaipur obtained their expertise in this craft by cutting garnets. In any case, Jaipur had not specialised in any particular gem until the latter part of the nineteenth century. Starting from the last quarter of the nineteenth century the city became one of the largest centres in the World for cutting emeralds. It is generally believed that the man who brought this fame to Jaipur was Banjilal Tholia. Banjilal, son of Kaluram Tholia, a cloth merchant, was born in 1857. He started his jewellery business at the age of 13 and by the time he was 28 years old, "he was reckoned as one of the foremost

27. Some emerald used to be mined in the Ajmer and Bhilwara district but the quantity was not significant. The production of emerald in pounds (lbs.) in various years as given in the *Memoirs of the Geological Survey of India* (Vol. 86) Calcutta, 1959, in various years was as follows:

1944-45	169	1947-48	480
1945-46	922	1948-49	198
1946-47	946	1949-50	123

28. Rajmahal was within the boundary of Jaipur State but is now in the Tonk District.

29. Supplement to the Jeypore Museum Catalogue (1896); Garnet and not emerald remained the speciality of Jaipure at least up to the end of the 19th century. *The Report of the Political Administration of Rajputana for the year 1882-83* states: "It may be noticed that there is now a large trade in garnets, which are collected here from mines mostly in other Rajputana States, though partly also in Jeypore and are exported to Europe, the smaller ones being for use in watches and the larger yielding, according as they are cut carbuncles or other ornamental forms of the Stones" (p. 10). The Census Report for the year 1901 also mentions garnet cutting and not emerald cutting. "Garnets and crystals-garnet, necklaces and other ornaments are made chiefly for Europeans. Good lapidary work is done here." (p. 9).

businessmen of the Jaipur city."[30] It is said that it was he who started the direct import of raw, that is, rough emeralds from abroad and made Jaipur internationally famous as a centre of emerald cutting. Banjilal Tholia died in 1928.

Another jeweller family who took active part in developing the emerald trade in Jaipur in the second half of the nineteenth century was the Phopholia family.

The city continues to attract jewellers from outside even now. Some of them coming from Gujrat have established themselves in the export trade of gemstones. The Durlabhji family is the most well-known among them. And there are other who have come from Delhi and Agra.

Banking

The administration report for the year 1869-70 quoted earlier makes mention of the importance of the banking business of Jaipur. It also mentions that the local trade and industry were not large enough to support banking business on such an extensive scale. It is thus not clear what trade or industry this extensive banking system was financing. There was of course the large-scale buying and selling of precious metals and jewellery and this must have required large finances. But even this would not support banking business reckoned in crores of rupees.

It is possible that the bankers and financers had migrated from other places to Jaipur city when it was founded because of the safety and security of this walled city. These bankers financed the local trade of grain and cotton. In the latter part of the eighteenth century when the trade route to the north-west passed through Jaipur, their business increased. The more important of the bankers also gave loans to the ruler to enable him to pay the tributes to the Maratha raiders. These loans were given against the security of the revenues of some assigned territory of the Jaipur State. A large number of documents acknowledging such debts exist in the Kapaddwara Records whose list is available in the Bikaner Archives. One such document is in possession of Shri Swarup Narain Purohit whose ancestor gave a loan of Rs. 16,000/- to the ruler, Pratap

30. *Jaipur Album* (1935), Ch. XVIII, p. 7.

Singh, for paying the tribute to the Holkar. The translation of the documents reads as follows:

Seal
Maharajadhiraj
Shri Sawai Pratap Singhji

Shri Maharajadhiraj Shri Sawai Pratap Singhji sends his cordial wishes to Purohit Lachmandas. Further, Rs. 16,000/- be paid to subedar Rao Tukaji Holkar as part of the tribute payable to him by the State. through Raja Khushaliram Daulatram Bohra. This amount shall be chargeable against the first instalment of Shekhawati revenue in our account.

Miti Mangsir Badi 6, Samvat 1848 (A.D.1791)

The bankers also lent money to the Jagirdars for meeting the marriage expenses of their children and for other purposes.

Apart from these, the bankers also financed the general trade. The main trade of India has always been in food-grain, cotton and cloth. In so far as these commodities entered Jaipur for consumption and re-export the trade was financed by the Jaipur bankers. But there were at least two commodities which did not necessarily pass through Jaipur city, though the bankers here financed them. The first was the salt trade of Sambhar. Sambhar[31] was the second largest[32] source of salt in northern India and trade in this commodity was extensive. Another trade financed by the Jaipur bankers was opium. Opium does not grow in the Jaipur territory, but apparently the Jaipur traders took a keen interest in it. The Imperial Gazetteer (1908) mentions,[33] "Up to about 1896 a heliogarph from Jaipur to Fatehpur in Shekhawati was maintained by the opium merchants of the latter town for use in their business."

In the later half of the nineteenth century bankers like Bansidhar Khetan of Mehansar (Shekhawati), Seth Bihari Mal of Berath (Jaipur) and Baldeodas of Pilani had established

31. Sambhar lake was jointly owned by the Jaipur and Jodhpur States, but under a treaty of 1869, the salt sources were worked by the British Government. Aitchison, *op. cit.*, pp. 56, 74-78; See *Imperial Gazetteer*, Vol. XIII, p. 396.

32. The largest inland source of salt in the Indian subcontinent is the Salt Range in Pakistan.

33. *Imperial Gazetteer*, Vol. XIII, p. 393.

their firms in the city of Jaipur.[34] The *Jaipur Album* also mentions them among the important firms doing banking business in Jaipur in the thirties of this century. The list is given below. Considering that it takes a number of generations to accumulate the capital required to do banking business, it may be surmised that the ancestors of these persons were the important bankers of the period under discussion:

1. Baldeo Dass Brijmohan Birla.
2. Bansidhar Shiva Prasad Khetan.
3. Bansilal Abir Chand.
4. Biharilal Kodiwala Bairathi.
5. Brijlal Zirawarmal Banthia.
6. Chandrabhan Bansilal—This was the branch of the firm whose main office was in Bikaner.
7. Chhogamal Surajmal.
8. Gokaldass Jiwandas — Main office of the firm was in Jabbalpur.
9. Ganeshdeo Narsinghdass.
10. Jawaharmal Suganchand—Proper: Seth Bhagchand Soni (M.L.A.). The main office of the firm was in Ajmer.
11. Jhoomarlal Swarooplal.
12. Kanwalnain Hamir Singh—The main office of the firm was in Ajmer.
13. Khetsidass Sadasukh.
14. Shriram Nanagram.
15. Suraj Bux Nirbhairam.

Raja Baldeodass Brijmohan Birla of the Birla family had his banking office in Johari Bazar at that time.

Rousselet's Description of the Ganesh Chaturthi Fair

Ram Singh died in 1880. Jaipur at this time was a growing and prosperous town. One Louis Rousselet who came to Jaipur

34. C.R. Bhandari, B.L. Soni, K.L. Gupta, Ed. *Introduction of Indian Merchants*, Pt. I (in Hindi), Calcutta, 1985, (Rajputana Section), pp. 61-62.

near about this time has described[35] the goods sold in the Ganesh Chaturthi Mela.[36] If the common people of Jaipur could afford to buy all these things, they were a prosperous people indeed.

> "Towards the middle of August the Jeypoorians celebrate with great magnificence the festival of Ganesa, the God of Science and Wisdom. For several days the five boulevards of the capital are covered with picturesque crowds, drawn from all parts of the kingdom; the houses and palaces are decorated with gaudy flags and draperies, and the public squares adorned with poles covered with flowers. The fair or mela which is held on the occasion round the royal palace, forms the chief attraction to the crowds of country people. There all the products of Rajasthan and of Hindustan, as well as of Europe are collected. Magnificent shawls from Thibet, scarves from Bundelcund, figured kincobs from Benaras and gauzes from Bengal are found side by side with shirtings from Manchester, printed calicoes from Belgium and Turkey reds; while armouries offer you daggers from Herat, Gorkha Krisses, Katars from Mewar, and cutters from Sheffield and Chatelherault. The principal products of Jeypur industry which are exposed for sale are embroidered turbans, marble idols, copper stoves, embroidered shoes, the salt of Sambhar and enamels of fine gold."

The Map of Jaipur in 1881 A.D.

A map of Jaipur city and its environs was given with the Census Report for 1881.[37] This is perhaps the first printed map of the city. The following points are worth noting in this map:—

1. All the *Chowkris* of the city except *Chowkri* Topkhana Hazuri had practically fully developed by 1881. They had straight roads and lanes. However, Topkhana

35. Louis Rousselet, *India and its Native Princes*, London, 1882, p. 236.
36. The Mela is not mentioned in the list of fairs given in the *Jaipur Gazetteer* of 1876.
37. A photocopy of the map is reproduced on p. 143.

Hazuri had the look of an unplanned area with crooked lanes and scattered clusters of houses here and there. Rajamal ka Talao known then as the city lake existed at that time actually as a lake. It has since then been filled up.

2. There were few buildings outside the walls. Among them were the Railway Station, the Residency and the Hathroi fort. Ram Newas Garden had been built and is shown in the map.
3. The Hindu cremation ground near Adarsh Nagar existed even at that time, but the present cremation ground on the Jhotwara road west of the Chandpole Gate was not there at that time. There was however a cremation ground about half way between the Chandpole gate and the Government Hostel. This ground has now come within the built-up area.

CHAPTER V

The Period of Stagnation—1880-1922

Ram Singh died in 1880 without leaving a son. In spite of his love of learning and interest in cultural matters, he selected a successor who had received little education. This youngman, originally named Kayam Singh, and aged about 19 years at that time, was employed in the Tonk Cavalry as a Sepoy. On becoming the ruler of Jaipur he took the name Madho Singh III.

The Development of Irrigation Sources under Kanti Chandra Mookerjee

For the first two years of his rulership, the State was managed by a regency council. In 1882 Madho Singh was given full powers on attaining the age of 21 years. Kanti Chandra Mookerjee,[1] who was from 1876, the Private Secretary

1. The following information about the early life of Kanti Chandra Mookerjee was available from his grandson A.C. Mookerjee:

   "Kanti Chander Mookerjee was born probably in 1836 in Rahuta —a small village in the district of 24 Parganas. He was the only son of his mother who was widowed when he was young. To supplement their income from a small piece of land which they possessed his mother stitched mosquito nets for sale He first studied in the village primary school in Shamnagar near Calcutta and then went to the High School in Chandernagore. He was one of the early graduates of the Calcutta University. He started as a school master at Janai, a village near Calcutta. Hari Mohan Sen was at that time the Private Secretary to the young Maharaja Ram Singh of Jaipur. He met Mookerjee when he visited his father-in-law in Janai and invited Mookerjee to take over as the head-master of the School in Jaipur. He came to Jaipur in 1865."

of the Maharaja, was made the Chief Member of the Council in 1885. From this time onwards the development of Jaipur city received less attention of the State Government. Mookerjee, it appears, thought more of the development of irrigation of the State. This would be evident from the figures realised from irrigation during the various years during Mookerjee's period:[2]

Year	*Revenue from Irrigation* (*Rs.*)
1880-81	80,000
1885	1,35,000
1896	3,23,000

The revenue from irrigation varied from year to year also, with the amount of rainfall during the year. If there was a good rainfall the tanks would fill up, and more area would be irrigated. This would bring in more revenue. But the fourfold increase in irrigation revenue was mostly due to the fact that many new irrigation sources were created by constructing storage dams across the rivulets.

One of the most important irrigation projects started during the time of Mookerjee was the Ramgarh Irrigation Dam. The foundation stone of Ramgarh Dam across the Banganga river was laid on the 30th December 1897. Later, this lake became the most important source of water for the city.[3]

2. *Public Works Report for the year ending 31-12-1897.*
3. The river Banganga has its source near Bairat about 65 Km. north of Jaipur city. After flowing through hilly part for about 40 Km. it passes through a narrow gorge about 3 Km. long near Gopalgarh about 5 Km. east of Ramgarh village. After emerging from the gorge, it flows for about 90 Km. through the territory of the erstwhile Jaipur State and then enters the territory of the erstwhile Bharatpur State. In Bharatpur the river is also known as Utangan.

A project to built a dam at the site where the river enters the Gopalgarh gorge was first prepared in 1872. But the project was delayed by 25 years because the Bharatpur State objected to this project as soon as they came to know of it. Bharatpur said that all the water of this river which was used for irrigation purpose in that State would be held back by the dam proposed by Jaipur. The Jaipur State explained that the dam proposed was not in Mowha Ramgarh but in Jamwa Ramgarh which was 50 miles upstream. The loss to Bharatpur would not be as great as they feared; and in fact less than 20 per cent of the total flow of the Banganga river would be held back by the

The Famine of 1899-1900

Jaipur suffered one of the most serious famines in its history in the years 1899-1900. The scarcity of food in the city was avoided by importing food-grains for the permanent residents. But a large number of starving villagers who moved into the city in search of food, died of hunger because they had no money to purchase the food.

It will be recalled that this year was the year of the great Rajasthan famine. There was practically no crop throughout western Rajasthan and the famine was so severe that many parts of Bikaner and Marwar were depopulated. The famine is known as "CHHAPANIA KAL". Famine was severe in the areas around Jaipur City also, but thanks to the supplies which could be brought from other States by railways, the prices of food-grains did not rise very high in the city. The following table gives the prices of food-grains each year from 1898 to 1902:

Year	*Food-grain in seers per rupee*		
	Wheat	Barley	Bajra
1898	12.61	19.61	18.53
1899	11.00	15.51	13.68
1900	9.73	13.76	12.67
1901	11.75	19.64	21.72
1902	12.12	16.21	16.21

proposed dam. Bharatpur was not satisfied with this answer. The matter was referred to the British Government who stopped the construction of the dam till Jaipur gave an assurance that they would indemnify Bharatpur for any future loss. Jaipur refused to give such an assurance. The Government of India then ordered the work on the dam to be stopped by their letter dated 22-9-1875.

The ban on the construction of the Ramgarh Dam imposed by the Government of India was not removed for twenty years. At the end of this period, the report of the Agent to the Governor-General for 1895-96 states as follows:—

> "The Durbar have decided on proceeding with the construction of the reservoir at Ramgarh. The Project which was designed by Col. Jacob, C.I.E., who has conferred so much benefit to the State by his work as Chief Engineer is calculated to supply water for the irrigation of a large area. The opposition raised by Bharatpore Durbar which delayed the construction of the reservoir for

In other words, while the countryside was famine-striken, there was no serious shortage of food-grain in the city. After some time the starving people from the villages started moving towards the city. The result was reminiscent of the scenes in Calcutta during the 1943 Bengal famine. Pierre Loti, the famous French novelist, came to Jaipur in that year. He has left a vivid description of the condition of these people some of whom were not allowed to enter the city and were stopped at the gates. Loti saw them while approaching the city. He wrote:[4]

> "But what can be the meaning of those miserable heaps of rags lying at the foot of ramparts? There are human shapes hidden under them. What can all these people be doing on the ground? Are they ill or are they drunk? Ah! these are heaps of bones, or the withered and mummified caracasses of the dead. No, it cannot be that, for there are some who still move, their eye-lids tremble and they can see, and there are some who can even stand on the tottering bones that serve as legs."

When Loti entered the city he again found these starving people.

> "But there are also many hideous vagrants—graveyard spectres like those lying at the rampart gates. For these have actually dared to enter the rose-coloured city and to drag their skeletons through the streets. There are more of them than I should have thought possible . . . . There are horrible heaps of rags and bones lying on the pavements hidden amongst the gay booths of the merchants, and people have to step aside so as not to tread upon them. These phantoms are peasants who used to live in the surrounding districts . . .
>
> "They are hungry and they wish to eat, that is why they have come into the city. They thought that people

many years has fortunately been overcome, and work will now commence." (p. 7)

Reports on the Ramgarh Irrigation Projects (1) 1883, (2) 1888, and (3) 1892.

Correspondence relating to Ramgurh Bund.

4 Loti, Pierre, *India*, translated by G.A.F. Inman (3rd ed., London, 1913), pp, 190, 192, 193.

would take pity on them, and would not let them die, and they had heard that food and grains were stored here, as if to resist a siege; they had heard, too, that every one in the city had something to eat . . .

"But though there is food it cannot be had without money. It is indeed true that the King gives food to the poor who dwell in his capital,[5] but as to helping the peasants who die by thousands in the surrounding fields, how can that be done if there is not a sufficiency. So all heads are turned aside from the poor wretches who wander through the streets, and who haunt the places where people eat, still hoping that a few grains of rice may be thrown to them, till at length the time comes when they must lie down anywhere even on the stones of the streets, to wait for death's deliverance."

These starving peasants must have searched for food in the street garbage and as a result died of stomach disorders. This is perhaps the reason for the high number (2296) of deaths recorded due to cholera in that year.

The Government of India appointed a Famine Commission to report on the methods of mitigating the effects of the Famine. Kanti Chandra Mookerjee was appointed a member of this Commission. He died on 15 January 1901 in Nagpur during the sittings of the Commission there.[6]

The only major improvement in the city during this period was the building of a trolley line over which the garbage of the town was carried. The maps show that the line had a gauge of 15 inches. The line that went along the wall started at the mid-point between the Ghat gate and Sanganeri gate, where the first depot was situated. The second depot was near the Sanganeri gate and the third near Ajmeri gate. Thereafter the line turned south, ending somewhere near the present Secretariat building, where the refuse was dumped. It may be mentioned

5. Grain was supplied in the city by the State at 10 seers a rupee—*Census Report of Jaipur for 1901*, p. 14.

6. The next permanent incumbent in the office of the Prime Minister of Jaipur was Sansar Chandra Sen. Sen had also come to Jaipur as a teacher in the Maharaja's College.

that even today refuse is dumped behind the Secretariat building near about the Ganda Nala. The line was constructed[7] in 1887-88 and was used until the forties of this century.

A Period of Stagnation, Decay and Decrease in Population

The whole period of the rule of Madho Singh (1880 to 1922) was a period of stagnation and decay for the Jaipur city. This will be evident from the figures of population of the city and its environs during these years:

YEAR	POPULATION			
	City within the walls	outside the walls	Total	Increase (+) or decrease (—)
1881	1,25,785	16,793	1,42,578	
1891	1,32,421	26,366	1,58,787	+11.4%
1901	1,32,091	28,076	1,60,167	+00.9%
1911	1,11,585	25,513	1,37,098	—14.4%
1921	94,216	25,991	1,20,207	—12.3%

It will be noticed that so far as the walled city was concerned the population increased from 1,25,785 to 1,32,421 or 5.3% from 1881 to 1891 and thereafter it steadily decreased to 94,216. The decrease in population in these 40 years, 1881-1921 was slightly over 25%.

Conditions were not very much better outside the walls either, where, after indicating an increase of 60% from 1881 to 1891, the population remained almost stagnant.

It must have been very depressing to live in the city in those years when, as shown in the chapter on Public Health, year after year more people died in the city than were born. Immigration, which used to make up this deficit, also dwindled after 1891.

Increase in the Number of Mohallas

Though the population of the city fell so steeply during

7. *Public Works Report for the year 1888*, p. 4.

this period, it is interesting to note that the number of Mohallas within the city increased in number. According to the 1881 Census report there were 221 Mohallas within the city. *Notes on Jaipur* (1916) on the other hand puts the number at 407. In the report of the 1881 Census, the names of the Mohallas in the various Chowkris is given. According to this list there were the following numbers of Mohallas in each Chowkri:

Chowkri	Number of Mohallas in 1881	Population in 1881	Population in 1921
1. Gangapol	15	7,750	11,145
2. Sarhad[8]	9	4,174	*
3. Puranibasti	50	18,263	
4. Topkhana Desh	43	20,182	14,723
5. Modi Khana	8	8,822	2,650
6. Visheshvarji	19	13,435	7,783
7. Ghat Darwaja	44	22,127	15,138
8. Topkhana Hazuri	13	12,297	10,251
9. Ramchandarji	20	28,729	12,545
Total	221	1,25,785	94,216

Decrease in Population, Sickness and Prevalence of Diseases

It will be noticed that for some unexplained reason the population of Chowkri Gangapole increased during these forty years. In all others, the population fell, in some of them quite precipitously. For example, in Chowkri Visheshvarji it fell by 42%. The tables above show that the population of the city within the wall fell by 29% in the twenty years i.e. during

8. Sarhad Chowkri consisted of the population living in the environs of the palace. It had, according to the 1881 Census Report, the following Mohallas:—

1. Chelon Ka.	4. Sriji Ka	7. Bazar Gangori Darwaja.
2. Kanwalgatta.	5. Anjir Darwaja.	8. Tripolia Bazar.
3. Jaleb Chouk.	6. Mahron Ka.	9. Bazar Sire Deodi.

In the 1921 census, the population of these Mohallas was presumably counted along with that of the nearest Chowkri. For instance, Bazar Gangori Darwaza was included in Chokri Purani Basti, and Bazar Sire Deori in Chowkri Ramchandarji.

1901-1921. In 13 of these 20 years, plague was prevalent in the city in a mild or severe form. The great world-wide influenza epidemic of 1918 also took a heavy toll in the city. The total number of deaths from fever alone within the city that year was 5898, which would mean 5% of the total population.

Caste and Occupation of the People

The 1901 Census of India was one of the most detailed attempts to find out the caste and means of livelihood of the people. We therefore know a great deal about these two aspects of the life in the city from the census report of that year. The total population of the city in 1901 was 1,60,167. The population of the first 16 castes in descending order of their total numbers was as follows:[9]

1. Brahman — 24,365
2. Sheik (Musalman) — 24,223
3. Pathan (,,) — 9,859
4. Mali — 9,569
5. Agarwal (Hindu) — 8,106
6. Rajput (Hindu) — 5,338 There were a few hundred Muslim Rajputs also. In most of the castes the numbers of males and females were almost equal, but among the Rajputs living in the city there were only 1,799 females compared to 3,539 males. It is likely that most of the Rajputs in the city were in the army or Police and had left their families in their village homes.
7. Koli — 4,806

9. *Census Report for Jaipur State for 1901*, pp. 144-149.

8.	Khandelwal (Hindu)	— 4,718
9.	Kumhar	— 4,313
10.	Khandelwal (Jain)	— 3,635
11.	Kayastha	— 3,397
12.	Saraogi	— 2,927
13.	Nai	— 2,661
14.	Mina	— 2,633
15.	Sayad (Musalman)	— 2,444
16.	Sunar	— 2,253

Muslims thus comprised a little less than one-fourth of the total population of Jaipur in 1901. Among others, Brahmans had the largest population being 15% of the total. It is noteworthy that four of the Mahajan castes (Agarwals, Khandelwals —Hindus and Jains—and Saraogi) were among the first 16, and comprised together about 12% of the population. As noted in an earlier chapter, after including other Mahajan castes such as Oswal, Maheshwari etc., their number was about 14%. Jaipur thus continued to remain a city of Brahmans and traders with more than a quarter of the population belonging to these two communities. It may be mentioned that among the 24,365 Brahmans, the largest number was that of Gaur Brahmans (10,131) followed by Pariks (2,773).[10] Half of the Rajputs (5,338) in the city were the Kachhawas (2,526) i.e. belonging to the clan of the ruler, followed by the Chauhans (926) and the Rathors (576).[11]

It was found[12] that out of the total population of 1,60,167, the number of workers were 83,318 (62,131 males and 24,494 females) and the rest 76,843 were dependants. The number of workers was thus about 52% of the total population.

Government services, both civil (10,267) and military (8,524), employed more than 30% of the working males. Most of the persons (over 10,000) in civil employment were either Darbar officials or menials. This was to be expected in the capital of a native state which was still not quite out of the medieval age.

Another big group (8,658 males and 3,283 females) rendered

10. *Census Report for Jaipur State for 1901*, p. 164.
11. *Ibid.*, p. 165.
12. *Ibid.*, Occupations or Means of livelihood, pp. 180-215.

personal services and served as domestic servants, cooks, barbers, washermen etc.

Among the non-productive people were those working as priests. Their numbers were 2,117 males and 642 females. Their dependants numbered 2,968. The number of beggars in the town appears to have been quite large. There were 1516 male and 1411 female non-religious mendicants in the city and their dependants numbered 1236. And there were 210 prostitutes in the city apparently too few for a city of such a large size.

The industry which engaged the largest number of people in the city was that connected with cotton weaving, spinning and dyeing and printing of cotton cloth. Cotton weaving engaged 3353 people and calendering and dyeing and printing of cotton cloth 2483. Spinning of yarn which was practically confined to women, engaged 2870 persons. It may be mentioned that in the whole of the Jaipur State there were nearly 19,000 cotton spinners in that year. This shows that even in 1901 this industry was flourishing and mill spun yarn had not till then made it obsolete.

Compared to the workers engaged in processing cotton, the number of workers in gold, silver and precious stones was not large. There were in the city only 835 workers engaged in this industry, but there were as many as 716 dealers in these precious commodities. Clearly, gem stone cutting had not till then become an important industry; but from the number of jewellers it is apparent that the city was a big market for gold and silver ornaments and jewellery.

The number of bankers and money lenders was also quite large. There were 502 males and 182 females engaged in this trade.

The handicrafts of Jaipur were an attraction for the tourist at that time as they are now. There were a large number of shops[13] selling handicrafts and jewellery in the early part of this century.

Low Cultural Level

The general cultural level of Jaipur remained low even by

13. For list of the shops see *Notes on Jaipur* (1916).

the end of the Madho Singh's reign. As shown in the chapter on Education, among the five largest towns of Rajasthan—Ajmer, Jodhpur, Alwar, Jaipur and Bikaner—in percentage of literate population, Jaipur occupied the fourth place, being slightly better than Bikaner only, in 1921.

The Census Report of the Jaipur State for the year 1911 gives[14] a list of periodicals published in the city in that year. This list is reproduced below and it shows that there was practically no interest in creative writing here.

> "There are two printing presses in Jaipur City.
>
> "A weekly paper, entitled the "*Jaipur Gazette*" is published by the Jaipur Government in English, Hindi and Urdu; its circulation is very limited (about 25).
>
> "A Sanskrit monthly named "*Sanskrit Ratnakar*" is published at the Balchandra Press. About 300 copies of this magazine are circulated.
>
> "A Hindi monthly, named "*Abla Hitaishi*" is also published at the Balchandra Press and 300 copies of Hindi magazine are circulated.
>
> "Balchandra Press also published a Hindi and Urdu combined monthly, named "*Dharma Tattwa Probodhini*". It has a circulation of 250 copies."

Editing of Sanskrit Texts

On the other hand the period of the ruler Madho Singh was one of revival of Sanskrit learning in India, and Jaipur Pandits played an important role in this. Three Mahamahopadhyayas were writing and editing many books in Sanskrit in Jaipur at this time. Mahamahopadhyaya Pandit Durga Prasad Sharma edited the famous *Kavyamala* series published by the Nirnaya Sagar Press. Mahamahopadhyaya Pandit Shivadatta Dadimath was a great Sanskrit grammarian. He edited *Siddhanta Kaumudi*, *Nirukta* and Patanjali's *Mahabhasya*. This last published by the Nirnaya Sagar Press is probably still the standard work on the subject. Near about the end of the period under discussion, Mahamahopadhyaya Pandit Durga Prasad Saryooparin was

14. *Op. cit*, p. 196.

writing books on astronomy.

However, this group of learned Sanskrit scholars working in the Jaipur Sanskrit College could not effectively raise the cultural level of the citizens. Jaipur, whose system of general administration was still almost medieval, remained in the backwaters of Indian cultural renaissance and out of contact with modern civilization.

Balabux Khawas

The people in the town passed their time gossiping about the latest exploits of Balabux Khawas. Balabux Khawas popularly known as Khawasji was the personal attendant of the ruler Madho Singh. His official designation was *Muntazim Kapaddwara* (Superintendent of the Household). *Khawas*—an Arabic word—means attendant. In Jaipur *Khawas* generally means barber. But Balabux was a tailor by caste and was a descendant of Rodaram Khawas. Rodaram was also the personal attendant of the then ruler Jagat Singh (1802-1818). Since Jagat Singh spent most of his time in his harem, Rodaram, his confidant, is said to have become almost the defacto ruler of Jaipur. Balabux, his descendant, exercised great influence on the ruler Madho Singh. Though he interfered in all matters of the State, his special mischief was seen in those cases where the ruler had complete personal discretion to act. These would be mostly in the ruler's relationship with the jagirdars, especially in the *Matmi* cases. In the case of the important jagirdars, it was customary for the ruler to go to the houses of the jagirdars in succession cases and recognize the successors. This recognition was called *Matmi*.

It is said that until Khawasji's palms were properly greased he saw to it that the ruler did not find it convenient to go to the house of the jagirdar. Many stories about the doings of Balabux Khawas can still be heard from the older residents of the city.[15]

15. *Dastur Komwar*, Serial Order 'b'.

Chandradhar Sharma

Here we may mention two illustrious persons of Jaipur during this period who brought renown to their native city. These were Chandradhar Sharma Guleri who was a distinguished scholar, and Arjunlal Sethi, who took a prominent part in the liberation movement.

Chandradhar Sharma Guleri was a versatile genius. His father Pandit Shivram was a resident of Guler in Kangra. Maharaja Ram Singh of Jaipur had heard of his learning in Sanskrit language and literature and had brought him to Jaipur. Chandradhar was born in Jaipur in 1883. He was a bright student and he stood first in the Allahabad University both in the Entrance Examination and in the B.A. Examination (1903). The sensation he created all over Northern India by his result in the B.A. examination has been described in the chapter on Education. In 1902, he collaborated with Lt. Garret in writing "The Jaipur observatory and its Builder".

Chandradhar was not able to proceed with his M.A. studies, because the Maharaja of Jaipur wanted that he should go to Ajmer and be a guardian of the Raja of Khetri who was studying in the Mayo College there. He however continued his studies privately and became a master of Sanskrit, Pali and Prakrit. He also learnt Bengali, Marathi, Latin, French and German. He was appointed the senior teacher of Sanskrit in the Mayo College. Madan Mohan Malaviya heard of his learning and brought him over to the newly established Banaras Hind University as Manindra Chandra Nandi Professor of Indian History and Culture as also the Principal of the Oriental College. Chandradhar Sharma died in 1922 at the age of 39 while serving on these posts.

About 1905 he started from Jaipur a journal in Hindi called *Samalochak*. His writings which covered many subjects such as history, philosophy, philology, etc. were witty and free from obscurantism. Later he became the editor of the Nagari Pracharini Patrika and also the editor of a series of books called *Surya Kumari Pustakmala* published by the Sabha. In 1915, the *Sarasvati* of Allahabad published his short story "*Usne Kaha Tha*". This story has made him an immortal figure in Hindi literature. His two other stories *Sukhamaya*

Jiban and *Buddhu ka Kanta* are also well known.[16]

Arjun Lal Sethi

Arjun Lal Sethi, the father of freedom movement in Rajasthan, was born in Jaipur on 9 September 1880. He was the son of Jawaharlal Sethi of Gheewalon ka Rasta and he passed his B.A. examination in 1902. In 1907 he established Shri Jain Vardhman Vidyalaya in Jaipur. The main objective of the school was to impart nationalistic education to the boys. In 1913 there was a dacoity in the Jaina Upashraya in Arrah where the Mahant was killed. The purpose of the dacoity was to collect funds for the national movement. It was alleged that a teacher and some boys from this school were involved in this dacoity. One of the boys of the school Motichand was hanged on the murder charge. After some time Arjunlal Sethi was also arrested on suspicion and he was detained without trial for more than five years, mostly in Vellore in South India. He was released only in 1920. Sethi died on 22 December 1941 in Ajmer in the house of a Muslim friend.

In the twenties, the leadership of political movement had passed into the hands of Jamnalal Bajaj and others who followed Gandhiji's method of non-violence.[17]

16. Ram Chandra Shukla, *Hindi Sahitya ka Itihas*, p. 514; *Hindi Vishva-kosh*, Vol. XI, p. 229.
17. For details of Arjun Lal Sethi see Dr. K.S. Saxena's "*The Political Movements and Awakening in Rajasthan*", pp. 78, 128, 129, 203, 271, etc.

CHAPTER VI

Modernization—1922-1940

Maharaja Madho Singh died on 7 September 1922. He had five *ranis* and 18 concubines but none of his *ranis* had any son. He had adopted on 24 September 1921 a ten-year old boy, Mormukat Singh, from the family of the jagirdars of Isarda, from which he himself had been adopted. This boy renamed Man Singh II became the ruler of Jaipur at the age of eleven.[1] The administration of the State was carried on by a State Council, some of whose members were British Officers, until Man Singh was a major.

Modernization of the Administration

It was only after the death of Madho Singh and after the administration had been taken over by the State Council that Jaipur finally left the medieval age behind and entered the modern era. It has been mentioned earlier that except for some departments like the Public Works Department or the Medical Department, the general administration of the State was carried on by the Revenue and Police Departments in the old traditional manner. These old departments which could have given employment to a large number of young people with modern education, were in the hands of people with traditional training. In fact, in the last few years of Madho Singh's rule, the government was said to be effectively in the hands of one Balabux Khawas, a half-educated man who had somehow come close to the ruler.

1. The dates etc., are as given in the *Jaipur Album*.

What gave the city a somewhat medieval look was the fact that all the gates of the city were closed at 11 P.M. in the evening. Nobody could enter or leave the city after this time until the morning. The purpose of closing the gate at night however is not clear. A hundred years earlier it was perhaps necessary to close the gates to protect the citizens from bands of robbers who might suddenly swoop down upon the city and after robbing the citizens vanish in the jungles outside. But nodody thought of changing the system when such dangers had disappeared. This practice was particularly inconvenient for people leaving or arriving by trains after 11 P.M. They had either to wait at the railway station for the train, or for the day break, for going out or coming into the town. On winter nights this was quite an uncomfortable experience.

One of the first acts of the new administration was to order the opening of the Chandpole gate throughout the night. This was done in 1923. Since Chandpole gate was on the way to the railway station, one great inconvenience was thus removed. After sometime a similar order to keep the Sanganer gate also open throughout the night was issued.[2]

An early act of the State Council to modernize the administration was to introduce the system of preparing annual budget of the State. This was also done in 1923. Accounts rules were codified in the same year. Up to this time civil and criminal procedure and law in Jaipur had not been codified. Circulars (Hidayats) were issued from time to time which instead of simplifying the procedure further confused it. In 1923 Pandit Seetla Prasad Bajpai was appointed the Special Law Officer to prepare the various law orders.

The Jaipur Municipality was reorganised in 1926 and a new Municipal Act was prepared in 1929.

In 1928 the old feudal system under which all the jagirdars had to furnish a certain number of horses and sawars for the service of the State was commuted into cash payment.[3]

In Madho Singh's time the police force of Jaipur was in a medieval state. It was divided into a number of departments: the Girai, the Kotwali, the C.I.D. and the reserve force. During

2. *Jaipur Album* (1935), Ch. IV, p. 6.
3. *Ibid.*, p. 5.

the minority regime these departments were amalgamated and the police force was reorganised by a British Officer of the Indian Police.

The powers of the district magistrate of a British Indian district were given to the Faujdar of the Jaipur city. The Faujdar did not have any civil powers. Later the name 'Faujdar' was changed to 'City Magistrate'. Thus within a short period of ten years, the administration of Jaipur was radically transformed. Instead of the old system, where the word of the ruler was final, an administration based on codified law was introduced. Citizens were also given some say in the civic affairs.

In June 1942, Sir Mirza Ismail took over as Diwan of Jaipur and he brought in more modernization. As a man coming from outside the state, he was not tied down by local sentiments. One of his early acts was to move the main offices of the State government outside the city wall to a building originally occupied by a hotel (and now used as the hostel for the State legislators). Till then these offices were in the Jaleb Chowk within the precincts of the city palace. This closeness to the Palace strengthened the image of personal rule by the Maharaja.

Mirza Ismail divided the territory of the State into a number of districts and placed magistrates in charge of each district. The feeling of a personal rule by the Maharaja thus started disappearing from the rural areas also.

Planning of the City Outside the Walls

In 1921 the population of the town was 1.20 lakhs. It rose to 1.44 lakhs in 1931. In other words, it increased by 20%. In the next decade, the increase was 22% and the population in 1941 rose to 1.76 lakhs.[4]

It was in the decade 1931-1941 that the major growth of the city took place outside the city walls, specially in the south. This southern area had a population of 14,905 in 1931. It was 27,308 in 1941. One reason was that the State government also considered this as the most suitable area for future growth. The new building of the Maharaja's College, and the new hospital building were both built in this decade here. What gave an

4. From the *Census Reports* of 1931 and 1941 respectively.

added importance to this area was the fact that the new ruler after his investiture started using Rambagh Palace as his chief place of residence. The building had been built as a guest house by Maharaja Ram Singh (1835-1880) in about 1840. The guest house had been remodelled and built into a palace[5] by Madho Singh (1880-1922) in about 1915.

Though many people were keen to build houses outside the city walls, it was in practice difficult for them to do so. The land outside the walls was mostly agricultural and even if one got permission somehow to build a house, there were no roads and other civic conveniences available. About 1941 land development schemes were prepared and plots of land of suitable sizes were sold to prospective house builders. In order to induce people to build houses, the plots were priced in the beginning at Rs. 0.25 to 0.50 a square yard. This method of allotment of plots at nominal prices continued up to 1957.[6]

Of the five schemes that were prepared in 1941, four were on the southern side of the city wall and only one of the schemes, the E Scheme or the Bani Park was to be built on the western side. The schemes were:—

A. Fateh Tibba.
B. The Medical College and the Gangwal Park area.
C. This is still called the 'C' Scheme, though it has the official name of Ashok Nagar.
D. New Colony and Jalupura.
E. Bani Park.

The first scheme which was taken in hand was the 'D' Scheme. After Sir Mirza Ismail took over as the Diwan of the State on 19 June 1942, emphasis was laid on implementing the 'C' Scheme quickly.

The new city has now come up quite well. Unfortunately in the haste to build up the new city quickly, care was not taken to construct an underground sewage system simultaneously. Another shortcoming is the lack of sufficient number of public parks.

5. *Notes on Jaipur*, pp. 44-45.
6. The present writer obtained a plot of about 1500 square yards in 1957 at the price of Rs. 1.75 a square yard.

Setting up of the Modern Industries

In the second half of the decade 1940-50, that is, immediately after the second World War, serious attempts were made to bring in modern industries here. Until that time there were no such industries in the city. Many types of artistic handicrafts were manufactured in Jaipur and for these the city was justly famous. But production by power-driven machinery was practically non-existent. Some oil mills, a cotton ginning factory, a few ice making plants were the only exceptions.

So Jaipur had to start from scratch. It had no supply of skilled labour and there was no market for the produce of sophisticated industries either. It was, therefore, difficult to induce the businessmen to come and open factories here. An appeal was made to the patriotic instinct of the businessmen whose home was in the Jaipur State, but who had migrated to the metropolitan cities. There was some response and by the time of the integration of the states, Jaipur had four large factories. They were:—

1. The National Ball-bearing Company Ltd., the first ball-bearing manufacturing plant in India (The name has now been changed to the National Engineering Industries).
2. The Man Industries Ltd. (Steel Rolling Mill specialising in door and window sections).
3. The Jaipur Spinning and Weaving Mills Ltd.
4. The Jaipur Metals and Electricals Ltd. (Non-ferrous Rolling Mill and House Service Electricity Meters).

II

THE CONTROVERSY ABOUT THE-SUITABILITY OF JAIPUR AS THE CAPITAL OF RAJASTHAN

When independence came in 1947, the Jaipur State, like the other native states of the country, continued as a separate entity for some time. Nobody thought at that time that the state would merge into some larger unit. Rajputana, Rajasthan or Rajwara had always been a historical and cultural unit, but there was no idea of a political integration of the princely states of the area. Indeed each state ardently desired to guard its separate existence.

However, even before independence, Sir Mirza Ismail, the Diwan of Jaipur, wanted that at least in the matter of higher education, the States of Rajasthan should not depend on the Universities of the British Indian provinces, but have a University of their own. He thought of a University of Rajasthan with Jaipur as its centre, and invited the other States of Rajasthan to join. Among the first states to agree to the formation of the University and adopt the necessary legislation were Udaipur, Jaipur, Jodhpur, Bikaner, Kota, Kishangarh, Bundi and Shahpura. Later Dungarpur, Banswara and Tonk also agreed to join. The University of Rajputana was inaugurated[7] by V.T. Krishnamachari, Diwan of Jaipur on January 8, 1947.[8]

The formation of the University of Rajputana with Jaipur as its administrative centre gave a hint of what was to come later. In less than two years after independence the State of Rajasthan was formed by the integration of all the 23 princely states. The State was, however, not formed all at once. Nine native states of the southern and the eastern Rajasthan formed the first Rajasthan Union on 25 March, 1948. Within a month Mewar also joined the Union to form Greater Rajasthan on 18 April 1948 with Udaipur as the capital of the new state. In the north-east, the four states of Alwar, Baratpur, Dholpur and Karauli had formed the Matsya Union on 18 March 1948. Only four large states of Jaipur, Jodhpur, Bikaner and Jaisalmer remained outside these groups. Attempts were continuously made by Sardar Patel to draw these four also in. Finally these four large states and the states of Greater Rajasthan formed the Rajasthan Union. This new state was inaugurated by Sardar Patel on 30 March 1949 in Jaipur which was chosen as its capital. Matsya Union joined Rajasthan on 15 May, 1949.[9]

Thus except for Ajmer which remained a separate state until November 1956, Rajasthan in its present shape, came into existence before the middle of 1949.

7. *Speeches of Sir V.T. Krishnamachari*, Jaipur, 1948, p. 82.
8. Mirza Ismail had left Jaipur by this time.
9. *White paper on Indian States*, New Delhi, 1950, pp. 53-54.

One of the reasons for the hesitation of the rulers of the four states to join the union was the question of the choice of the capital. V.P. Menon, wrote in his *Story of the Integration of the Indian States*:[10]

> "On 11th January (1949) I went to Jaipur and discussed the question with the Maharajah and Shri V.T. Krishnamachari, the Diwan. The Maharajah said that he was quite agreeable of the formation of the Union, provided it could be guaranteed that Jaipur would be the capital of the Union and that he would be the permanent hereditary Rajpramukh."
>
> Menon goes on to say, ". . . we now (January/February 1949) started working on the details of the proposed Union and the provisions to be included in the covenant. Three sets of parties were concerned: the first being the Maharajahs of Jaipur, Jodhpur, Bikaner and Jaisalmer and their respective advisers; the second, the rulers of the existing Rajasthan Union, and the third, the popular leaders of Rajasthan particularly, Hiralal Shastri, Jai Narain Vyas, Maniklal Verma and Gokalbhai Bhatt. I had discussions with all of them, separately and jointly.
>
> "The first question raised was, who should be the head of the new Union. The popular leaders endorsed the selection of the Maharajah of Jaipur as Rajpramukh. The city of Jaipur was the obvious choice for the capital."

Menon was however not correct in saying that Jaipur was the obvious choice from the very beginning. It is possible also that doubts were raised later by some of the parties concerned, and the choice of the location of the capital and also of the High Court both became open questions.

To assist the Government in coming to a decision on the matter, Sardar Vallabh Bhai Patel appointed a Committee consisting of Shri B.R. Patel, I.C.S., the then Chief Secretary to the Government of PEPSU, as Chairman, Lt. Col. T.C. Puri of the Directorate General of Health Services, and Shri H.P. Sinha, Superintending Engineer, C.P.W.D. They were asked to submit

10. V.P. Menon, *Story of the Integration of Indian States*, Paper-back edition, 1961, p. 251.

recommendations as to the suitability of the existing towns in Rajasthan for the location of the capital. The Report of the Committee dated 27 March 1949 was submitted to the Government. The Committee made the following recommendations:—

1. Jaipur should be made the capital of the new State.
2. The High Court and the Customs and Excise departments should be located at Jodhpur.
3. The possibility of locating the headquarters of the Armed Forces at Jodhpur should be considered.
4. The question of making Jodhpur the seat of Rajasthan University should also be considered.
5. The new government should consider the question of further decentralisation by locating some of the heads of the departments at other places in the Union.

The recommendations of the Committee that the capital should be at Jaipur and the seat of the High Court at Jodhpur were accepted by the Government.[11]

Three days after the Committee submitted the report Jaipur became the capital of Rajasthan. Luckily for Jaipur the Government of India did not accept the recommendation of the Committee that the seat of the Rajasthan University should be Jodhpur. Besides it is quite clear from the recommendations of the Committee that while other cities in Rajasthan such as Bikaner and Udaipur were also trying to be the capital of Rajasthan the main contestants were Jaipur and Jodhpur. (The Committee had however said that if a new capital city was to be built Udaipur due to its picturesqueness was the most suitable place).[12] Their decision was influenced by the following circumstances which were in favour of Jaipur for the location of the capital here:—

1. Jaipur is the oldest planned city in the country with wide roads and fine houses and has also underground drainage system existing in some parts of the city.
2. From the point of view of climate, Jaipur in summer is

11. *Report of the Rajasthan Capital Enquiry Committee*, 1958, pp. 2-3.
12. *Report of the Rajasthan Capital Enquiry Committee*, 1958, p. 26.

better than Jodhpur, although there is not much to choose between the two.

The decisive point, however, according to them was that "While Jaipur is surrounded on all sides by cultivated and populated areas, Jodhpur is surrounded by the desert and to the west of Jodhpur lies the Rajasthan desert."

For six and half years thereafter, nobody challenged the right of Jaipur to be the capital of Rajasthan; but on 1 November 1956 Ajmer was merged in Rajasthan and this latter city immediately claimed that the capital should shift from Jaipur to Ajmer.

The matter had, therefore, to be re-examined. The Government of India set up another committee on 11 July 1957 to re-examine the question of location of the capital and High Court of Rajasthan. The Committee that consisted of Shri P. Satyanarayana Rao, Shri V. Viswanathan, Shri B.K. Gupta submitted its report on 26 February 1958 and came almost to the same conclusion as the Patel Committee set up in 1949 and recommended that the capital should not be shifted from Jaipur and that the High Court should remain at Jodhpur.[13]

III
EDUCATION

Modern education started in Jaipur with the opening of the Maharaja's College in 1844. This was the only institution in Jaipur which imparted some knowledge of the English language. Though called a College, in the beginning it was merely a school with an insignificant number of students.

A Sanskrit College was opened in 1845 and in 1849 a branch of the Maharaja's College was opened in Chandpole. In 1874-75, the number of students in these schools were as follows:—

Maharaja's College	—	825
Sanskrit College	—	208
Chandpole Branch School	—	70

13. *Report of the Rajasthan Capital Enquiry Committee*, 1958, p. 43.

There were no other State schools for boys till then.[14]

Indigenous Schools

The vast majority of boys, who merely learned to read and write, received instructions in the indigenous schools. At the end of the 19th century when some sort of official recognition began to be given to these schools, they were divided into two categories, advanced and elementary.[15] Advanced schools were those in which printed books were used. These indigenous schools did not have any buildings of their own. The teacher who owned the schools, held the classes in some temple or mosque which were the only public buildings available in those days. Since Jainas as a business community were more interested in education than others, almost all the Jaina temples were used as school buildings by teachers who were in most cases the priests of the temple. The majority of these schools were elementary in the sense that they did not use any printed books for teaching the children. In Jaipur city there were 148 indigenous schools in 1905 of which 39 were advanced and 109 were elementary schools. In the Jaipur State as a whole there were 596 elementary and 85 advanced schools in that year.[16]

The details of the curriculum followed in these schools in Jaipur in the early 19th century are not available. It can, however, be safely conjectured that the curriculum was more or less the same throughout northern Rajasthan and perhaps beyond, and not much change has occurred during the course of a century and half. We have a report of the education system of Bikaner and Soojangarh Agency Report[17] for 1869-70:—

> "The only places of education which exists in Biccanere are the temples, Jain Monasteries, and pathashalas. At the last, the sons of the wealthy merchants of India, whose

14. Baylay's *Gazetteer of Jaipur* (1876), Appendix 8.
15. *Report on Public Instructions in the Jaypur State* for the year ending 31-3-1898, p. 17.
16. *Report on Public Instructions in the Jaypur State* for the year ending 31-12-1905, p. 20.
17. *Report on the Political Administration of the Rajpootana States*, 1869-70, p. 82.

homes are in Biccanere, are taught to read and write and cipher; their whole school equipment is a board and a bit of wood, and their studies are conducted in the streets. The pathashalas are not so well attended as formerly, for within the last ten years it has become the fashion to take the boys from schools immediately after marriage, and send them to their parents' distant houses of business, so fitting them to take part in mercantile operations, lately so extended, at an age when they used to begin their apprenticeship. In the pathashalas a course of letter reading and accounts takes about three years. The school fees amount to six maunds of bajra and eight rupees in cash for the whole period. The wealthy pay in the shape of a present of rupees one hundred additional.

"At the upsaras or monasteries Sanskrit is studied, and in one that I entered, I found the priest, who was courteous and communicative, and ready to permit access to his large Sanskrit library, teaching geography from a curious map,[18] which showed the concentric oceans and continents, lakhs of coss across, and history to match."

Clearly reading, writing and arithmetic were the three things that were taught. The method of teaching in the Pathashalas or *Chatshalas* as ascertained from the older residents of the city was as follows: so far as reading and writing was concerned it was taught by the teacher or a senior student writing the alphabet with ink on a wooden board brought by the student. The young pupil was then asked to copy the letters by writing over these letters again and again by a reed pen, until the whole thing was blurred. The board was then washed, and the process started all over again. Arithmetic was generally taught orally. It meant memorising long multiplication tables, all the children following in chorus the senior student. Multiplication tables

18. These maps are still seen in the older Jaina temples. A few of them are preserved in the Lun Karan Pandya's temple in Jaipur. According to the Indian mythology, the Universe consists of a central island called Jambu-Dvipa surrounded by alternate rings of seven seas and six lands. According to the Jaina mythology only the first 2½ dvipas or islands are habitable by human beings. The maps show only the first three dvipas.

up to 40×10 were generally learnt. The proficiency obtained in business calculations in this manner was quite high.[19]

Besides, all the boys were made to commit to memory a long piece about 250 syllables of nonsense words called *Seedha*. This went on as follows:—

सिधो वरणा, समा मुनाया, चतरु चतरे दासा, दऊ सवारा, दसो समाना

These are actually a badly corrupted version of the first *Pada* of the *Katantra Vyakarana*. This reads originally as follows:—

सिद्धो वर्णसमाम्नाय: तत्र चतुर्दसादौ स्वरा: । दश समाना:

This grammar of the Sanskrit language is now read only in parts of Bengal. How a badly mauled version of its first portion had become a compulsory learning in the schools all over the former Jaipur State and Marwar is a mystery.

Fortunately for the boys, they did not have to practice writing these nonsense words. They only had to repeat the whole thing standing when the classes ended for the day. It is learnt that in former days, boys from all the schools would go to the City Palace on the *Ganesh Chaturthi* day each carrying two sticks in their hands and which they would beat rythmically (this was called beating the *Danka*), while repeating the *Seedha*. Afterward sweets were sent from the Palace to be distributed among them.

Learning the *Seedha* continues even today in the *chatshalas* that exist all over Northern and Western Rajasthan.

In 1924 it was thought that these indigenous schools could be improved and utilised for spreading primary education in the city. The report of the education department for that year mentions:[20]

> "In order to encourage Primary Education in the city, the system of grants-in-aid to indigenous schools of *Maktabs* and *Chatshalas*, which number more than 60 in the city has been also introduced for which a sum of Rs. 4,000/- a year has been set apart. . . . The grant of *Joshis* and *Mullas* is calculated in a sliding scale at the rate of 10 boys per rupee

19. The author tested some of these boys in Barmer in 1954, by asking such questions as, "What is the cost of 37½ yards of cloth, if one yard of it costs Rs. 2/4/3?"

20. *Report on Public Instruction in the Jaipur State* for the year ending 31st August 1924, p. 16.

per month, to encourage them to admit large number of boys to their *Maktabs* and *Chatshalas*. . . . It is not intended at present to have any kind of strict control over the teaching in the *Chatshalas*, although the *Joshis* and the *Mullas* are persuaded to introduce gradually regular courses of Hindi and Urdu in their *Chatshalas* and *Maktabs* in addition to Arithmetic which is the only subject they are now mostly teaching. It is hoped that in about two or three years time many of these instructions will grow up into so many regular Lower Primary Schools. There were about 1,600 boys in the *Chatshalas* and *Maktabs* of the city when the grant system was introduced in March 1924, by the end of August it rose to about 1800. . ."

An attempt[21] had been made nearly 30 years earlier i.e. about 1898 to 'departmentalize' some of these indigenous schools in Jaipur State. This probably meant that the salary of the teacher was paid by the State. These departmentalized schools were called lower primary schools. The 1898 Report says:

"The 26 Lower Primary Schools (5 of these were in Jaipur City) were village *Chatshalas* or *Maktabs* of a little advanced nature, in which there was no systematic method of teaching. A few years ago it was thought advisable to raise the status of these schools by incorporating them to the Department. These schools now generally teach the Lower Primary standard and send up boys for the departmental examination."

There were, besides these State schools, 34 primary schools under private management in the whole of the Jaipur State. Of these, 10 were in Jaipur city—7 Mission primary schools and 3 Jaina primary schools in 1898.

By 1924, the number of State primary schools in the city came down from 5 to 2, whereas the private primary schools went up to 21.

21. *Report on the Public Instructions in the Jaipur State* for the year ending 31st March 1898, p. 16.

It will thus be seen that so far as primary education was concerned, the State did not make much effort even up to the 1st quarter of this century. This was left to indigenous schools and private efforts, mainly Christian or Jaina.

In August 1946, the Jaipur Legislative Council passed the Jaipur State Primary Education Act, as a result of which primary education was made compulsory in Jaipur city and primary schools were opened in every ward of the city.

Primary Education of Girls

There was no indigenous system of education for the primary education of girls. And it was left to the State to make some effort in this direction. Female education had received encouragement from Maharaja Ram Singh. In April 1866 a girls' school was opened in the city, where 25 girls enrolled themselves as pupils.[22] In 1867 one Mrs. Ockalton was brought from Calcutta to organize the girls' schools. She started a class for teaching sewing and embroidery in the school. This became quite popular, so other branches were also opened in 1875,[23] and some girls were appointed teachers in these. A Normal school for training women teachers was also started. In 1875 the number of pupils was 564. The branches of girls' schools were established at Hathroi, Gangapole and Ghat Darwaja. A separate industrial school for girls also was established near about that time.

By 1899 the Chandpole branch had been closed, and a new branch opened in Amer. A private girls' school was started in the city by the Digambar Jainas in that year (this school was closed in 1904). The number of pupils in the various schools were as follows:—

Main Schools	*Number of pupils in 1898-99*
Normal School	11
Central School	421
Industrial School	10
Total	442

22. *Report on the Political Administration of Rajpootana* for the years 1865-66 and 1866-67, Pt. II, p. 186. See also, Shyamaldas, *op. cit.*, p. 1330.
23. *Notes on Jaipur* (1916), p. 94.

Branch Schools	
Ghat Darwaja School	45
Gangapole School	45
Hathroi	40
Amer	40
Total	170
Jain Girls' School.	32
GRAND TOTAL	644

Evidently there was not much improvement in the number of pupils in a period of 25 years.

"The course of studies in the Girls' Schools during the year (1899) under report was generally the same as that prescribed for the Primary Examination in Hindu and Urdu, with an optional course in needle work."[24]

By 1924, the number of private girls' schools had gone up to 10 in the city. The Jainas had opened 4 girls' schools, the Christian Missionaries three, one each at Purani Basti, Dariba and Hathroi, and one school was opened by Mohammadans. This last had 35 students in 1924. And one school was started by a Seth Phoolchand. Thus among the local residents Jainas had taken a lead in promoting primary education of girls.

There was however no increase in the number of State Schools for girls which remained four (Central, Ghat Darwaja, Hathroi and Gangapole.)

The increase in the number of private girls' schools, specially those run by persons other than the Christian Missionaries shows that by this time (1924) the middle class people had also begun to take some interest in the education of their daughters. The State Schools were mainly used by the poorer section, because it was profitable to send their daughters to them; all the girls were given scholarships or daily prizes for attending the schools.

> "The system of giving scholarships to practically every girl who comes for receiving instruction in State Girls School does not seem to be very sound in principle, but perhaps it will be necessary to continue the old practice for some years

24. *Report on the Public Instruction in Jaypur State* for the year ending 31-3-1899, p. 16.

more until the parents of the girls begin to show a real interest in the education of their girls and do not require the bait of scholarship and daily prizes, which are now looked upon as a source of income by poorer parents, who alone in the majority of cases, now send their girls to the schools. If the practice of giving daily prizes is stopped abruptly, the number of girls is likely to fall down at once, especially in the lower classes of the schools which will take a very long time to fill up."[25]

Perhaps this very system of scholarship and daily prizes was a disincentive for the middle class parents who did not want to accept the charity. There thus arose some demand for private schools for girls.

The Central girls' primary school which had been originally started in 1850 was raised to the Middle level in 1927-28. In that year the total number of scholars in this school was 245.[26] It was called the Jaipur Central Girls' School. The Board of High School and Intermediate Education, Rajputana and Central India, granted provisional recognition to it as a High School in 1931. The first batch of seven girl students appeared in the High School Examination of 1933. Of these seven, three passed in the examination.[27]

In the forties of this century, a school for the education of the daughters of Jagirdars and other rich people was started in Jaipur. This school called the Maharani Gayatri Devi Girls' School was formally declared open on 4 July 1943 and started functioning on 12 August 1943.[23] This school has now become quite a well known institution in India.

Jaipur's Backwardness in Literacy

It is evident that no serious effort to make people of the city literate was made up to the first quarter of this century. The literacy figures for the city as given in the various census reports are as follows:

25. *Report on Public Instruction in the Jaipur State* for the year ending 31-8-1924, p. 22.
26. *Administration Report of the Jaipur State* for the years 1926-27 and 1927-28.
27. *Administration Report of the Jaipur State* for 1930-31, p. 56.
28. *Administration Report of the Jaipur State* for 1942-43.

YEAR		Actual No. of literates	Total population	Percentage of literates	Percentage increase in the decade of No. of literates
1		2	3	4	5
1901	Male.	12995	83845	15.5	
	Female.	443	76313	0.6	
	Total.	13438	160158	8.4	
1911	Male.	13466	70846	19.0	1.3
	Female.	822	66252	1.3	99.1
	Total.	14288	137098	10.5	6.8
1921	Male.	13645	64382	21.2	1.3
	Female.	1259	55825	2.3	43.0
	Total.	14904	120207	12.4	3.9
1931	Male.	17057	77933	21.9	25.0
	Female.	2144	62246	3.4	70.3
	Total.	19201	140179	13.3	28.3
1941	Male.	30196	93479	32.3	57.3
	Female.	5362	82331	6.5	150.1
	Total.	35548	175810	20.2	85.2
1951	Male.	64903	153631	42.3	114.9
	Female.	21315	137499	15.5	297.5
	Total.	86218	291130	29.6	142.5
1961	Male.	117981	217422	54.3	81.8
	Female.	53329	186022	28.7	150.2
	Total.	171310	403444	42.5	98.2

These figures show that up to 1921, there was practically no increase in the number of male literates. The number began to increase in the decade 1921-31, perhaps with the start of national regeneration, when Gandhiji brought politics to the masses. The growth of national aspiration was highest in the decade 1941-51, and the number of male literates also showed a very high increase—almost 115% in that decade; but perhaps the increase in this decade was also due to the influx of refugees from Sindh who were mostly businessmen and thus literate. The effect of the Compulsory Primary Education Act of 1946 had also begun to be felt.

In the case of females, though the percentage increase was high in all the decades, this starting from a small base was not significant. The real increase in literacy of the females started in the decade 1941-51. The reason assigned in official publication for the low literacy rate among the females was that, 'an educated or literate female was looked upon as not a very desirable member of the household'[29]. This, however, does not explain why both in male and female literacy Jaipur city lagged behind most of the principal cities of Rajasthan. The following table taken from the Census Report[30] of Rajputana and Ajmer-Merwara for 1921 shows :

CITY	Population	Percentage of literacy among all ages 5 & above.		Rank from the literacy point of view
		Males	Females	
Ajmer	113,512	32.3	7.7	I
Jodhpur	73,480	29.4	5.5	II
Alwar	44,760	27.8	2.5	III
Jaipur	120,207	23.2	2.5	IV
Bikaner	69,410	20.1	2.3	V

There was not much difference in the social outlook of the people in these different cities of Rajasthan either. Actually one of the main causes of Jaipur lagging behind others was the official inaction in promoting a demand for education here.

29. *Census Report of the Jaipur State*, 1911, Part I, p. 191.
30. *Census Report for Rajputana and Ajmer-Merwara*, for 1921, p. 176.

Indeed, the backwardness of the Jaipur State in education had been noted earlier by the Director of Public Instruction (Sanjiban Ganguli) in his report for the year ending 31-12-1905. He wrote:

> ". . . it is very strange that, in point of literacy of population, Jaipur State as a whole stands very much below many of the Rajputana States, which from educational point of view cannot for a moment hold comparison with it. Why is it so? Why Jaipur with its many educational facilities stands fourteenth among the twenty Rajputana States as disclosed in the Rajputana Census Report of 1901? Since I came to know this fact I have often thought over the matter, and I consider that two of the chief reasons are: (1) the inadequate provision for education in the districts chiefly owing to the utter apathy of the jagirdars in educational matters, and (2) the use of Urdu as the State language although it is not the language of the people. As it is not the time to press for more schools when all the resources of the State as well as of the jagirdars are severely strained to cope with the dire distress of the present famine, I would not dilate upon the first point. As to the second, I last year showed from the census report that in the Jaipur State only one in 2,000 speaks Urdu. But as knowledge of it is the passport to the State Service, the State educational system cannot altogether do without it. Were it not so, the money now spent on Urdu can be usefully utilized in opening more schools in the districts which are so urgently needed. From the old records in my office I learn that the use of Urdu is not a long standing custom, as I at first thought it to be. Before the seventies I find almost all the official correspondence were made in Hindi. But it is now very gradually ousted from all the offices of the State excepting the Treasury and the Account's Departments. Until this tendency can be checked and Nagri characters substituted for the Persian one, the prospect of mass education can never touch the common people, who invariably prefer the Hindi language and are mostly ignorant of the Persian characters."

In other words, people if they wanted their children to be

literate at all, were interested in getting them literate in Hindi, and Hindi was of no use in the official business of the State. There was therefore no effective demand for primary education in Jaipur for a very long time.

Maharaja's College

Though primary education had been neglected by the government, Jaipur was far in advance of other States in providing facility for secondary and higher education. Long before education up to the undergraduate standard was available in the other States of Rajasthan, the Maharaja's College had classes up to the postgraduate standard in several subjects. In fact postgraduate classes were started in Jodhpur and Bikaner only just before independence in 1947.

As stated earlier, the Maharaja's College came into being in a small way in 1844 at the instance of Colonel Ludlow who was the Political Agent at Jaipur at that time. Its object was to impart to the people of Jaipur, the rudiments of English education along with a knowledge of the vernacular. Shortly afterwards, Sanskrit and Hindi classes were added.[31] In the beginning there were three teachers in this College viz. Pandit Shiva Deen, Munshi Krishna Swarup and Pandit Vansidhar.[32] English was taught by Pandit Shiva Deen.

Shiva Deen died in 1865. He was educated at the Government College at Agra, and in 1845 was appointed tutor to the present Maharajah. By his zeal, integrity and ability he obtained the confidence of Maharaja Ram Singh, and was nominated Private Secretary; and eventually in May 1862, on the death of Thakoor Lachhman Singh succeeded to the office of the Prime Minister which post he held till his death in June 1864. During the brief period that he was in power, "the administration was carried on with vigour and wisdom."[33]

From the very beginning then Pandit Shiva Deen got involved in the administration of the State and could devote

31. *Notes on Jaipur* (1916), p. 91.
32. Shyamaldas, *op. cit.*, p. 1329.
33. *Report on the Political Administration of Rajpootana for the year 1866-67*, p. 190.

little attention to the College which also he headed until 1856. In that year Munshi Krishna Swarup was appointed the head-master. According to the *Vir Vinod*, the College languished until 1867 when the Maharaja brought three Bengalis over from Calcutta and appointed them in the institution. Due to their hard work and good administration, the college improved and the number of students also increased. "Now it is the premier educational institution of Rajputana."[34] "*Notes on Jaipur*" records: "In 1865 the College was reorganized by the Late Rao Bahadur Kanti Chandra Mukerji, C.I.E., who had then just been appointed Head Master, and its success as an educational establishment of the highest class may be said to date from this period."[35]

The date given in the *Vir Vinod* is wrong. Mukerji became the Head Master of the College in 1865. The standard of education rose and the first batch of candidates for the Entrance examination of the Calcutta University was sent up in 1867. In 1873 the college was raised to the F.A. standard of that University and so became a second grade College. When the University of Allahabad was founded in 1888, the Jaipur College was affiliated to it up to the B.A., but the B.A. classes were not actually opened until July 1890. In 1891, it sent up its first candidates for the B.A. degree of the Allahabad University, three of its candidates being successful. Harinarayan, B.A. was the first among these three. In 1897 the College was affiliated to the Calcutta University as a first grade College. The M.A. course of the University in those days took only a year. In 1898 four candidates were sent up for this examination, two in English and two in Philosophy. Of these only Surajnarayan Sharma was successful. He obtained a second class in M.A. (English).[36]

One noteworthy examination result of 1898 was that of Chandradhar Sharma from the school section of this College. He stood first among all the 3,000 candidates who appeared that year in the Entrance Examination of the Allahabad University from Uttar Pradesh (then known as N.W. Province and Oudh) and Rajputana. He then went on to secure the first

34. Shyamaldas, *op. cit.*, p. 1330.
35. *Notes on Jaipur*, p. 91.
36. Report on Public Instruction in the Jaipur State, 1899, p. 6.

position in the B.A. examination of the same university in 1903.[37] Chandradhar Sharma's feat in the entrance examination was repeated next year in 1899 when Gangabux Gupta from this school topped in the University.

In 1900 the College had teaching facilities in the following subjects: English, Sanskrit, Persian, Logic and Philosophy, Mathematics, History and Political Economy, Physical Science and Chemistry. Lectures in all the subjects were delivered in English, and Persian or Sanskrit was taught as a second language.

In 1900 the College was affiliated to the Allahabad University up to M.A. In the same year the College was recognized to teach up to the B.Sc. standard.

The Principal of the Maharaja's College continued to hold the charge of the office of the Director of Public Instructions also up to 1923. In June that year the two offices were separated.

37. Chandradhar Sharma was the only candidate to get a first division among the 228 candidates who appeared in the B.A. examination of the Allahabad University that year. The teachers in most of the Colleges in Uttar Pradesh in those days were Englishmen. It was perhaps thought that Indians were incapable of teaching in the College classes. There was general public satisfaction, therefore, when a student from Maharaja's College, Jaipur where all the teachers were Indians topped the list of successful candidates for the B.A. examination. Many newspapers commented on this. Among them were 'The Advocate' of Lucknow (17.5.1903); 'The Hindustan Review' and 'Kayastha Samachar' of Allahabad (June 1903), 'The Madras Standard' (20.5.1903) and 'The Bengalee' of Calcutta (3.7.1903). These comments were reprinted in the *Report on Public Instruction for Jaipur State for 1904.* Here is an extract from *The Bengalee*:

"Indian Principals and Professors"

Is it not a fact that notwithstanding a European Principal and a superabundance of European Professors, not a single Government College in the United Provinces could manage to pass even a solitary candidate in the first division at the last B.A. Examination? Is it not also a fact that the only successful candidate who was placed in the first division came from the Jaipur Maharaja's College? Lastly, is it not equally undeniable that the Jaipur College, which achieved this unique distinction last year, is an Institution, the professorial staff of which consists exclusively of Indian educationists? The Principal and Professors are all Indians, all veterans in their own line and some with a European reputation. . ."

Shri N.K. Ray who was holding both the posts was made the Principal. The degree classes, viz., B.A., B.Sc., and M.A. classes were separated and the College was renamed the Associated College; Pandit Shyam Sunder Sharma was made the Director of Public Instructions. He was also in charge of the Maharaja's Intermediate College.[38]

This experiment of bifurcating the College did not last long.

> "In the interests of efficiency and economy it was found necessary to re-amalgamate the two Colleges in August 1927, and they were placed under one Principal who worked under the direct orders of the Education Member, the Director (of Public Instruction) remaining in charge of the Secondary and Primary education in the State."[39]

The Agra University Act of 1926 came into force on 1 July 1927, from which date the Maharaja's College which was associated with the Allahabad University (external side), became affiliated to the Agra University.

In 1929, the Intermediate section came under the Rajputana High School and Intermediate Education Board with the formation of that Board in Ajmer. Since 1923, the Intermediate section had been affiliated to the U.P. Board.

The new building of the College came up in 1934 near the Ram Niwas garden. The old building of the College in Manik Chowk now house the police station there.

No tuition fees were charged in the schools and Colleges run by the State in Jaipur up to 1938. In that year the following schedule of fees was introduced—M.A. Rs. 5/- per month, B.Sc. Rs. 4/8/- p.m., B.A. Rs. 4/- p.m., Intermediate Rs. 3/8/- p.m. and 9th and 10th classes Rs. 1/8/- p.m. Persons not belonging to the State, had to pay double the fees.[40]

By 1947, post-graduate teaching was imparted in the Maharaja's College in a large number of subjects both in

38. Report on Public Instruction, 1924, p. 1.
39. Report on the Administration of the Jaipur State for 1926-27 and 1927-28, p. 54.
40. *Jaipur Hitaishi* (1941-42), Jaipur number, p. 231.

Humanities and Sciences. It therefore easily became the nucleus of the teaching department of the newly established University of Rajputana.

From the history of the Maharaja's College it will be apparent that right from the year 1865, the attempt was to adopt the system of education which was developing in British India. No innovations were tried and in fact the attempt was to conform to the British Indian system as much as possible. Perhaps the State Government did not have any conscious policy on higher education. They had opened a college and thereafter it was for the teachers to look after it. Moreover, there was the difficulty about the medium of instruction. The official language of the State was Urdu, the mother tongue of the people was Hindi, whereas the senior teachers were mostly from Bengal[41] who found it easier to talk in English. And it was in the interest of these teachers to maintain the system in which they themselves had been brought up. Higher education thus did not catch on in Jaipur.

Another reason why higher education was not popular was that the system of administration of the State was medieval until late in the twenties of this century. For getting government jobs, family connection mattered much more than education or personal merit.

The number of students in the Maharaja's College in 1926-27 was only 295. It showed a sudden and welcome increase to 418 in the next year.[42] Perhaps, we may say that the modern age started in Jaipur in this year i.e. 1927-28, for, incidentally, this was also the first year when the number of students in the Maharaja's College exceeded the number of students in the Sanskrit College where the enrolment was 402.

Sanskrit College

The large number of students in the Sanskrit College,

41. In the 40 years from 1865 to 1903, there were ten Principals in the Maharaja's College. Eight of these were Bengalis and one was a Parsi. In 1898, out of the seven Professors in the College, five were Bengalis. (*Reports of the Director of Public Instructions for 1903 and 1898 respectively*).

42. *Report on the Administration of Jaipur State for the years 1926-27 and 1927-28*, pp. 56 and 57.

Jaipur was due to its fame as a centre of Sanskrit learning and students came to it from all parts of India.

The College imparts a complete course of instruction in the various branches of Sanskrit learning viz., Grammar, Philology, literature, Vedanta, Nyay, Jyotisha, Vedas and Vedic literature and also Ayurveda until 1946 when a separate Ayurvedic College was established for Hindu Medicine. "It was first started in or about 1852, as the Sanskrit department of the Maharaja's College with six Pandits and there were classes for Byakaran, Sahitya, Nyaya, Aurveda and the Vedas. In 1866 this Sanskrit department was separated from the Maharaja's College, and transferred to its present building, the temple of Ramchandraji in the north-eastern part of the city. Since then it has been known as the Sanskrit Pathashala or the Sanskrit College. In 1870 a class of Jyotish or Hindu Astronomy was opened and a new Professor appointed to teach the subject. The method of teaching in this institution continued to be the old orthodox one, in which memory played an important part. Discipline in the modern sense was unknown. There was no regularity either in teaching or in attendance, and pandits gave lessons at pleasure. It took a long time to systematize the teaching in the Sanskrit College, especially owing to the opposition of some of the pandits of the old school. It was in 1886-87 that any real organization of the Sanskrit College commenced under Babu Hari Dass Shastri, M.A., who was himself a learned scholar and at that time the Director of Public Instruction in the State. He revised the curriculum, fixed the textbooks in consultation with the pandits, and also introduced Sanskrit Title Examinations, which gave a fresh impetus to Sanskrit learning in Jaipur. In 1893 Pandit Lakshminath Shastri was transferred from the Maharaja's College to the Superintendentship of the Sanskrit College; and he brought to bear on the latter institution his ideas of discipline and training formed from his long connection with the English College of which he was the Professor of Sanskrit for more than eight years."[43] Thus the main reason why the College flourished was because the system of education and

43. *Report on Public Instruction in Jaipur State* for the year ending 31.3.1904, p. 16.

the manner of giving diplomas had been modernized.

Sanskrit Title Examination

The boys entered the College after passing the Praveshika examination the course for which was taught in the School department attached to the College. In the College the student was expected to choose a special subject for study. There were Title Examinations for each subject: (1) the Upadhyaya or Proficiency Examination, (2) the Shastri or High Proficiency Examination and (3) the Acharya or Honours Examination, on the results of which the title of Upadhyaya, Shastri and Acharya were conferred on the successful candidates.

The number of students in various subjects in the year 1903-04 were as follows:

Vyakarana	16
Nyaya	4
Vedanta	2
Jyotisha	19
Ayurveda	16
Vedas	35
Total	92

The point to note here is that out of the 92 students only 16 were studying Ayurveda, the only subject which could give a person a vocation. One wonders how the others made their living. Some of them would no doubt get jobs as Pandits in the courts of Hindu Princes and Zamindars. Others perhaps joined the teaching profession. However, the number of students of Ayurveda continued to increase, until the Ayurveda Department required a separate building for itself.

The College continued to maintain a good reputation for instruction in different branches of Sanskrit learning, specially in Ayurveda, and it used to attract students from all over India. In 1928, the number of students enrolled was 402.[44] In the thirties and the forties, the Colleges used to have four to five hundred students with about 35 professors and lecturers.

44. *Report on the Administration of Jaipur State* for the years 1926-27 and 1927-28, p. 57.

The Principal at that time was Mahamahopadhyaya Pandit Girdhar Sharma. These were the best days of the College both for the fame of its Principal and for the number of students on its roll. In 1941-42, the students were over 500 in number.[45] In course of time Ayurveda became the most popular subject in the Sanskrit College.

Ayurvedic Education

Courses in Ayurveda were taught in the Sanskrit College since the beginning in 1852, but it was only about 1886 87 that the syllabus was properly organized. Rajvaidya Krishnaramji Bhatt was made the head of the Ayurvedic Department in 1890 As in the other subjects, there were three title examinations in Ayurveda.

The syllabus in 1904 was as follows:

Upadhyaya Examination

First day — Madhavnidana; Rasa Manjari
Second day — Bhavaprakasa up to Dravyaguna
Third day — Chakradattachikitsasara Sangraha, Paribhasa by Gangadhara Kaviraj.

Shastri Examination

First day — Kalpasthana, Chikitsasthana from Charak Sanhita.
Second day — Susruta Sanhita—Sarirasthana; Rasendrasara Sangraha.
Third day — Vagbhata Sanhita.

Acharya Examination

First day — The remaining portion of Charaka Sanhita, not prescribed for the Shastri Examination.
Second day — The remaining portion of Susruta Sanhita.

45. *Jaipur Hitaishi*, December-January 1941, p. 235.

Third day — Rasendra Chintamani,
Fourth day — Literature (Sisupalavadha, canto I to IX; Kadambari Purvabhaga).

As is clear from the above, the syllabus at that time was based exclusively on the classical texts.[46]

One of the most famous teachers of Ayurveda in this College was Lakshmiram Sadhu who was incidently the first person to pass the Acharya examination (in Ayurveda in 1896) of the Sanskrit College in any subject. The list[47] of the first seven Acharyas of the Sanskrit College is as follows:

1. 1896—Lakshmiram Sadhu (Ayurveda)
2. 1898—Vishnudatta Brahmachari (Ayurveda)
3. 1899—Madhoprasad (Ayurveda)
4. 1902—Durgaprasad Sharma (Ayurveda)
5. 1904—Girdharlal (Vyakaran)
6. ,, —Chandra Datta (Vyakaran)
7. ,, —Surajnarain (Vyakaran)

Lakshmiram Sadhu later became a very famous Ayurvedic physician of India. He was the head of the Ayurvedic department of the Sanskrit College, Jaipur for a long time. And it was during his period that attempts were made to modernize the syllabus of Ayurveda. A laboratory for practical work in Ayurveda was opened; and the services of a doctor were secured for the teaching of Anatomy and Physiology in 1928.[48] Lakshmiram Sadhu retired in 1934 and died on the 10th July 1939.[49]

The titles of the diplomas for the Ayurveda in the Sanskrit College were changed to 'Bhisak', 'Bhishagvar' and 'Bhishagacharya' in 1933.

In 1946 the Ayurveda department of the Sanskrit College was moved to Madhav Vilas Palace.[50]

46. *Report on Public Instruction in the Jaipur State* for the year 1904, pp. 42-43.
47. *Ibid.*, p. 41.
48. *Report on the Administration of Jaipur State*, 1926-27 & 1927-28.
49. *Jaipur Hitaishi*, December-January 1941, p. 300.
50. Information obtained from the District Ayurvedic Office, Jaipur.

IV

WATER SUPPLY FOR THE CITY

To be able to prosper a city needs to have an assured water supply round the year. Jai Singh, when he built Jaipur, gave early attention to this problem. He built canals to bring in water to the city from a river nearby, and it appears that these made a plentiful water supply available to the city. Girdhari mentions in his *Bhojanasara*:[51] "There are in the city large canals and reservoirs, and fountains throwing up sheets of water."

Later, when the canals dried up because of the silting up of the river, water supply for the city became a problem. This perhaps happened early in the nineteenth century. The people then had to fall back on the supply from wells. This source was not good for drinking purposes because perhaps most of the wells in the city contained brackish water. Whether it was always so, or whether the water in the city wells, in course of time, became brackish is not clear. The following quotation from Hendley in *The General Medical History of Rajputana* is interesting: "In all the principal cities of Rajputana the water is brackish and nearly undrinkable. Even in the modern city of Jaipur which is only 170 years old, out of 820 wells only 40 contained sweet water a short time ago."[52] Hendley states elsewhere that "up to 1872 people who could afford it were in the habit of sending for their drinking water to certain wells which were reported to contain pure supply. They were chiefly situated outside the city."[53]

A dam was built in 1844 on the Amani Shah Nala which flows by near the city, and the water from this dam supplied the needs of the city for sometimes. The dam is said to have cost 4½ lakh rupees, according to Hendley. The canals built by Jai Singh were utilized to bring the water from the dam to the city. The then ruler Ram Singh had gone to see the dam and was standing on the embankment. As he went down, water[54] got round the west abutment and carried away part of

51. *Bhojanasara*, couplet No. 185. See Appendix VII.
52. *The General Medical History of Rajputana* (Calcutta, 1000), p. 63.
53. *A Medico-Topographical Account of Jaipur* (Calcutta, 1895), p. 3.
54. Fateh Singh, *A brief History of Jaipur*.

the dam. The water supply from the dam which had continued for eight to ten years was stoppēd. The remains of this masonary dam can be seen even today.

"Nothing further was done until 1874, in which year steam pumps were erected on the side of the streams just above the side of the old embankment, and water was pumped up from the river bed into a reservoir, whence, it was at first through the old masonary duct, and fiom December 1875 by pipes, to the city. All objections to the water except those of the most conservative inhabitants were met by the approval, in the first place of a committee of priests, pundits, etc., appointed by the Maharaja, and in the end, by the self interest and convenience of the people "[55]

Some orthodox people, especially among the Jainas and the Vaishnavas still object to drink water brought by pipes. One reason perhaps is that the washers of the taps are made of leather. For drinking and cooking purposes, therefore, they use such wells whose water is not too brackish. In Chowkri Modikhana, for instance, there are two or three such wells from where the more orthodox persons of this Chowkri draw their water for drinking and cooking.

Shortage of Water in the Amani Shah Nala

At the time these pumps mentioned by Hendley were fitted, Amani Shah Nala was a perennial stream and the supply of water was sufficient for the city. Later, the flow used to shrink during the summer months. "From about the middle of May (1882) till the 12th June the river was often pumped dry, and the pumps had to be stopped. and it was necessary on the 29th May to shut off the water from the city from 10 A.M. to 4 P.M. and from 9 P.M. to 4 A.M , to prevent wastage."[56]

Water was supplid both to private houses and public taps. In 1883 the number of private houses getting the supply was 80, and the number of public taps on the roadsides which generally also had cattle troughs for the waste water, was

55. Hendley, *Medico-Topographical Account of Jaipur*, pp. 3-4.
56. *Jeypore State Public Works Report* for the year ending 31st March 1883, p. 32.

563.[57] The private houses were charged at the rate of one rupee per month per tap for the first tap and eight annas for every other tap.[58] The supply in the public taps was free.

No efforts for augmenting the water supply of Jaipur were made until the twenties of this century and Amani Shah Nala pumping station remained the only source of piped water supply to the town. The source, however, was very uncertain and dependant on the annual monsoon rains.

The Ramgarh Lake as Source of the City Water Supply

In the twenties a large plan for increasing the water supply of the town was prepared. The scheme was to draw the supply from the Ramgarh lake that had originally been made by damming the Banganga river for irrigation purposes. But the increasing need of the town combined with the uncertainty of the Amani Shah Nala made it necessary that the lake be used for town water supply also.

The new water works were completed in 1931. The Administration report for that year recorded:

> "The new Ramgarh Water Works were in operation for the whole of the year and the pipe-line successfully passed through its first monsoon. The supply from Amani Shah Works was in a precarious condition during the height of the demand and the Ramgarh Works afforded a welcome relief."[59]

There was, however, no phenomenal increase in the number of water connections given. The figures given in the corresponding administration reports are as follows:

Connections	*1936-37*	*1937-38*
Private.	1,005	1,103
Public Stand Post.	300	302
Water connection to Raj buildings.	180	143

57. *Jeypore State Public Works Report* for the year ending 31st March 1883, p. 34.
58. *Notes on Jaipur* (1916), p. 74.
59. *Report of the Administration of Jaipur State* for the year 1931-32, p. 46.

For a town with a population of about 1,25,000 the number of connections appear to be too few. Either the people were too poor to afford connections to their houses, or they preferred to use well water.

The Ramgarh water works with the filtration plant on the Lachman Dungri continued to serve the city until the late 1950s. At that time the shortage was again felt due to the very high increase in the population of the town. The water supply was therefore supplemented by tapping underground water sources by deep tube-wells. Their number in April 1974 was 117. Besides this, 32 open wells had also been fitted with pumps for increasing the water supply.

The Problem of the Identification of the Darbhavati River

As mentioned earlier, the masonary ducts or canals which brought water to the city in 1844, were built by Jai Singh.[60] We may examine now the sources of water for these canals. *Ishwaravilasa Mahakavya* (7/52) mentions that Jai Singh brought inside Jainagar the strongly flowing stream Darbhavati from a great distance. Since Shri Krishna Bhatta the author of *Ishwaravilasa Mahakavya* was a contemporary of Jai Singh and composed his work only a decade after the foundation of the city, there is no reason to doubt his statement that these canals were built by Jai Singh to bring the waters of Darbhavati inside the town.

The identity of the river Darbhavati, however, is not clear in *Ishwaravilasa Mahakavya.* Hanuman Sharma, in his *Nathawaton ka Itihas*[61] has described the attempts of Jai Singh to bring water by canals to his city.

> "First of all Jai Singh constructed a 16 miles long canal from the Bandi river to Jaipur. He cut the canal through the hill near Harmara, and then built aquaducts a few miles long to bring this water into the city; but since the level of the city was higher, not much water reached the town. After this Jai Singh built a large tank on the high

60. The Engineer-in-charge was Vidyadhar. He was awarded a 'Siropao' for this work in 1735 A.D. See Appendix IX.

61. Hanuman Sharma, *op. cit.*, p. 166.

ground behind Balanandji's temple and connected it to the various channels within the city, but this again was unable to supply water to places other than those within the palace grounds. Lastly he constructed a dam across the Amani Shah and also a canal which ran from west of the city through the bazars and went up to the east of the city. The canal was built of masonary and was plastered; and it was so wide that 5 or 7 horsemen could ride abreast along it. It was roofed and at many places along it there were openings from which the public could get water for their use. This canal or tunnel like structure might also be described as a secret Ganga or a secret canal. Many parts of the town could get plenty of water from this canal; but after S. 1901 (1844 A.D.) that is, after the construction of metalled roads within the town, and after the destruction of the masonary dam, and with the starting of water supply through metal pipes, this canal got buried within the markets, and its deep wells got filled up."

According to Hanuman Sharma, therefore, Jai Singh had at first tried to bring water all the way from the Bandi river about 25 km. away, and across the hills near Harmara. There is no indication near Harmara that Jai Singh made any such foolhardy attempt. But the editors of the printed edition of *Ishvaravilasa Mahakavya*, after giving reference to the statement of Hanuman Sharma, have identified Darbhavati with the Bandi river.[62] Since according to Hanuman Sharma water was not brought to the city by Jai Singh from Bandi, but from the Amani Shah Nala on his final attempt, it would be more rational to identify Darbhavati with Amani Shah Nala. There is, however, another reference to Darbhavati in a document of the time of Jai Singh. The *Dastur Komwar* preserved in the Bikaner archives records that a rivulet named Darbhavati was dammed in S. 1792 (1735 A.D.) and opened out into a lake called Mansagar, under the supervision of an architect Gaga Ram [63] Mansagar is the lake on the Amer road in which the *Jal Mahl* is situated. According to *Dastur Komwar* then, Darbhavati is the name of the small stream—practically a sewer now—which flows from the Brahmapuri side to Mansagar and crosses the Amer road just south of the government dairy. This stream flows towards the north of the town, while Amani Shah Nala flows at first south-west and then south towards Sanganer. Since apparently both the streams are described as Darbhavati in contemporary writings, there appears to be a paradox at first sight. Of course, there is the possibility that at one time the water of the Darbhavati mainly ran through a channel towards Mansagar and later on its bed was silted up and the main stream then joined the Amani Shah Nala. It turns out that this was what had actually happened.

The position will be clear from the Report of the Public Works Department for the nine months ending 31-12-1883. A shortage of water was felt at this time in the Amani Shah Nala due to the increasing demands of the city. The report considered methods of removing this shortage. It recommended digging of wells either in the bed or on the sides of the Nala. The report goes on to say:

> "Should both the above suggestions prove insufficient, there is another plan which would no doubt answer fully, viz., to bund up the river completely about a mile above the site of the pumping station.
>
> "The length of the bund would be 800 feet, average height 40.88 feet, the width at top 30 feet, outer slope 3 to 1, inner slope 4 to 1.
>
> "Every drop of water in the rains which came down the river would be caught, and when (if ever) the water rose to within 15 feet of the top of the bund; it would escape by a 50 feet wide channel, which would be cut for a short distance with an average depth of 5.92 feet to an old water course along which the river evidently once used to flow, and go past the foot of the Nahurgarh hill to the Raja Mull, Tal Katora and the Man Sagur Talaos."[64]

Evidently, therefore, Darbhavati was joined to Amani Shah Nala, but two hundred years ago, it ran north towards

62. *Ishvaravilasa Mahakavya* (Jodhpur, 1958), p. 133.
63. Dr. G N. Sharma: *A Bibliography of Medieval Rajasthan*, Agra, 1965, p. 41. The reference given is to *Dastur Komwar*, Vol. 23, for S. 1792.
64. *Jeypore State Public Works Report* for the nine months ending 31st December 1883, p. 6.

Mansagar, and even 90 years ago, its old bed was visible. The origin of the two tanks, Tal Kaltora and Raja Mal ka Talao (now filled up) is also explained.

V

PUBLIC HEALTH

Detailed statistics about births, deaths, epidemics etc., and about the medical facilities in Jaipur City are available only from 1875 onwards. We have no figures of any sort available on these matters prior to this date. It may, however, be surmised that conditions were not very much better in the earlier days.

High Death Rates in the Period 1875-1920

So far as the figures of births and deaths are concerned, those for the former are likely to be more unreliable than the figures of deaths, since many people even today fail to register the births of children, especially daughters. The number of births actually in Jaipur city varied from 20 to 30 per thousand during the years 1875-1930. We can, however, assume that the birth rate in Jaipur city was about 40 per thousand per year all through these years. This is approximately the birth rate in India today. On the other hand the average death rate recorded for the 48 years from 1875 to 1922 was 48.65 per thousand per year.[65] It is difficult to conceal a death and we can take the figures of death as more or less correct. The death rate in Jaipur was thus higher than the rate of birth all through these years i.e. 1875 to 1922; half the mortality occurred among children less than 5 years old. The other words, but for a steady rate of immigration, the population of Jaipur city would have shown a decreasing trend until about 1930. It is also clear that the city was a very unhealthy one.

Improvement After 1920

The position in the decade 1921-1930 was better. The number of deaths went down in this decade to 37.7 per

65. *Annual Report of the Jaipur Medical and Meteorological Institution* for 1922, p. 46.

thousand per year.[66] The recorded namber of births was only 28.4 per thousand, but if we assume that the actual births were about 40 per thousand, then in this decade the natural increase in the population also contributed to the total increase of the population of the city from 1.20 lakhs in 1921 to 1.44 lakhs in 1931. In fact it was only from this decade that the population of the city started growing steadily after declining or remaining static since the first census in 1870. The conditions continued to improve slowly and the death rate for the decade 1931-1940 came down slightly to less than 36 per thousand per year.[67] In the next two decades the conditions began to improve faster till in 1955-56 the death rate came down to 10.5 per thousand.[68]

The Census reports of 1931[69] and 1941[70] both state that there were no significant incidences of epidemic diseases like plague, cholera or smallpox during the decades preceding these census years. The high death rate during these twenty years (1921-40) were therefore solely due to causes which were endemic.

We may now note the diseases which took their toll in the Jaipur city.

Causes of Death

In the 48 years i.e. 1875 to 1922, 3,05,480 persons were recorded to have died in Jaipur city. Of these more than 47% i.e. 1,23,510 persons died of fever, 25,702 died of respiratory diseases, and 18,441 died of diarrhoea and dysentery. These were the main endemic diseases prevalent in Jaipur and every year a large number of people died of them. It will be noticed that the cause of death as recorded by the officials at the cremation grounds or places of burial were in layman's language. The exact diseases were not mentioned. If we go by the

66. *Census Report of the Jaipur State* for 1931, p. 50.
67. Calculated from the table of vital statistics given on p. 10 of the 1941 Census Report of Jaipur.
68. From Table No. 11.1, City Survey Report of Jaipur (1969), Rajasthan University.
69. *Census Report of 1931*, p. 8.
70. *Census Report of 1941*, p. 10.

experience of more recent years, the specific diseases were mainly malaria, typhoid and tuberculosis (in the cases of those recorded to have died of fevers), and dysentery. Of these malaria was by far the most prevalent disease. From the statistics given in the Annual Reports on Jaipur Medical and Meteorological Institution for 1908, 1911 and 1922 it may be seen that of all the infectious diseases recorded both among outdoor and indoor patients in the hospitals of the city the number of malaria patients exceeded the combined numbers of all the others.

Malaria

Strangely enough though malaria was year after year the biggest killer in Jaipur, people were not as much afraid of it as they were of cholera, which very rarely visited the city in a really epidemic form. Dr. Hendley commented (1895 A.D.) on this as follows:[71]

> "Although Cholera is universally dreaded, perhaps more than any other disease, it causes but a tithe of the sickness and mortality which are due to malarial fevers. It is true that death is not so sudden; but sometimes a man is struck down and is unconscious almost from the first, and dies after a very brief illness. Malarial disorders prevail all the year round. . . . There are however two periods in Jeypore of maximum prevalence—one to a less degree from the beginning of March to the beginning of May; the second, of far greater intensity, from the middle of August to about the middle of November. . . . At times almost every member of the family is indisposed, and even becomes completely unable to work. . . ."

Malaria was thus the greatest killer disease of Jaipur from the last quarter of the nineteenth century to the fifties of this century when the disease was almost eradicated from India. It killed either directly, or by debilitating a person and making him an easy victim of other diseases. There are no records

71. T. Holbein Hendley: *A Medico-Topographical Account of Jeypore* (Calcutta, 1895), p. 66.

to find out whether the disease was as common in Jaipur before 1875 as it was after that year. There is a possibility that malaria struck Jaipur and other parts of Rajasthan in the last quarter of the nineteenth century when it also started depopulating some districts of West Bengal, notably Hooghly and Burdwan.

Cholera

Of the three main epidemic diseases of India, cholera, plague and smallpox, the first two did not have much effect on Jaipur before the advent of the railways. The railways were built in Rajasthan mostly between 1874 and 1881. Indeed, cholera, killed more than 400 persons in a year in the following years only:—

1878	—	652
1890	—	457
1900	—	2296
1916	—	675

It is quite likely that many of the deaths recorded as due to cholera might have been caused by gastro-intestinal diseases with symptoms resembling those of cholera. These diseases are quite common in Jaipur, because of bad sanitary conditions. The high incidence of deaths in 1900 was exceptional. We have dealt with this year separately.

Cholera is a water-borne disease, and is never contracted until the excreta of a patient contaminates the food or drinking water. Also the incubation period of cholera is small and the death after the symptoms of the disease appear is quick. As such without a fast mode of travel, such as railways, cholera cannot travel far in sparsely populated areas like Rajasthan where drinking water wells are also deep. The reason for the widespread fear of cholera perhaps was that this disease was new to Jaipur in the days Hendley lived here (1874-1895) and the patients who contracted the disease died a quick and ugly death.

Cholera as an epidemic disease is rarely mentioned in history books. One of the few such mentions is that of the outbreak of this disease among the troops of Ahmad Shah Abdali while they were engaged in looting and slaughtering the people in the Mathura region in March 1757. "A cholera epidemic broke out at Mahavan and daily 150 of his soldiers began to die of it. There was no remedy, no medicine available; it cost Rs. 100/- to buy a seer of tamarind, a drink made of tamarind being prescribed with benefit."[72]

Plague

Bubonic plague first appeared in Jaipur in the 20th century. It appears that after raging in different provinces of India in the seventeenth century from the reign of Jahangir[73] up to about 1688 in Bijapur[74] where Aurangzeb's wife, Aurangabadi Mahal, died of this disease, it did not again appear in India throughout the eighteenth century. Records about plague epidemic in India are found again in the nineteenth century.

In 1836 there was a sudden and severe attack of plague in Pali. Hundreds, perhaps thousands of people died of this disease and most of the rest left the town in penic. These people in turn spread the disease in the neighbouring towns. Assistant Surgeon H. Maclean wrote a letter to his superior on 16th October 1836, after visiting Pali a few days earlier. The letter, because of its details, has become quite well known, and is also referred to in the Imperial Gazetteer (1909). People in Pali had practically all fled away when plague struck. Describing this Maclean wrote,

> "Although previously aware that the greater number of inhabitants had left the town, I had not imagined the desertion to have been so complete as I found it really to be on my first visit, on the 11th instant. Almost all the long narrow streets and alleys were tenantless, every shop shut, and in so far as I could form an opinion after visiting every quarter of the town on the 11th and 12th. I was disposed to think that not more than a thousand individuals, and those chiefly of the lowest caste, remained out of a

72. Sarkar, *op. cit.*, Vol. II, p. 88.
73. *Cambridge History of India* (Indian Edition), Vol. IV, p. 69.
74. *Ibid.*, p. 290.

population of probably fifteen thousand."[75] These people had gone away to villages and neighbouring towns like Sojat and Bhilwara, where this plague also spread. Fortunately for Jaipur, plague did not come to this place that year.

Plague raged in Maharashtra from 1896 onwards. Steps to control the disease there led to public agitation in which Tilak was imprisoned. This time also plague came only up to south-western Rajasthan. The *General Medical History of Rajputana* mentions, "It is known that the disease in 1897 was brought from Poona to the villages of Teuri in Sirohi, and that the man died the day after his arrival there."[76]

The dread disease entered Jaipur in a small way and for the first time in 1903. Thereafter it haunted the town up to 1918. Thereafter there has been no death from plague in Jaipur city. The number of deaths in the various years during which plague was prevalent here were as follows:—

1903	—	7	1911	—	34
1904	—	3	1912	—	3620
1905	—	2901	1913	—	598
1906	—	8	1914	—	NIL
1907	—	227	1915	—	NIL
1908	—	3459	1916	—	NIL
1909	—	25	1917	—	4417
1910	—	4822	1918	—	1191

The maximum deaths were thus in 1910 when nearly 3% of the people of the city died of this disease. Usual measures such as opening a plague hospital near Rawalji's Bund, attempts to have mass inoculation etc., were taken in all these years, but it does not appear that the people had much faith in these. To quote from the report for the year 1908,[77] when nearly 3500 people died of plague:—

75. The letter is quoted in full in Hendley's *General Medical History of Rajputana.*
76. *Cambridge History of India* (Indian Edition), Vol. IV, p. 155n.
77. *Annual Report on the Jaipur Medical and Meteorological Institutions* for 1908, p. 4.

"Prophylactic measures to check the epidemic were taken as far as possible by improvement of the sanitation of the city, disinfection of the infected quarters and encouragement of inoculation. Rat killing was not adopted owing to the ignorance or prejudice or both on the part of the inhabitants.

"Inoculation as a special measure was introduced; practically all the staff of the Mayo Hospital includiug the Superintendent, were inoculated, and amongst the nobles the chief of Chomu and his followers by submitting to the operations, helped to convince the public of the safety and painless character of inoculation. Notwithstanding this, however, inoculation as a prophylactic against plague, did not find favour with the general public. Only a few of the more intelligent of the population consisting of the European residents, some professors of the College, football and cricket team members, numbering altogether 454 persons were inoculated.

"A plague camp hospital remained open as usual near Rawalji's Bund but only homeless and deserted patients numbering 31 received treatment there.

"The Plague Camp Hospital remained open from 1st January 1908 to 16th May 1908, and was in charge of Assistant Surgeon Pannalal Dass and Assistant Surgeon Daljang Singh Khanka, M.B."

In all the years that plague occurred in the city it also occurred in the district. This perhaps meant that it was spread by the people running away from the city or the villages infected with plague and spreading it to other villages. However, not much mention of mass evacuation of the city is seen in the earlier medical reports. It occurs for the first time in the Medical Report for 1912.

"Compulsory segregation as a prophylactic measure was enforced at the commencement but was given up afterwards when the epidemic increased in vigour; the panic-stricken population who could afford and who had no prejudices, evacuated the infected city of their own accord."

What these prejudices were is not clear. However, there was no such prejudice in leaving the infected city or the villages when plague raged in the city and district for two years running in 1917 and 1918. This was evident from the sharp fall in the number of children reading in the schools that year. The annual report on Public Instruction in the Jaipur State for the year ending 31-8-1918 has the following:

> "The number of schools with that of scholars has this year fallen heavily by 329 and 11,763 respectively. This fall may be attributed to the spread of the epidemic plague throughout the length and breadth of the State, which was of so virulent a type that many of the Proprietors of Private Schools and teachers and taught of Indigenous schools had to fly for their lives and many of them had been a victim to the dire epidemic."

Smallpox

For the first seven years for which the records exist, the deaths due to smallpox in the city were as follows:

1875	—	123	1879	—	93
1876	—	517	1880	—	1451
1877	—	1367	1881	—	508
1878	—	286			

Thereafter the figures of death due to smallpox never touched 500. In a number of years there have been no deaths due to smallpox. The reason-perhaps was that mass vaccination started here quite early. In the beginning the people did not like to be vaccinated. The General Medical History quotes from a report by Dr. Edben for the year ending 30-6-1857, "The Jeypurians seem to have an insuperable aversion to be vaccinated on any terms." It is not quite clear whether there was any general facility available for vaccination in 1857, because the Medico-Tophographical account of Jeypore states,[78] "Vaccination was established at the end of 1860 by Dr. Burr, who

78. *Op. cit.*, p. 13.

taught four men and employed them in the city." The report quoted in the General Medical History for the year ending 30-6-1865 says: "Small Pox also prevailed in Jaipur, but prejudices against vaccination was diminishing."

Two Bad Decades

One frightening year in the history of Jaipur city was 1900 A.D. In that year 13,874 persons, which was nearly 10.5 per cent of the population of the city died. In fact the whole decade 1891 to 1900 was bad in the sense that death rate had exceeded 5% of the population twice more in this decade, once in 1892 (5.1%) and again in 1894 (5.2%). Another bad decade was 1911-1921, when the population of the city came down sharply from 1,37,000 in 1911 to 1,20 000 in 1921. This reduction in the population was mainly due to the effects of the plague (1912, 1917 and 1918) and the world-wide influenza epidemic of 1918. Compared to this decade the reduction in the population of the city in the ten years 1891-1901 was slight. This anomaly can perhaps be explained by the fact that the very high death rate of the year 1900 did not affect the permanent residents of the city and the larger number of deaths recorded are those of the starving peasants who came to the city in search of food.

VI

MEDICAL FACILITIES

The first medical dispensary for the public was opened in 1844 by the Regency Council which managed the State during the minority of the ruler Ram Singh. It is possible that even earlier to this some medical facility was available to the public from the dispensary attached to the British Political Agency. This Agency was established on 18 March, 1821 and one Dr. Simpson was posted as the Medical Officer to the Agency. "Bishop Heber mentions in 1825 that Dr. Simpson, the Agency Surgeon, took charge of a poor Brahman whose hand his own medica adviser, Dr. Smith, had amputed for a tumour of the wrist, so no doubt thus early European Surgical aid was available for those who cared for it."[79]

Generally speaking, however, medical facilities were available prior to 1844 only from private medical practitioners i.e. Vaids and Hakims. It can be presumed that by the end of the eighteenth century a tradition of learning in Ayurveda had grown among the Vaids of Jaipur city. At the time of the ruler Pratap Singh (1778-1803), two text books on Ayurveda, one in Sanskrit and the other in Hindi, were got compiled by the co-operative efforts of the local Vaids. The Sanskrit work was called *Pratap Sagar* and the Hindi one was called *Amrit Sagar*.[80]

The modern Hindi version of *Amritsagar* contains 630 printed pages. It is divided into four parts. The first part is Utpatti Khanda which besides giving the usual story of the origin of Ayurveda also briefly describes the physiology according to Ayurveda. The Khand is in 18 pages only. The second part is Vichar Khanda. It gives a brief description of the manner of examining a patient, but the main discussion in this Khand is about the various metallic compounds and their preparations and about the medicinal properties of various plants. The chapter comprises 98 pages.

The main parts of the book are the third i.e. the Nidan Khand and the fourth i.e. the Chikitsa Khand. These describe, as the names signify, the symptoms and diagnosis of various diseases and their treatment, and cover the rest of the more than 500 pages of the book. The important points to note in *Amritsagar* are the following:

1. Use of metallic compounds as medicines.
2. Description of 18 types of pulse. It appears that *Amritsagar* here followed the Unani system of describing the movements of the pulse as resembling those of the frog, gazelle, etc.

79. Hendley, *A Medico-Topographical Account of Jeypore*, p. 11. I have not been able to trace the reference to this surgical operation in Heber's "*Narrative of a Journey*, 1824-25".

80. *Amritsagar* was perhaps written in the Jaipuri. The currently available version is in modern Hindi language. This was published by Shyam Kashi Press in Mathura in 1938.

3. Mention of Syphilis (Phiranga Vata) and its treatment with mercury.
4. Prescriptions of Surgery for fistula.
5. Direction to use magic and mantras for diseases for which medicines did not exist such as mental diseases, rabies etc.

Amritsagar quotes a number of authorities such as Sharngadhar, Vagbhatta, Bhavaprakasha, Vaidyarahasya etc.

As a handbook of Ayurveda it is still used in the areas in proximity to Jaipur. This compilation from many standard books on Ayurveda at the end of the eighteenth century shows that Jaipur had at that time a tradition of academic discussions on Ayurveda. This tradition however rapidly disappeared.

Boileau reports that there were 250 Vaids (Bed or Baid) and 900 *Hakims* (*Hukeem*) in Jaipur in 1835.[81] Assuming that Boileau's estimated figures generally are about four times the actual numbers, we get about 60 Vaids and 225 *Hakims* in Jaipur in that year. This number of Vaids for a population of more than 80,000 Hindu seems small. On the other hand, considering that Muslim population was about 12 to 15 thousand in Jaipur at that time, the *Hakims* seem to be too many. Presumably the figure of *Hakims* also includes bone-setters and masseurs (*Pahalawans*) who even today are mostly Muslims. As stated earlier academic knowledge about Ayurveda had by this time declined in Jaipur. The science of medicine had gone into the hands of illiterate quacks.

No contemporary record, however, as to the mode of treatment by these half educated Vaids and *Hakims* exists. Some sixty years later Dr. Hendley conjectured as follows :[82]

> "The people of Jeypore, until the late Maharaja's accession (i.e. 1844), were treated when sick by—(a) *Baids* or Hindu physicians, of whom very few were learned. In fact most of them knew little more than a few Sanskrit verses or *shloks* which they recited as guides to the selection of particular remedies when they thought they were dealing

81. See Appendix IV.
82. Hendley, *op cit.*, p. 10.

with the disease to which these texts referred. State Baids are still subsidized in many villages.

2. Jain priest or jaties, and other priests. These depended chiefly upon the Amritsagar, an abridgement of *Susruta*, *Charaka* and other well known Sanskrit authors which was drawn up in 1779-1803 by order of Maharaja Pratap Singh, one of the chiefs of Jeypore.

3. *Hakims* or Mohammedan physicians, who practised the *Yunani* or Greek (more correctly Arabian or humoural) system of medicines. Very few of them were educated. One or two of these are still attached to each of the State regiments.

4. *Jarrahas* or barber-surgeons, a very poor and ignorant sort of men, who bled, drew teeth, applied the actual cautery, and bandaged limbs in cases of fracture. They have great influence still, specially with women.

5. *Sathyas* or couchers, who practised reclination of the crystalline lens in case of cataract.

6. *Bairagis* or Hindu, and *Fakirs* or Musalman devotees; wise women; clever persons who drive out diseases by the aid of the *jharu* or broom and charms.

7. *Pansaris* or Druggists, at whose shops *Baids* are accustomed to sit and practice. There are no regulations for the sale of poisons, hence there are great risks of accidents occurring. Something ought to be done in this matter."

A dispensary and hospital was established in the city of Jaipur in 1844 for the cure of poor and all other persons according to European principles.[83] This infant institution was believed to have attracted greater notice because it was thought that it was the revival of a hospital said to have been originally established by Maharaja Sawai Jai Singh, the founder of the city of Jaipur.[84]

83. J. Ludlow, Political Agent, Jaipur to Major C. Thoresby, Offg. A.G.G. Rajputana dt. 23 May 1844, No. 51, Foreign and Political Department, National Archives of India, New Delhi.

84. Lt. Col. Sutherland, A.G.G. Rajputana to F. Currie, Secretary to Government of India dt. 10 June 1846, Cons. 18 July 1846, No. 183, For. & Pol. Deptt., National Archives of India.

In his report of the 15th July 1856, H. Ebden, M.D., Rajputana Agency Surgeon observed:

"At Jaipur, the dispensary house, Dr. Ebden thought, was a large and as well arranged a place as any in India, and the Rajah supported it in the most liberal manner. The daily attendance under Dr. Burr was about 50."

"Indigenous drugs were largely used" and Dr. Edben adds, "our faces are strenuously set against any use of European medicines that are not absolutely required."

The fact that the doctor in charge of the dispensary, Dr. Burr preferred using indigenous medicines was not surprising. The state of medical science was not much different in Europe and India in those days, and the effectiveness of the medicines in both the systems was almost equal.

"The report for 1859-60 was only sent in on December 8, 1860.

"It was noted that a branch dispensary had been opened in the city for which returns would be available in the next annual statement.

"The Midwifery Hospital was highly commended, but the dispensary attendance was still small.

"Dr. T. Murray relieved Dr. Burr at Jaipur in 1861. The former officer reported that the Midwifery Hospital was chiefly filled with women who were sent by the police when it was suspected that they intended to procure abortion; other poor persons, chiefly unmarried persons, came willingly.

In 1968, Dr. Moore regretted to have to report that the Midwifery Hospital had also been closed."[85]

The facility for medical treatment in Jaipur was thus not satisfactory until 1875. The first general hospital in the city, called the Mayo Hospital was opened in 1875. This continued to be the main hospital for the city till the new hospital first known as Lady Willingdon Hospital and now known as the S.M.S. Hospital was formally opened in 1936 (but started functioning nearly 10 years later). The Mayo Hospital building was later converted into the district courts building and continued to be used as such until 1974. The Mayo hospital had 100

85. Quotations above unless otherwise stated are all from the *General Medical History of Rajputana.*

beds in 1895.[86] The hospital building was continuously expanded and in 1916 it had 180 beds.[87] The hospital had a female wing also attached to it under a lady doctor. By 1935 the Mayo Hospital had 170 beds for males and 50 for females.[88] Actually a separate hospital for women had been started in 1931 and to begin with, the Scottish Mission at Jaipur was asked by the Durbar to administer the hospital and provide the staff.[89] The Mission itself had started its own Women's Hospital and Dispensary, sometimes in 1909-10 in a rented building in Nahargarh-ka-Rasta[90] and had sent two qualified lady medical missionaries to look after it. Presumably this hospital was closed down after the opening of the State Women's Hospital.

The foundation stone of the Lady Willingdon Hospital (now known as S.M.S Hospital) was laid on 3 March 1934. The *Sardars* and rich merchants of the Jaipur State were asked to contribute towards its building. The largest donation of one lakh of rupees was from Raja Seth Baldeodas Birla.[91]

Thus Jaipur got a large and well equipped hospital just before the integration of the States. When shortly afterwards a Medical College was started in Rajasthan, there was no difficulty in making the S.M.S. Hospital its nucleus

VII

GAS WORKS AND ROAD LIGHTING

As mentioned earlier Maharaja Ram Singh (1835-1880) had tried to modernize and beautify the city in many ways. One of these was to light up the main streets of the city by gas. He perhaps wanted his city to vie with Bombay and Calcutta where gas lights had already been introduced. The project was started in 1876 and the gas supply commenced in 1878. The gas works were situated south of the town close to the wall-almost on the same site on which the present Gem Cinema is situated. All the main streets, the palace, the large public

86. *A Medico-Topographical Account of Jeypore* (Calcutta, 1895).
87. *Notes on Jaipur* (1916), p. 86.
88. *The Jaipur Album* (1935), p. 1.
89. *Ibid.*, p. 3.
90. *Notes on Jaipur*, p. 104.
91. *Jaipur Album* (1935), p. 3.

institutions and several of the more important roads, and the road from Sanganer gate to the railway station, the present Mirza Ismail Road were lighted by gas. There were a few private consumers also. The gas was manufactured from Kerosene oil. By 1892 there were 670 jets, about 200 of them being within the city palace campus.

The Superintendent of the gas works tried to induce the private citizens to have gas lights in their houses and shops, but the Jaipur public preferred to continue using primitive oil lamps in their houses. The Superintendent of the Gas Works reported:[92]

> "I am sorry to say that less progress was made in extending the gas to private houses. I tried very much to extend this and gave all possible facilities; but after five years trial, I have very little hopes left that the Jeypore public finds the necessity yet of a good light when it has to be paid for privately.
>
> "Five jets are the total of extensions made to private houses, and even in this in one shop the gas was only taken because I paid the pipe works out of my private purse, which I did in the hope that if once introduced others would possibly follow example.
>
> "Notwithstanding that we charge the gas only at our own cost, and that there are already 161 jets erected at private houses, only Rs. 118 10-11 were cashed on those for gas supplied during the year or 11 annas 9½ pies per jet. I think it will explain the cause sufficiently if I say that no gas but even candles are very seldom in use even in the best-to-do houses; the most primitive oil lamps of half candle power are in general use."

This reluctance to use bright lights can perhaps be explained. Jaipur was culturally very backward at this time. Few people read books, and there were practically no entertainments available in the evening. People would thus finish their meals early and go to sleep. Gas lights were not needed in the house.

The number of jets had gone up to 836 in 1915. By that year

92. Jeypore Gas Works: Annual Report for the year 1881, p. 10.

the Residency and the Jaipur Hotel (at present the M.L.A's hostel) had also been lighted up with gas.[93] It is, however, obvious that the number of gas lamps were too few to give any effective light in the streets.

The Durbar had in that year sanctioned the installation of a coal gas plant. It was thought that when ready, incandescent burners would be substituted for the ordinary jets and this would have three times the illuminating power.

The main reason for substituting oil gas by coal gas was the comparative cheapness of the latter. The coal gas plant was started on 1 June 1918.[94] However, since the ruler preferred to have oil gas lights within the palace both the plants were kept running. By the next year the palace lights except of the Chandra Mahal[95] were also converted to coal gas.

In 1923 it was decided to replace gas by electricity. An electric power house was constructed near the Railway Station and the installation was formally opened by the ruler on the 3 January 1927. "A number of public roads and also buildings both State and private, were lit with electricity, and progress in this direction continued. It was decided to close the gas works as soon this can be conveniently done."[96]

93. *Notes on Jaipur* (1916), p. 83.
94. *Jaipur Gas Works Annual Report* for the year ending 31-8-1918, p. 3.
95. *Jaipur Gas Works Annual Report* for the year ending 31-8-1919, p. 3.
96. *Report on the Administration of the Jaipur State* for 1926-27 and 1927-28, p. 47.

CHAPTER VII

Religious Life

I

THE TEMPLE OF GOVINDADEVA

The Govindadeva temple within the city palace premises is the most famous temple of Jaipur. The temple was built by Jai Singh in 1735.[1] The image of Govindadeva installed in the temple, is said to be the one that was discovered by Roop Goswami in Vrindaban in the 16th century. The legend is as follows:

Vrindaban, the scene of the boyhood days of Krishna, had become almost a jungle by the early 16th century. No trace of the original place was left at the site known as Vrindaban. Chaitanya had visited the site in 1514 A.D. and had discovered some of the places mentioned in the *Bhagvat Purana*, but he was not able to stay here long enough to discover the others. Two learned Brahmans, Roop and Sanatana, were high officials in the services of the Sultan of Bengal. Later the brothers became the disciples of Chaitanya and resigned from their posts. Chaitanya asked them to go to Vrindaban, settle down there and discover the lost holy sites. Roop and Sanatana came to Vrindaban and settled down there. Later they were joined by their nephew Jeeva and a few more disciples of Chaitanya. They

1. This is generally believed to be the year of construction of this temple. At the time of the integration of the States in 1949, the palace officials of Jaipur prepared a list of buildings constructed at various places in India by the rulers and the members of their families. In this list 1735 is mentioned as the date of construction of the Govindadeva temple: Appendix VI. However, there is mention of the Govindadeva's temple in *Siyaha Hazur Papers* of 1733 A.D.

were able to locate here many sites associated with *Krishna leela.*

"Nobody knew Vrindaban at that time. The two brothers Roop and Sanatana came here under the orders of Shri Krishna Chaitanya and pointed out the places described by Sukadeva Swami."[2]

These disciples of Chaitanya, who were all called *Goswamis,* also discovered a number of images of Krishna. These images had been hidden away for fear of desecration by Muslim invaders either by burying them underground or by keeping them in the private houses. The image of Govindadeva was discovered by Roop Goswami himself from a site called Goma Tila in Vrindaban.[3]

Roop Goswami died in 1563. In 1590 A.D., Raja Man Singh of Amer, an ancestor of Jai Singh, built a temple for Govindadeva in Vrindaban. This temple built of red sand stone is a massive structure. Both from inside, and outside it looks like a cathedral. From inside, the temple is in the form of a cross, the east-west arm being 117 ft. and north-south arm 105 feet.[4] It is perhaps the largest Hindu religious building built in the Mughal empire. There is a small stone inscription inside the temple. The translation of the inscription is as follows:

> "In the 34th year of the reign of Emperor Akbar, Maharajadhiraj Shri Man Singh Deva, descendant of Maharajadhiraj Shri Prithvi and son of Maharaj Shri Bhagvantadas built this temple of Govindadeva in the *yoga pitha sthana* of Shri Vrindaban. The chief builder was Shri Kalyandas, the architect was Manikchand Chopang, and the mason was Govindadas a resident of Delhi (signed) Ganeshdas Vimval."

The image of Govindadeva was kept in this temple from 1590 onwards. It seems likely that sometime between 1667 and 1670 the image of Govindadeva was taken out of the temple for fear of desecration by the Emperor Aurangzeb and hidden

2. *Vartika Tilaka* of *Chhappaya* number 445, in the Bhaktamala.
3. The years of the discovery according to the tradition of the sebait family of the image was 1525.
4. Percy Brown, *Indian Architecture* (Bombay, 1942), Vol. I, p. 157. Also see, Fergusson, p. 462.

away either somewhere in Vrindaban itself, or perhaps, as is believed by the family of the priests of this image, in Kama in Bharatpur district. It could not have gone to Amer since the rural of that place was not in a position to protect it against the Mughals. Mirza Raja Jai Singh of Amer, an ancestor of Sawai Jai Singh, had died in 1667. He and Jaswant Singh of Jodhpur were the two important Hindu generals of Aurangzeb and had some restraining influence on the Emperor's inconoclastic zeal. On Jai Singh's death, Jaswant Singh was left alone. He had himself become quite old, and perhaps felt unable to cope with Aurangzeb alone. On hearing of Mirza Raja Jai Singh's death, he is said to have uttered the *doha*—

> "The bells do not ring in temples, the emperor is not restrainable, come back once again my Jai Singh."[5]

Aurangzeb's iconoclastic fury burst out within two years of the death of Mirza Raja Jai Singh. "On 19th April 1669, he issued a general order to the governors of all the provinces to demolish the schools and temples of the infidels and put down their teaching and religious practices strongly.[6] Temples were destroyed extensively all over the Mughal empire according to these orders. The first extensive outbreak of Hindu reaction against this policy of persecution took place among the sturdy Jat preasantry of the Muttra district, where the local commandant Abdun-Nabi was a bigoted oppressor. In 1669 the Jats rose under a leader named Gokla of Tilpat, killed Abdun-Nabi, and after keeping the whole region in turmoil for a year, were suppressed by a strong imperial force under Hasan Ali Khan."[7] Practically all the Hindu temples of Vrindaban were destroyed during these years, but the priests were able to save most of the images by hiding them or taking them away from this area. The famous-image of Goverdhan Nath was taken to Nathdwara near Udaipur, during this time.[8] It is said to have been removed from Vrindaban in 1668 and to have reached the Sihad village, later known as Nathdwara

5. This oft quoted *doha* is no doubt apocryphal.
6. *Cambridge History of India*, Vol. IV, Indian Edition, p 241.
7. *Cambridge History of India*, Vol. IV, p. 243.
8. G.N. Sharma, *Rajasthan ka Itihas*, Vol. I, p. 619.

in 1669. The earliest document about the image in Mewar is dated 1672. The document is a grant for land for the maintenance of the temple. The translation of a part of it reads as follows:—

Shri Ram is Victorious Let Shri Ganesh be pleased.	Let Shri Eklingji be pleased.

Sahi

Maharajadhiraj Maharana Shri Raj Singhji commands from the auspicious Udaipur the jagirdar of Sihad and Brahmans and all inhabitants.

Be it known that Shrinathji residing at Sihad. Let uncultivated as many desire be cultivated till such time. When Shrinathji goes back to Brij the land of those to whom it belong will . . . . in fact. If any one of them obstructs in any way he will be rebuked grant Masani Loghs in Smt. 1729 on Asoj Sudi 15, Thursday.[9]

The image of Goverdhannath had therefore arrived in Mewar before 1672. Also from the wording of the grant it appears that it was understood then that the image was in Mewar for a short period only and ultimately it would go back to the land of Brija, i.e. Vrindaban.

Since the temple of Govindadeva was the largest temple in Vrindaban, it is unlikely that it escaped the fury of the Mughals. The image was saved but the temple building was destroyed and it was not repaired until the second half of the nineteenth century. The repair work was started[10] by Mr. Growse, the Collector of Mathura, in August 1873, and the initial finance (Rs. 5,000) for the repairs was provided by Ram Singh, the then ruler of Jaipur. The rebuilt temple does not have any image. The picture of Chaitanya is worshipped in this temple.

Just behind this Govindadeva temple in Vrindaban is a

9. Quoted in the paper book prepared in the appeal (Shri Govindlalji Maharaj of Nathdwara Vs The State of Rajasthan and others) to the Supreme Court, 1962, p. 200.

10. Growse, *op. cit.*, p. 226.

small temple containing a replica of the image of Govindadeva. This temple is said to have been built by one Nanda Kumar Basu in 1820. The priest in charge of this temple in Vrindaban and of the Govindadeva temple in Jaipur is the same person. The post of the priest runs in the family. A few years ago there was an appeal in a civil case in the court of the Additional District Judge Allahabad. The judgement was delivered on 28 December 1968.

The dispute was between Praduman Kumar Deo (Banerjee) the *pujari* or the *sebait* of the Govindadeva temple in Jaipur, on the one hand, and Sudha Chandra and others on the other hand. Praduman Kumar Deo claimed that he was also the *sebait* of the temple of Govindadeva in Vrindaban which was built by Nanda Kumar Basu. The appellate court upheld the claim and declared Praduman Kumar Deo as the *sebait* of this temple also.

One important evidence produced in the court was the genealogical tree of the priests of the Govindadeva temple. The tree starts from Roop Goswami himself. For the first nine generations the *sebait-ship* ran from *guru to chela*, until we come to Jagannath, the ninth *sebait*. Jagannath was the *sebait* or the priest at the time of Jai Singh. He was the first priest of the temple to get married perhaps under the general permission given by Sawai Jai Singh to all the *Vaishnava Bairagis* to marry. Since then the priesthood of the Govindadeva temple has descended from father to the eldest son.

The complete genealogical tree as produced in the court is as follows:—

Roop Goswami (1490-1563)

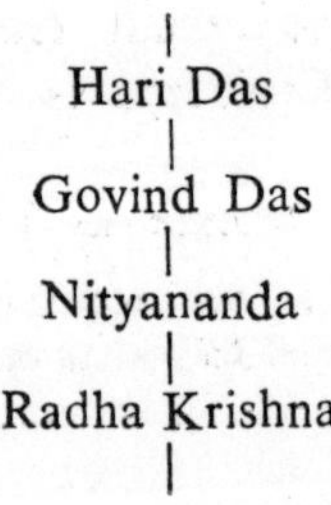

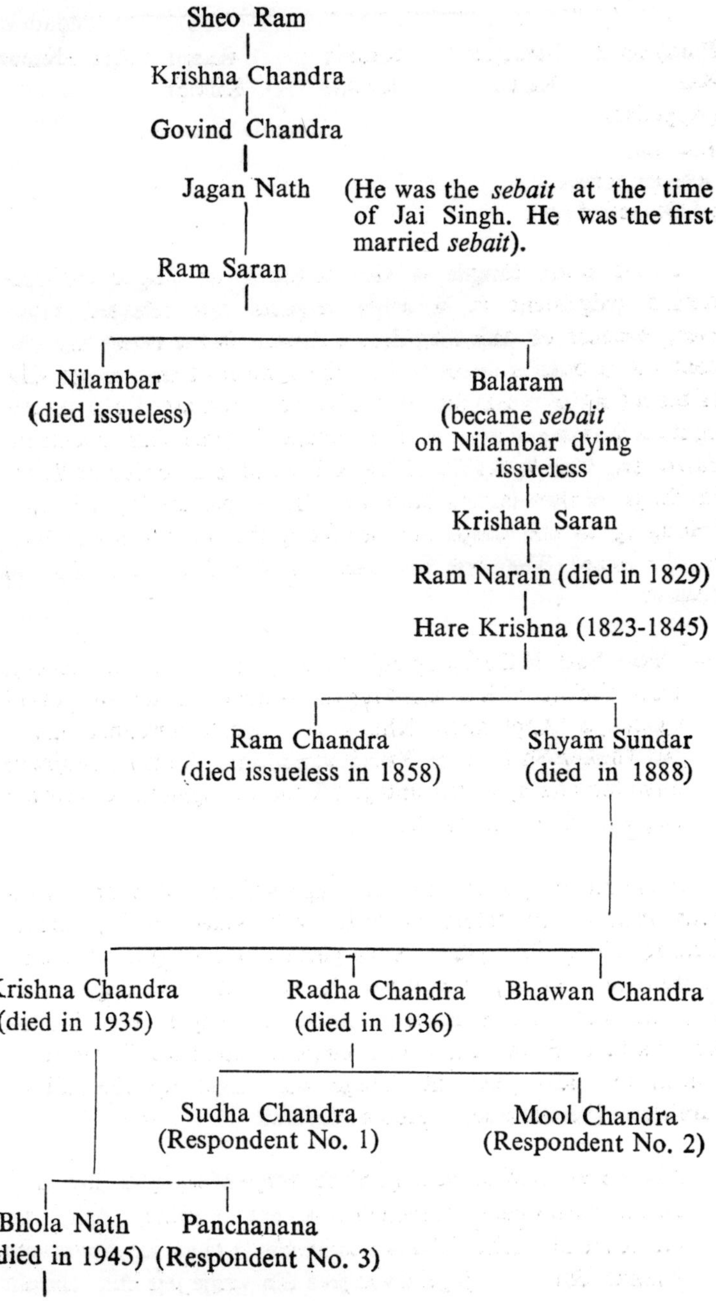
Sheo Ram
Krishna Chandra
Govind Chandra
Jagan Nath
(He was the *sebait* at the time of Jai Singh. He was the first married *sebait*).
Ram Saran
Nilambar
(died issueless)
Balaram
(became *sebait* on Nilambar dying issueless
Krishan Saran
Ram Narain (died in 1829)
Hare Krishna (1823-1845)
Ram Chandra
(died issueless in 1858)
Shyam Sundar
(died in 1888)
Krishna Chandra
(died in 1935)
Radha Chandra
(died in 1936)
Bhawan Chandra
Sudha Chandra
(Respondent No. 1)
Mool Chandra
(Respondent No. 2)
Bhola Nath
(died in 1945)
Panchanana
(Respondent No. 3)

Pradyuman Kumar (Appellant and the present *sebait* of Govindadeva).	Niranjan Kumar	Kaunit Kumar	Ranjit Kumar	Ajit Kumar

So far as the temple of Govindadeva in Jaipur is concerned judgement is in other respects not relevant. However, because of this long drawn dispute in the court, the two contending parties unearthed a large number of documents. One of them (in the possession of Pradyuman Kumar Deo) throws light on the time of arrival of this image in Amer. This document dated *Asoj Vadi* 9, S.1771 (1714 A.D.) and is an order by Sawai Jai Singh to allot certain land for use as pasture for the cattle belonging to the image and also fixing the periodical gifts etc., for the image. The first few lines of the document read as follows.

> "Sidhi Shri Maharajadhiraj Maharaj Shri Sawai Jai Singhji Dev Vachanat Kamaiti Pragane Amber ka disesu prasad vanchaya. Apparanch Khushvoi vagirah lawazma mafik jail Thakur Shri. . . .ji Vrindavanji nazik Amber Virajman huve tab charaya istak miti jail Khusvoi vagairah va lavazma bag vagirah mukarrar hoi. . . . ."

From this it appears that the image had arrived in Vrindaban near Amer shortly before the order was issued in September/October 1714. This place is the garden on the right hand side of the road from Jaipur to Amer between the Mansagar lake and the hills. There is even today a temple for Radha Krishna here. From another document dated S.1772 appears that in the next year the image was taken up the hill to Jainiwas. The document reads as follows:

> "Sidh Shri Shah Sewaramji Shah Meghrajji jogya likhitang Divan Kishoredas Tarachand Kenya Vanche. Athe ka samachar bhalache. Thanka sada bhala chai je. Aparanchi Thakur Shri . . . . ji jainiwas jeta din viraje jeta din chouki

rati ne deva ke vaste mali vagirah nephar 9 rakhiwa ke. . . ."

Jainivas[11] was perhaps the garden just below the Amer.

The image of Govindadeva presumably stayed on in the Jainivas garden until the present temple was built in 1735 in the city palace of the newly-built capital, Jaipur.

We may thus summarize the itinerary of the image of Govindadeva as follows:

1590 to some time between 1667-1670—In the Govindadeva temple at Vrindaban (in Mathura District)

1670-1714—Either in Kama in Bharatpur District or hidden in Vrindaban itself. The image was taken to Amer in 1714 when the fear of Mughal intervention in that place had disappeared.

1714-1715—In the Vrindaban garden near Amer.

1715-1735—In the Jainivas garden.

1735 to date—In the present temple in the City Palace, Jaipur.

The temple, it may be presumed, was in the beginning maintained at the cost of the ruler of Jaipur. Within a few years, that is from the time of Maharaja Madho Singh, part of the cost of maintenance of the temple was met by a cess on the land revenue or tribute paid by the Jagirdars. An order[12] dated *Kartik Vadi* 9, S. 1808 (November 1751) issued by Madho Singh states that Jagirdars and Ijaradars would pay a cess of Rs. 1/4/- per one thousand rupees of land revenue. Out of this amount one rupee would go towards the maintenance of the temple and the balance four annas for the maintenance of the *Sebait* of the temple.

Later, some villages were given in jagir to the temple itself. Many other temples of Jaipur were also given jagirs. Some of

11. The garden which is known as Jainivas, now-a-days, is the large ornamental garden, between the Chandra Mahal and the present temple of Govindadeva. This garden was built in 1726, according to the City Palace records. (See Appendix VI).
12. Document in possession of Pradyuman Kumar Deo.

these were called *Guru* Jagirs. Their list in 1935[13] was as follows:

	Name of Thikana	*Name*	*Caste*
1.	Shri Balanandj	Mahant Ram Krishnandji	Brahman
2.	Shri Gobinddeoji	Gushain Krishanchandraji	Bengali Brahman
3.	Shri Gopinathji	Gushain Madholalji	Bengali Brahman
4.	Shri Galta	Acharaj Hari Sharanji	Brahman
5.	Shri Binodilalji	Gushain Gokal Laldeoji	Bengali Brahman
6.	Shri Ladliji	Gushain Radheylalji	Brahman
7.	Lakshman Dwara	Mahant Gopi Dasji	Brahman

With the abolition of Jagirs, the revenue from jagir villages has been converted into cash annuity. The annuity of the Govindadeva temple now is Rs. 32063.93.[14]

The Govindadeva temple in the city palace in Jaipur is a flat-roofed building. It is situated within the precincts of the city palace about 200 metres due north of the main palace building. This flat-roofed structure later became the model for most of the temples, both Hindu and Jain, in Jaipur.

The worship of Govindadeva is carried on here in the Gaudiya Vaishnava manner since the priests of the temple belong to that sect. However, so far as the devotees are concerned there is no sectarian bias and this temple is the most popular temple in the city. Practically, all religious-minded Hindus of Jaipur visit the temple periodically, and there are many people here who make it a point to go to this temple at least once in a day. The image of Govindadeva is shown to the public only seven times a day for fixed periods. Two of these periods are of one hour each and the other five are of 15 minutes each. The timings of these periods which vary with the seasons are called *jhankis.* The people gather at the temple at the appointed times and enthusiastically break into *bhajans* when the curtain is removed and the image is made visible.

13. *Jaipur Album* (1935), Ch. XIV, p. 20.
14. Information obtained from the office of the Jagir Commissioner.

The *bhajans* and *kirtans* sung at each *jhanki* are fixed. The total number of these songs is twenty-five.

The singing of these *bhajans* and *kirtans* daily at the Govindadeva temple is one of the few community worships practised by the Hindus of Jaipur and perhaps has some effect on the religious thinking of the people. The themes of these songs are therefore important. Since it is a Gaudiya Vaishnava temple, the importance of Radha as a consort of adolescent Krishna of Vrindaban is emphasised in these songs. Vrindaban *leela* of Krishna has therefore gained significance among the Vaishnavas of Jaipur. This is most obviously seen in the names of persons in Jaipur. For instance, names like Radha-ballabh, Gopinath, Ladli Mohan etc , are quite common here. (The contrast may be seen in Eastern Uttar Pradesh and North Bihar where Rama as a part of the name of a person is ubiquitous). Two of the songs, one of which is in Bengali (भालि गोरा चांदेर श्रारती बनी) mention Chaitanya and his immediate disciples. Some songs mention Krishna in his post-Vrindaban life, but no song mentions Lakshmi Narain. A song by Surdas, (यशोदा मैया खोल किवड़िया) about Krishna's childhood days, shows that there was no sectarian bias in selecting the songs. (Surdas was one of the *Ashtachhapa* poets of the Vallabhacharya *Sampradaya*). In fact, a song even in praise of Ramchandra is included in the list of songs. This is sung at the second *Jhanki* and is entitled, श्रीधूप श्रारती श्री रामचन्द्रजी ।

The Bengali song mentioned above is by an obscure poet Birballabhadas. Nothing is known about him, but this song and the only one by this writer finds place in the famous collection of Bengali *Vaishnava* songs, *Pada Kalpataru* (*Pada* number 2868). *Pada Kalpataru* was compiled in the last years of the eighteenth century. The song was originally composed for the evening *arati* of Chaitanya, and is sung in the Govindadeva temple also at the time of the evening *arati*.

The mention of the *Ishta Devatas* of practically all the sects of *Vaishnavas* in the *bhajans* sung at the Govindadeva temple in Jaipur shows that there is no sectarian controversy among the *Vaishnavas* here. It also shows that the good work done by Jai Singh in bringing together all the *Vaishnava* sects in his time, has continued to remain effective uptil now.

The Story of a Religious Debate

An important event in the history of *Gaudiya Vaishnavism* is associated with the Govindadeva temple in Jaipur. *Gaudiya Vaishnavism* did not start as an offshoot of one of the four official sects of Vaishnavism known as the *Chatuh-Sampradaya*. Legend and history are mixed up in this story of the formation of these four sects.

Vedanta among the six systems of Indian philosophy has been the most dominant school at least from the time of Shankara in the 8th/9th century The main teachings of *Vedantism* are found in three sets of books. The first consists of the twelve accepted *Upanishads*, namely, *Isa*, *Kena*, *Katha*, *Prasna*, *Mundaka*, *Mandukya*, *Taittirayi*, *Aitareya*, *Chhandogya*, *Brihadaranyaka*, *Kaushitaki* and *Shvetashvetara*. The second is the *Vedanta Sutra* or *Bhrahmasutra*, and the third is the *Bhagvadgita*. These are also known as *Shrutiprasthana*, *Naya-prasthana* and *Smritiprashana* respectively. One could not start a religious sect unless one wrote the commentaries on these three Prasthanas—the *Prasthanatrayas*, based on one's religious theory.

The first great commentator of these three *Prasthanas* was Shankaracharya. Shankara believed in *Advaitu*, i.e. monism or non-dualism, and he interpreted these books accordingly.

Vaishnavism was a protest against non-dualism and its associated theory of *Maya* or Illusion. There were four great commentators of the *Prasthanatrayas* among the Vaishnavas, and thus four *Sampradayas* of *Vaishnavas* started after them. These commentators of *Acharyas* were Ramanuja, Madhva, Vallabha and Nimbarka. The followers of these four *Acharyas* formed the four sects or *Sampradayas* in which the *Vaishnavas* were divided. Other *Vaishnava Sampradayas* formed in later days tried to invoke the authority of one of these four to gain respectability.

Gaudiya Vaishnavas were followers of Chaitanya. Chaitanya himself did not belong to any of the four *Vaishnava* sects. In fact he was initiated in his ascetic life as a *Sanyasi* of the *Bharati* order by Keshva Bharati of the Shankaracharya school. In the famous dialogue with Rai Ramananda at Raja

Mahendri in Andhra, he is said to have stated[15]—"What to say of others, I who am a *Mayavadi-Sanyasi*, I too am carried away in the waves of adoration of Krishna at seeing your love."

Thus to start with, the *Gaudiya Vaishnavas* did not belong to any of the four authorised *Vaishnava Sampradayas*.

There is a tradition[16] among the *Gaudiya Vaishnavas* that sometimes in the eighteenth century the *Vaishnavas* belonging to the Ramanandi sect at Galta near Jaipur found out that the *sebaits* or the priests of the Govindadeva temple did not belong to any of the four sects of *Vaishnavas*. They were, therefore, asked to desist from the duties performed by them in the temple. Vishvanath Chakrabarti was at that time the head of the *Gaudiya Vaishnava* community in Vrindaban. He sent his disciples Krishnadeva Sarvabhauma and Baladeva Vidyabhushan to Jaipur to look into the matter. These two came to Galta and entered into a debate with the Jaipur *pandits* and got the better of them.

The Bengali priests were thus restored to their duties in the Govindadeva temple. However, the Jaipur *pandits* demanded to see the commentary of the *Gaudiya Vaishnavas* on the *Brahma Sutra*. On this Baladeva asked for a month's time. Baladeva wrote his commentary within this month according to the directions he received in his dream from Govindadeva himself. The commentary is thus called the *Govinda-bhashya*.

It is difficult to say how far this story of the religious debate in Galta is true. *Govinda-bhashya* as the *Gaudiya Vaishnava* cammentary of the Brahma Sutra, does no doubt exist, but there is no memory of this religious debate in Jaipur, not even in the family of the priests of the Govindadeva temple.

II

RELIGIOUS BELIEFS OF THE SUCCESSORS OF JAI SINGH

Ishvari Singh (1743-1750) was the eldest surviving son of Jai Singh. Though Jai Singh was celebrated for his wide intellectual interests, it does not appear that his son had much

15. *Shri Chaitanya Charitamrita—Madhva Leela.*
16. S.K. De: *Earlv History of Vaishnava Faith and Movement in Bengal*, 1961, p. 22.

interest in non-mundane matters. The *Ishvaravilas Mahakavya* written during his reign and eulogising his martial qualities does not mention anything about his religious beliefs. There is an image of *Hanuman* in blackstone in a temple near the place where Jai Singh had performed his *Ashvamedha*. This image is said to have been installed by Ishvari Singh. From the black colour of the image it is surmised that Ishvari Singh believed in *Tantrik* rites. Ishvari Singh's short reign of seven years was almost completely occupied in defending his throne from his step-brother Madho Singh who was helped both by his uncle, the Rana of Mewar, and the Marathas. No wonder Ishvari Singh tried to invoke supernatural help for himself.

Madho Singh (1751-68)

Madho Singh appears to be the only ruler of Jaipur who had a *guru*.[17] Balananda who was the head of a sect of Ramavat *Vaishnavas* is mentioned as his guru by J.N. Sarkar.[18] The *Buddhi Vilas* which was composed shortly after Madho Singh's death mentions[19] that for a short while, one Shyam Tiwari had displaced even Balananda from the position of the guru by some incantations.

Galta was the headquarters of another sect of Ramavat *Vaishnavas*. It may be surmised therefore that Madho Singh's leanings were more towards the Ramavat form of *Vaishnavism* than the Krishnavat form which appealed to his father, Jai Singh.

Prithvi Singh (1768-78)

Madho Singh's elder son Prithvi Singh became the ruler of Jaipur at the age of five but died when only fifteen years of age.

17. There was always a number of Rajgurus in Jaipur. Important religious persons and persons learned in religious matters were appointed to these posts as Rajgurus. These posts were sometimes hereditary. Balananda on the other hand was a personal religious guru of Madho Singh.
18. Sarkar, *Fall of the Mughal Empire*, Vol. III, p. 234.
19. See p. 282 infra.

Pratap Singh (1778-1803)

He succeeded his step-brother at the age of fourteen. Like his grandfather, Jai Singh, this prince was also deeply interested in religion; but his approach towards religion was different. While Jai Singh's interest was mainly intellectual, Pratap Singh's religion was emotional and his approach towards God was through poetry.

Pratap Singh wrote a large number of poems practically all dealing with the *Vrindaban-Leela* of Krishna and Radha. His pen-name was Brajanidhi.[20] Attempts have been made to find out the *Vaishnava* sect to which Pratap Singh belonged from these poems. There are numerous lines in the writings of Pratap Singh where he has given an important place to Radha:

कृपा करो बृंदाबन रानी ।

or

कृपा करो बृषभान-नंदिनी 'ब्रजनिधि जीवन जी की ।।

From such lines, it has been inferred that Pratap Singh's thinking was on the lines of the Radha Vallabhi[21] sect. On the other hand, an affinity is traced to the Vallabha Sampradaya also.

Though Govinda Deva, the palace deity, belonged to the *Gaudiya Sampradaya* and poems addressed to Govinda Deva appear frequently in his writings, there is no trace of the influence of this sect in his poems. One of the surest signs of the influence of the Gaudiya sect is the mention of Chaitanya and his immediate disciples in songs. Not one poem of Pratap Singh does this. One of his court poets Rasarasi Ramanarain, however, mentions Chaitanya and his disciples in the first few lines of his *Vamsa Prasansa*:[22]

20. The writings of Pratap Singh were collected and edited by Harinarain Purohit, and published by the Nagari Pracharini Sabha, Varanasi, under the title "*Brajanidhi Granthavali*". The number of poems in this book are about 1400. Though called a Granthavali, the Granthas in this volume are 23 sets of short poems.
21. The Gurus and Radha Vallabha Sampradaya have been the recipients of jagirs in Jaipur, vide Devasthan Records, Bikaner Archives, V.S. 1800-1872 etc.
22. Umesh Shastri, *Mahakavi Rasarasi* (Jaipur, 1972), p. 128.

जयति कृष्ण चैतन्य महाप्रभु, प्रगट स्याम घन ।
जय जय नित्यानन्द जयति जय रूप सनातन ॥

Apart from composing poems on *Krishna Leela*, Pratap Singh also constructed a temple where the deity, again, was the Krishna of Vrindaban. This was the temple of Brijnandji in Jaipur. It was constructed in 1792.[23] Other such temples constructed during his period were the following:[24]

1. Ananda Krishna Behariji	Within the *Sarhad* of the City Palace.
2. Pratapeshwarji	
3. Goverdhan Nathji	
4. Madan Mohanji	Opposite the Hawa Mahal.
5. Anandbihariji	
6. Gyangopalji	At Galta.

Hawa Mahal itself was constructed by Pratap Singh. The purpose of this building is not clear for it has apparently little utility. From the manner in which it is dedicated to Radha-Krishna, it was possibly meant to be a religious building.

Jagat Singh (1803-1819)

Very little can be said about the religious beliefs of Jagat Singh who is better known for his shameless harem life.[25] He must have been like his predecessors, a *Vaishnava*, at least formally. The temple of Brijraj Bihariji in Tripolia Bazar was established by him in 1813.[26] This temple as the name signifies is a *Vaishnava* temple. Another *Vaishnava* temple called Radha Agar Shiro Maji's temple was built -by one of his wives, Rathori Udai Bhanotji in Vrindaban in 1819.[27]

23. The date is given in the palace list of buildings and temples constructed by the rulers of Amer and Jaipur. Appendix VI.
24. *Brajanidhi Granthavali*, p. 43.
25. *Vamsa Bhaskar*, pp. 3984-3986.
26. List of temples and buildings, Appendix VI.
27. *Ibid.*

Jai Singh III (1820-1835)

Jai Singh was a posthumous son of Jagat Singh and died at the age of fifteen. In January 1832, the Jaipur Darbar had reluctantly sent him to attend the Darbar of Lord William Bentinck at Ajmer[28], as it was believed that the Europeans did not know the precautions which were necessary to be taken in respect of food (*Khanpan*).[29]

Ram Singh (1835-1880)

His son Ram Singh was born in 1833, and became the ruler before he was two years old. The State was managed by a Regency Council until Ram Singh was given ruling powers in 1851 when he was eighteen years old.

A number of *Vaishnava* temples were established by the widows of the previous Maharajas during the period 1820-1851. But all these temples were in Vrindaban except for one in Pushkar near Ajmer.[30]

A temple of Ramchandraji was established by Chandravatiji, mother of Ram Singh, in Sireh Deori Bazar in 1854.[31]

Vaishnavism is an emotional religion. The image of Krishna in many cases (for instance, that of Govinda Deva in Jaipur) is treated almost as a human being. It is woken up, bathed, dressed and given food as if it were a human being and the image itself is treated with adoration. Ram Singh's approach towards religion on the other hand was conservative. He wanted that people should follow the *Smarta Dharma*, that is, the more orthodox form of Hinduism based on the *Smritis*. In fact he established a Council of Pandits, called the *Mouj Mandir*, to give authoritative directions on religious and ritualistic matters. The local population on the other hand was overwhelmingly *Vaishnava* and did not appreciate the ruler's attitude. It was thus during Ram Singh's time that a

28. Har Bilas Sarda, *Ajmer Historical and Descriptive*, 1941, p. 209.
29. Memorandum of H.T. Prinsep's meeting with Jhota Ram at Muhair dated 12 January 1832, Cons. 14 May 1832. No. 3, For. & Pol. Dept., National Archives of India, New Delhi.
30. Appendix VI.
31. *Ibid.*

controversy which greatly agitated the public mind took place in Jaipur.

This religious agitation started with a judgment of the Supreme Court of Bombay in the *Maharaja* Libel Suit in 1862.[32] The *Maharajas* were the spiritual guides of the sect of Vallabhacharya. From the early 19th century many allegations of the immoral practices of these *Maharajas* were being aired in Bombay and Gujarat. The judgment of the court revealed that these allegations were correct. The *Maharajas* were committing adultery with female disciples who felt honoured by this act and even paid them for this. The Poona Observer of May 20, 1862[33] editorially commented, "The religion of the Vallabhacharyas will not survive this blow." It further hoped that "the worship of Krishna is indirectly but more decisively struck at in the judgment of the Supreme Court of Bombay". There are temples of the Vallabhacharya sect in many places in Rajasthan. In fact the principal temple of this sect in India is in Nathdwara in Mewar. However, the priests of the sect in Rajasthan perhaps did not indulge in these immoral practices within Rajasthan. For, Tod, who had an intimate knowledge of the votaries of the sect here, wrote[34] "The predominance of the mild doctrines of Kanhya over the dark rites of Siva is doubtless beneficial to Rajput society."

So far as Jaipur was concerned the sect had little influence here. There was only one important temple, that of Gokul Chandramaji (in Purani Basti) belonging to this sect in Jaipur. It appears, however, that the judgment of the Supreme Court of Bombay greatly disturbed the ruler Ram Singh. He started questioning the very system of *Vaishnava* worship. What subsequently happened is given in detail in the Jaipur Agency Report of the 30th March, 1867.[35]

> "During the past year His Highness has had several public discussion in his palace, on which occasion all the priests of the several temples in the city of Jeypore have been assembled together. The subject discussed was with reference

32. *History of the Sect of Maharajas or Vallabhacharyas of Western India*, London, 1865.
33. *Ibid.*, p. 151.
34. Tod, *op. cit.*, Vol. I, p. 423.
35. *Report on the Political Administration of Rajpootana* for the years 1865-66 and 1866-67, Part II, pp. 195-196.

to the present form of *Vaishnava* worship, which His Highness maintains is opposed to the ordinances laid down in the *Shastras.* Many of the leading priests in the principal temples of Jeypore held opposite views and their minds as well as those of the people who frequent the temples of the *Vaishnava* sect, were much disturbed and alarmed, as rumours got abroad that the Maharajah intended to expel all those from the city who entertained views opposed to those of His Highness. The Maharajah took every favourable opportunity, however, to impress on the priests and people that such was not his intention, and that, although he held his own views of what he considered the true Hindu religion, they were at liberty to follow their own doctrines.

"In spite, however, of these assurances of toleration the alarm increased, when in the month of July last the priest of the temple of Gokulji marched out of the city, taking the idol with him, and was followed by thousands of the inhabitants crying and giving vent to their feelings by loud and frequent expressions of grief and sorrow at the great calamity which had befallen the city of Jeypore."

"The priest remained encamped for a week within two miles of the City, when he was visited daily by all of the *Vaishnava* sect imploring him to return, and it is said that he would have returned had the Maharajah given him any encouragement to do so. His Highness's reply on the question being put to him is said to be "he has left of his own accord, and he is quite at liberty to return in the same manner, and remain without being interferred with."

"Several other priests belonging to temples, in Jeypore of the *Vaishnava* sect have also gone away quietly from fear of persecution."

"Rumours have got about that His Highness's conduct towards the *Vaishnava* party has been harsh, and that the priests who left were expelled or obliged to leave from the persecution they received; such, however, I am enabled to state from His Highness's own assurances, as well as from what others have told me who are in a position to know the real state of matter, is not the case."

"The Maharaja has been most tolerant in all his proceedings, and though it is said prayers were offered for Maharaja's death, and incantations and charms employed nevertheless the villages given in grant to these temples and other privileges enjoyed by the priests or their servants who left the city, are still continued to them, and they are free to return whenever they feel inclined."[36]

People of Jaipur still talk about these incidents which happened a hundred years ago. The common version is that Maharaja Ram Singh was a *Shaiva,* unlike his predecessors who were all *Vaishnavas.* Ram Singh, it is said, wanted that all the priests should put the *Tilak* on their forehead in the *Shaiva* fashion and this the *Vaishnavas* resented. This is said to have caused fear among the *Vaishnava* priests, some of whom left Jaipur with the images of their gods.[37] Hanuman Sharma in his *Nathawaton ka Itihas*[38] has brushed aside the story summarily:—

उनके सम्बन्ध में शैव वैष्णव और शाक्त आदि की जो विवादास्पद बातें कही जाती हैं वे अधिकांश में भ्रान्तिमूलक और तथ्यशून्य मानी जा सकती है।

On the whole, Hanuman Sharma was correct. As is clear from the extract given above from the Administration Report, Ram Singh does not appear to have had any anti-Vaishnava feeling. He was perhaps perturbed somewhat on the publication of the judgment of the Supreme Court of Bombay and

36. The subsequent history of the Gokul Chandrama temple and its priests is found in Powlett's *Gazetteer of the Bikaner State* (1874), p 101:—
"Balabacharyas: The Maharaj Vishnu Gosains of Balabhacharva sect, whose foul practices were exposed in a great libel case in Bombay some years ago have many devotees in Bikaner and when two of them, offended by the discountenance they met with from the Maharajah of Jaipur, abandoned that State, they were invited to Bikaner, and were received there with great honour, the late Chief himself going forth to meet them and running beside their palkis fanning them. In their presence he used to stand with folded hands, and for years the cost of their maintenance was a grievous burden to the State. They at length left for the neighbourhood of Mathura."
37. As related to me by Shri G.N. Bahura.
38. Hanuman Sharma, *op. cit.*, p. 302.

took precautions to see that the *Vaishnavas* of his territory were free from this taint. After the departure of the priest of Gokul Chandramaji temple which was the only important temple of the Vallabhacharya sect in Jaipur, the cause of his irritation was removed.

Madho Singh (1880-1922)

Madho Singh was the adopted son of Ram Singh. Unlike Ram Singh he was an uneducated man and had little intellectual curiosity. He practised the ritualistic religion of an ordinary uneducated Hindu.

Madho Singh had gone to England in 1902 for three months. A whole ship 'S.S. Olympia' was chartered for this voyage. The ship was thoroughly washed and ritualistically purified. He took water from the Ganges for d inking and also some earth for ablutions. In England, he got a well dug for his drinking water.[39]

Man Singh (1922-1949)

Man Singh's religious leanings were not obvious. The one important thing he did in this direction was the renovation of the Shila Devi temple in Amer. He was also a regular visitor to this temple. From this it might be inferred that he had *Shakta* leanings. If so, he was the first ruler with such leaning in this strongly *Vaishnava* family. It may be mentioned though that both he and Madho Singh before him had taken *Deeksha* according to the *Nimbarka Sampradaya*.[40]

The ruling family of Amer/Jaipur from the sixteenth century onwards were generally *Vaishnavas* either of the *Ramavat* school or of the *Krishnavat* school, the majority following the latter school. Though from the time of Sawai Jai Singh, the palace deity was Govindadeva, there was not that commitment to this god as, for instance, Mewar had for Eklingji. The rulers of Jaipur maintained a very liberal outlook towards religion.

39. *Jaipur Album*, Ch. II, p. 26.
40. Information obtained from Shri Pradyuman Kumar Deo, *Pujari* of the Govindadeva temple.

The religious beliefs of the ruler influences the religious belief of the people also and the vast majority of the people of Jaipur are *Vaishnavas.* But the people of Jaipur also worship fervently two folk gods. In the city practically in every lane there is a shrine for *Hanuman.* Similarly in every village in the State in addition they have the temple of *Shitala*, the goddess of small-pox. The rulers of Jaipur are not known to have been ardent worshippers of these folk gods. They also never came under the popular religious sects such as the *Nath Panthis* or the *Dadu Panthis.*[41] How damaging could religious interference be for the State can be seen in the history of Jodhpur where Maharaja Man Singh was obsessed with his regard for the Naths, and the whole State of Mewar suffered for nearly forty years (1803-1843) because the Naths obtained a dominating position in the administration of the State.[42]

III

THE JAINAS

The Jainas have held important positions both in the administration and in business in Jaipur from the very beginning. Indeed, in the other important States of Rajasthan also, such as Jodhpur, Udaipur, Bikaner, etc., Jainas have occupied high posts in the government from time to time. We hear of Tejpal and Vastupal, the ministers who built the famous temples of Abu. We have Bhamashah, the merchant and financer of Rana Pratap and many other famous Jainas. It is noteworthy that while most of the prominent Jainas of Mewar, Marwar and Bikaner were *Svetambara* Jainas, the Jainas who were prominent in the history of Jaipur were mostly *Digambar* Jainas or *Saraogis.*[43]

Most of the old Jaina families of Amer came down to Jaipur when the capital shifted here. Other Jainas came from Sanganer, Chaksu and other neighbouring places. One of the oldest Jaina families of Jaipur is that of Mukimji of Dariba Pan. The

41. Of course, respect was shown to the *Dadu Panthis* by the rulers of Jaipur, vide *Dastur Komwar*, classed in 'D'.
42. Zabar Singh, *the East India Company and Marwar*, pp. 61-83.
43. G.N. Sharma, *Social Life in Mediaeval Rajasthan*, pp. 211-18.

family came here from Amer at the instance of Jai Singh and have a *patta* from him.

Bakhtram Shah who wrote *Buddhivilas*, a book mainly dealing with Jaina rituals emigrated to Jaipur from Chaksu. Sanganer about 12 kilometres south of Jaipur has been an important Jaina centre for a long time. Among the several Jaina temples here one built of marble and sandstone is very beautiful. It was built in the 17th century. According to Bakht Ram Singh and one or two other authors of the eighteenth century, *Tarapanthism* among the Digambar Jainas originated in Sanganer. In other words, in the area around Jaipur there were many Jaina settlements.

In spite of their importance in business and administration for a number of decades, the number of Jainas in the city has never been large. They are roughly 5 to 6 per cent of the total population of the city. Most of them live in the *Chowkris* Modi Khana and Ghat Darwaja. According to the census report of 1911, out of a total population of 1.37 lakhs of the city, Jainas numbered 7,503 or roughly 5.5% in proportion. Again out of these Jainas, 3,510 lived in *Chowkri* Ghat Darwaja and 2,032 in *Chowkri* Modi Khana. Another 878 lived in *Chowkri* Bisheshwarji. Jaina population in other *Chowkris* of the town was therefore negligible.

The importance of the Jainas in the bureaucracy of Jaipur and other States of Rajasthan will be apparent from the classification of this community in the census reports up to the end of the nineteenth century. The Jainas were generally considered as writers up to this period. In the 1891 census tables of Rajputana, the following five castes were shown under the occupational heads of writers: -Kayasthas, Khatris, Dhusars (Bhargavas), Oswals and Saraogis. Later perhaps, it was thought that the matter needed correction and in the main body of the report Oswals and Saraogis were placed in the Mahajan group.

Jainas were of course, comparatively more literate. According to the census report of the Jaipur State of 1911, more than 50% of all the male Jainas in the State were literate. Among the other castes Kayastha males came next with 40% literacy, whereas only 14% of the Brahman males and only 5% of the Rajput males were literate. Since 50% of the Jaina males included people of all ages including children, one might say that practically all Jaina male adults were literate. The Jainas also took a leading part in the last years of the nineteenth century and early years of this century in establishing primary schools both for boys and girls.

No wonder, therefore, that the Kayasthas and the Jainas held most of the government jobs, the latter due to their wealth occupying the higher echelons.

The editors of *Veer Vani*, a journal published from Jaipur and dealing in matters of interest to the Jainas have compiled a list of Jaina ministers of Jaipur. According to this list there were the following Jaina ministers in the court of Jai Singh (1700-1743):—

1.	Ram Chandra Chhabra	1692-1722
2.	Phatah Chandra Shah	1708-1714
3.	Choudhari Jagram Pandya s/o Ghasi Ram	1717-1733
4.	Tara Chand Villala s/o Keshav Das	1716-1733
5.	Rao Kripa Ram Pandya s/o Jagram	1723-1733
6.	Phatah Ram Pandya s/o Rao Jagram	1733-1756
7.	Bhagat Ram Pandya s/o Rao Jagram	1695-
8.	Nayan Sukh Terapanthi	1712-1713
9.	Shri Chand Terapanthi	1713-1714

Among these, Ram Chandra Chhabra and Rao Kripa Ram Pandya were well known. Kripa Ram is said to have been a worshipper of Sun. He is said to have built 120 temples dedicated to Sun in various parts of the country. The Sun temple on the hill due east of the town was built by him. The number of Jaina ministers in the court of Madho Singh, son of Jai Singh, was also large. The invitation letter of the *Indradhvaja Puja* dated February 1764 proudly mentions:—

दरबार के मुतसद्दी सर्व जैनी हैं और साहुकार लोग सर्व जैनी हैं । यद्यपि और भी हैं परि गौणता रूप हैं, मुख्यता रूप नाहीं । छः सात व आठ व दस

हजार जैनी महाजनों का घर पाइए हैं। ऐसा जैनी लोगों का समूह और नग्र बिषै नाहीं। और यहां के देश बिषै सर्वत्र मुख्य पणे श्रावगी लोग बसे हैं॥

> "All the courtiers are Jaina; and all the merchants are Jainas. Though others are also there but they are in a minority, not in the majority. Six, seven or eight or ten thousand Jaina traders live here. Such a large gathering of Jainas would not be found in other cities; and mainly the Saraogis live in this country."

The letter paints the picture of a self-satisfied community exaggerating its own importance, but it confirms the fact that many of the court officials were Jainas. This *Indradhvaja Puja* was celebrated with great *eclat* in Jaipur in 1764. Letters were sent to Jainas in Delhi, Agra and other cities inviting them to join in the celebrations.[44] According to this letter a platform 64 yards square was constructed near Moti Doongri for the Puja. The then rular of Jaipur (Madho Singh) had offered that all the things that were required for the Puja could be taken from the palace stores. The letter also mentions that one of the attractions of the Puja was that the great Pandit Todarmal was to give his commentary on *Gommatsar*, an important and voluminous book on Jaina religion, within the Puja premises.

In the middle of the eighteenth century there was a great sectarian controversy among the Digambar Jainas in the Jaipur-Agra area. A reformist sect called *Terapanthi* was becoming popular among the more educated people. This was opposed by the orthodox Jainas who were in their turn called *Beespanthis*. Todarmal was a *Terapanthi* while his son Gumaniram started a new sect called *Gumanpantha*. *Gumanpanthis* are no longer important but the present Digambar Jaina population of Jaipur consists of *Terapanthis* and *Beespanthis* in the ratio of 40:60. This however is only a rough estimate. Most of the families of Agarwal Jains are *Terapanthis* while the Khandelwal Jainas are *Beespanthis*.

Bakhta Ram Shah the author of *Buddhi Vilas*, was a great antagonist of *Terapanthis*. About *Terapanthis* he wrote:[45]

44. The letter is quoted in full in the Todar Mal number of the *Veer Vani* of March, 1957.

45. Quoted in the Introduction to '*Ardha Kathanak*' by the Editor in the Hindi Grantha Ratnakar, Bombay Edition, 1957, p. 50.

कपटी तेरा पंथ है, जिन सौं कपट करंत

"The *Terapanthis* are frauds, they cheat even the Jina (Mahaveer)". He also said that *Terapanthis* and *Beespanthis* fight like cats and mice.

As it is, there is not much difference between the two sects, so far as the religious beliefs are concerned. The difference is mainly in regard to the rituals to be followed in the temples, the *Terapanthis* tending to be more puritanical. For instance, *Terapanthis* offer their *Puja* standing, they do not offer *Puja* at night, nor do they touch the feet of the priest. *Terapanthis* do not offer *Kesar* at the feet of the image, nor do they worship with flowers.

The *Indradhvaja Puja* mentioned above was celebrated by the *Terapanthis*.

Todarmal as one of the Early Writers of Hindi Prose

Pandit Todar Mal is said to have been born near about 1740 A.D. in Jaipur. The year of his birth is, however, uncertain. He died in 1767. Considering the number of his writings it is quite possible that he was born earlier than 1740, for it is unlikely that he could have produced so much in such a brief span of life.

Todarmal and his son Gumaniram wrote many books on Jainism. Todarmal's fame rests on his commentaries in Hindi on a number of Jaina books. The most famous of these are *Gommatsara* (38,000 slokas), *Labdhisara* and *Kshapansara* (13,000 slokas) and *Trilokasara* (14,000 slokas). He wrote in Hindi prose a commentary on these 65,000 slokas which were written in some form of *Prakrita*. Todarmal wrote these works near about 1760 A.D. These were the early days of prose writing in Hindi Khari Boli. It was quite a feat on his part to write the commentaries of these abstruse Jaina books in a language which had not until then reached maturity. Yet Todarmal's language was not weak. He also translated a Sanskrit work on aphorisms called *Atmanushashana* and also wrote a commentary on it. One example from this might be quoted.

भाषा टीका—अर्थ—पाप से दुःख होता है, और धर्म से सुख ऐसे ये वचन सर्वजनों विषें भली प्रकार प्रसिद्ध हैं, सर्व ही ऐसे मानते हैं। इसलिए जो सुख का

अर्थी है, जिसको सुख चाहिए, सो सदा पाप को छोड़कर सदा काल धर्म को अँगीकार करे।

भावार्थ—पाप का फल दु:ख का है, और धर्म का फल सुख, ऐसे केवल हम ही नहीं कहे हैं बल्कि सर्व ही मतानुयायी कहे हैं। इसलिए सुख चाहो तो पाप को छोड़ो धर्म करो।।८।।

This is practically modern Hindi prose. It might be said therefore that Todarmal who wrote his works in Jaipur city was one of the originators of Hindi prose.

Another well-known Jaina writer of the eighteenth century was Daulat Ram Kasliwal. He was born in Baswa, a small town near Bandikui in the Jaipur district. He came to Jaipur in search of a job and was appointed the agent (Vakil) of Jaipur in the court of Jagat Singh, the Maharana of Udaipur.

बसुवा को बासी यहै अनुचर जय को जाति,
मंत्री जय सुत को सहि जाति महाजन जानि।

जय को राखे रण मे, रहे उदयपुर माहि, जगतसिंह कृपा करे राखे अपने याहि।

It was necessary to quote the above because Ram Chandra Shukla in his well-known "Hindi Sahitya ka Itihas" has taken Baswa to be in Madhya Pradesh and discussed Daulat Ram Kasliwal accordingly.[46] Shukla has mentioned Daulat Ram as one of the first writer of Hindi prose and quoted an example of his style from his book, *Padma Purana.* Another quotation from *Padma Purana* is given below[47] from which it would appear that Daulat Ram's prose had not yet reached the maturity of Khari boli style of his contemporary Todarmal:

जब रावण ने ऐसा कहा तब इन्द्रजीत पिता की आज्ञा से पीछे बाहुडा। अर सर्व देवों की सेना शरद के मेघ के समान भाग गई जैन पवन कर शरद के मेघ विलय जाय। रावण की सेना में जीत के वादित्र बाजे, ढोल नगारे शंख झांझ इत्यादि अनेक वादियों का शब्द भया।

Daulat Ram wrote about 15 books, mostly on Jaina mythology. His most voluminous book is *Adhyatma Barahkhari.* The only copy of this book has been found in a *Shastra*

46. R.C. Shukla, *Hindi Sahitya ka Itihas*, Revised edition. S. 1999, p. 448.
47. *Jaina Grantha Bhandars in Rajasthan*, p. 249.

Bhandar in Jaipur. From this it would appear that he spent a part of his literary life in Jaipur.

Jaipur then occupies quite a prominent place in the history of Hindi prose.

Todarmal's son, Gumaniram, wrote in *Dhundhari*, that is in the dialect of the Jaipur region.

Both Todarmal and Gumaniram worked mostly in the library attached to the Jain temple Badhi Chand. This temple, situated at Gheewalon ka Rasta, Johari Bazar, was constructed in 1738. The *Shastra Bhandar* (Library) attached to the temple contains at present 1278 manuscripts.[48]

Dr. K.C. Kasliwal in his book *Jaina Grantha Bhandars in Rajasthan* has listed about 18 such libraries attached to the various Jaina temples in the city. It is noteworthy that whereas the Hindu collections of manuscripts are generally found in the private libraries of princes, rich persons or learned people, the Jaina collections are mostly found in the libraries attached to Jaina temples. This is perhaps because the Hindu temples were treated as private properties whereas the Jaina temples were in many cases treated as belonging to the community, where others could donate books and manuscripts for preservation and study by the learned persons in the community.

Death of Todarmal

It is commonly believed that Todarmal was killed during an anti-Jaina riot either by a Hindu mob or under the orders of the ruler. A number of such riots are said to have occurred during the period 1861-1869. They are described in *Buddhi Vilas*.[49] According to this book in S. 1818 (1761 A.D.) there was a rascal called Shyam Tiwari. He was a low type of Brahmana, but with the help of some magic practices had obtained complete influence over Madho Singh, the ruler of Jaipur. He became the *guru* of the ruler and became more important than even Balananda. For sometime he persecuted the Jainas, forced them to eat at night and destroyed some of the Jaina temples. In some Jaina temples he installed *Shivalingas*.

48. *Jain Grantha Bhandars in Rajasthan*, p. 49.
49. Verses No. 1289 to 1326.

Suddenly one day the ruler got annoyed with him and turned him out of his kingdom. The Jainas breathed a sigh of relief and within one and half years were back in their original prosperous state. The Brahmanas did not like the revival of Jaina prosperity. They went and falsely complained to the ruler that the Jainas were uprooting the *Shivalingas*. The ruler was misled by such accusations and put some *Saraogis* in prison and imposed fines on others. There was an important *Terapanthi* gentleman known for his ability. Some people incited the ruler against him and the ruler got him killed and his body was buried in garbage.[50] Later there was again a revival of Jainism, but in S. 1826 (1769 A.D.) the Brahmanas again accused them of uprooting the *Shivalingas*, and attacked the Jaina temples.

The *Buddhi Vilas* was written in S. 1827. The sporadic attacks were continuing even at that time.

There are no other contemporary records of such incidents. There is one Jaina temple, namely, the temple of Bara Diwanji in *Chowkri* Modi Khana in the precincts of which there is a Shiva temple. This perhaps partly confirms the incidents described in the *Buddhi Vilas*.

However, there is no reason to doubt the main description of *Buddhi Vilas*. The book itself was written when the incidents had not completely died off and we may take it that there were several anti-Jaina riots in the decade 1760-1770.

The most obvious reason for these anti-Jaina riots was the fact that Jainas were a wealthy community and many of them were ministers of the ruler. This naturally made the non-Jainas envious of the Jainas.

The point may be examined whether the eminent *Terapanthi* Jaina, mentioned in couplet number 1304 to have been killed was Todarmal. Only two manuscript copies of the *Buddhi Vilas* have been found. The first dated 1770 A.D. was by the author himself. Here the couplet occurs as follows:—

यक तेरह पंथिनु में भ्रमी, हो तो महा योग्य साहिमी
कहे षलनि के नृप रिसि ताहि, इति को धरयो ग्रसुचि थल वाहि ॥१३०४॥

The second manuscript is dated 1806 i.e. 38 years later. Here the couplet reads:—

50. *Buddhi Vilas*, Couplet No. 1304.

गुर तेरह पंथिनु को भ्रमी, टोडर मल नांम सांहिमी
ताहि भूप मारयो पत नांहि, गाडयो मद्धि गंदगी तांहि

Thus Todarmal's name as the important person killed occurs in the latter document only. It is likely therefore that the name was interpolated later. Todarmal was an important person among the *Terapanthis* of Jaipur. If he died in such unnatural circumstances, it should have found mention in other Jaina writings, specially in the literature of the *Terapanthi* sect. Moreover, it appears unlikely that the ruler Madho Singh would suddenly get so enraged with an eminent scholar as to order him to be killed, and his body buried in garbage.

Jhootharam Sanghi and the End of Jaina dominance in the Administration of the State

Though the Jainas were always quite important in the administrative set-up of Jaipur specially during the 18th century, they never became a dominant force until the third and the fourth decades of the nineteenth century. At this time one Jootharam Sanghi became for all practical purposes the regent of Jaipur during the minority rule of Jai Singh III (1819-1835). Jootharam was a *Saraogi* but he was not a local man. He had come to Jaipur from Agra. The mother of the boy-ruler was the regent and Jootharam Sanghi was the principal minister. Jhootharam was very powerful but he was opposed by the *Thakurs* of Chomu and Samod and some other important *jagirdars* of Jaipur. The constant friction between Jootharam and his party on the one hand and the *jagirdars* of Chomu and Samod on the other led to misrule in Jaipur, the effects of which have been described by Boileau. Jootharam had been able to induct some of his close relations, such as his brother Hukam Chand, Amar Chand etc., in high position in the State administration. The boy-ruler died suddenly on 4 February 1835. People opposed to Jootharam spread the rumour that he had poisoned the ruler. Immediately after the funeral of the ruler an anti-Jaina riot flared up in which some Jaina temples were attacked and images were destroyed. Though the incident has been mentioned in the *Nathawaton ka Itihas*,[51] it is not

51. Hanuman Sharma, *op.cit.*, p. 262.

mentioned in other histories of Jaipur such as by Gehlot, M.L. Sharma and others.[52] In fact in a letter[53] published in the *Calcutta Courier* of 29 March 1837, it is mentioned,

> "On the funeral day the Brahmuns of Jeypoor turned out en masse, and headed the crowd, openly proclaiming treason and demanding to see their Sovereign's corpse; nor could they be dispersed till five or six of these Brahmans had been shot by the mercenaries of Jhootharam."

Jhootharam fell from power shortly after the death of this boy Maharaja in 1835 and from then onwards the domination of Jainas in the higher posts of the Government of Jaipur also ended. Throughout the rest of the nineteenth century with the exception of Seth Manik Chand there was no Jaina Minister in the Jaipur Government. The British sources mention Seth Manik Chand, as the Finance Minister of the State[54] during the time of J. Ludlow, the Political Agent of Jaipur (1844-48). He was a resident of Bikaner who uniformly rendered valuable assistance to Ludlow. He helped Ludlow in the abolition of Sati in the State.[55] During the minority administration (1922-1931) of Man Singh II (1922-1970), Jaipur was ruled by a Council of State with six full members and five other members who were called *Sigha* members. One of the *Sigha* members was Munshi Pyare Lal Kasliwal B.A.[56] He also officiated as Revenue Member for six months when the incumbent was on leave.

52. The incident is not mentioned in British records, not even by Brooks in his *History of Jaipur*.
53. Reprinted in the *Jeypoor Trials*, pp. 315-330.
54. John William Kaye, *The Administration of East India Company*, p. 543n J. Ludlow mentioned Seth Manik Chand as the "State Treasurer". Cf. Ludlow to Sutherland, dated 8 December 1847, Cons. 25 February 1848, No. 24, For. & Pol. Dept., National Archives of India, New Delhi.
55. John William Kaye, *op. cit.*, p. 543n.
56. Pyarelal Kasliwal's son Dr. Rajmal Kasliwal (b. 1906) is a well known physician of Jaipur. He retired a few years ago as the Principal of the Jaipur Medical College.

Jaina Grantha Bhandars

The largest Jaina Grantha Bhandar[57] among the older libraries of Jaipur is in the Bara Mandir. This Mandir is a *Terapanthi* temple situated on the Gheewalon ka Rasta. It is a *Panchayati* or a community temple. The date of foundation of this temple is not correctly known but Todarmal is said to have patronised this library. This would mean that the temple was in existence by the middle of the eighteenth century.

The total number of manuscripts in this library is 2630 (including 324 *gutkas* or abridged versions). Most of these relate to Jaina religion and mythology, but there are also works by Jaina authors on grammar, prosody, lexicography, astrology and *Ayurveda*. There are many works written by non-Jaina authors also. These are mainly on *Kavya*, grammar, *Ayurveda*, astrology, *Kama Shastra*, etc. There are 13 manuscripts of *Raghuvansa* of Kalidas and two Sanskrit commentaries on *Kiratarjuniva* of Bharvi. Works of famous Sanskrit authors such as Kalidas (*Raghuvamsa*, *Kumarsambhava*, *Meghaduta* etc.), Bhavabhuti, Sriharsa, etc., appear to have been kept in almost all of these Jaina Grantha Bhandars. The works of Kabir, Bihari, Kesava, Vrinda and others are also found in this Bhandar.

The next large collection in Jaipur city is in the *Grantha Bhandar* in the Jaina temple of *Patodi* in *Chowkri* Modi Khana. According to Dr. Kasliwal this Bhandar was established in 1737, i.e., shortly after the foundation of Jaipur city. The number of manuscripts including *gutkas* in this Bhandar is 2565. This library specialises in works on various aspects of Jainism such as Jaina Purana, Charita, Grammar etc. in Prakrit, Apabhramsa, Sanskrit, Hindi and Rajasthani. The number of works on non-Jaina authors in this Bhandar is not many.

On the whole it is seen that the Grantha Bhandars in the Jaina temples in Rajasthan serve a wide variety of readers, both Jaina and non-Jaina. They are not by any means sectarian libraries.

57. All information on Jaina Grantha Bhandars are taken from Dr. K.C. Kasliwal's *Jaina Grantha Bhandars in Rajasthan*, Jaipur, 1967.

The other 16 temple libraries of Jaipur noticed[58] by Dr. Kasliwal are as follows:—

	Name and place of Library	*No. of MSS*
1.	Amar Sastra Bhandar (17th Century collection of Amer recently shifted to Jaipur)	2755
2.	Pandya Lunkaranji's temple (circa 1735)	1032
3.	Baba Duli Chand's temple (1854)	850
4.	Tholia temple (18th century)—Gheewalon ka Rasta.	783
5.	Chandra Prabha Saraswati Bhandar (early 19th century)—Chowkri Modi Khana.	830
6.	Jobner Temple—Chandpole Bazar.	340
7.	Parshvanath Digambar Jaina Saraswati Bhawan (1748).	558
8.	Godha temple (late 18th century).	718
9.	Badhi Chandra temple (1738).	1278
10.	Sanghiji's temple (19th century)—Bordi ka Rasta.	979
11.	Laskar temple (19th century)—Bordi ka Rasta.	828
12.	Naya Mandir or Bairathiyan temple in Moti Singh Bhomia ka Rasta.	150
13.	Chandhariyan ka Mandir—Chowkri Modi Khana.	108
14.	Kala Chhabra Jaina Mandir.	410
15.	Megharajji temple	249
16.	Yasodanandji temple (1791)	398

IV

THE BALANANDIS

A sub-sect of the *Ramanandi Vaishnavas* are the *Balanandis*. There is a temple belonging to the *Balanandis* in the south-western part of the Jaipur city. There are three groups of images in the temple. The main group is *Ram-Janaki*. The others are *Vijay Raghunath* and *Ram-Lakshman-Janaki*. The temple is situated in a very large building on a hillock. The building looks like a small fort. The site is said to have been allotted to the Balanandis who built their temple here in 1753

58. Dr. Kasliwal, *op. cit.*

A.D. There is said to have been a small temple of Radha Vinodi Lal at this site before.

According to the tradition maintained in this temple, Balananda Naga, a Rajput from the Delhi district, and his *guru* Brijananda or Virjananda Naga were brought to his state by Jai Singh. They were originally given a site near Jhalana. This place was called Jhalana Mahal.[59]

Balananda is generally thought to have organised the *Vaishnava Bairagis* into a militant body. G.S. Ghurve mentions :

> "In a Jaipur chronicle (*Tawarikh*), according to the information given by the Nimbarki Pandit Rajavallabha Sharanji, there is some information about Vaishnava Akhadas recorded in the year 1713 A.D. . . . One Balanandaji of the Ramanandi sect was entrusted with the task of organising the Naga section of the Bairagis in an appropriate manner to enable the Vaishnava Bairagis to withstand the onslaughts at the holy places of pilgrimage made by Shaiva Sannyasis, who were already well organised. He is said to have formed three 'Anis' 'Ani' is evidently a short form of the Sanskrit work anika meaning an army. Balananda also established seven Akhadas."[60]

Nothing much is known about Jai Singh's connection with Balananda or with militant *Vaishnavism*. However, it shows that all types of Hindu sects specially *Vaishnava* sects were given shelter in Jaipur by Jai Singh.

In course of time, Balananda became quite important in Jaipur and at the time of the rule of Jai Singh's son, Madho Singh (1750-1767), Balananda became his *guru*.

Madho Singh treated Balananda with great respect:

> "On Chet Vadi 8, S. 1809 (1752 A.D.) the Maharaja himself went to the camp of Balananda to pay him his

59. The Present Jhalana Mahal near the railway crossing on the Sanganer road is a much later building built at the time of Madho Singh II in the early years of this century.

60. G.S. Ghurye, *Indian Sadhus*, Bombay, 1953, pp. 202, 203. Ghurye has given no clue about this *Tawarikh*.

respects, and gave him his offering of ten Mohars and two coconuts. The Maharaja received the blessings of Balananda and a '*dupatta*' and '*Prasada*'. Thereafter the Maharaja used to go to Balananda every year to give his offerings and receive Balananda's '*Prasada*'."[61]

Balananda, it seems, also took part in the political affairs of the State. Sarkar mentions Balananda in connection with Maharaja Pratap Singh's negotiations with Mahadji Sindhia. He writes,

> "The Rao Rajah of Macheri had been sent to Jaipur in advance (for negotiating the amount of tribute by Jaipur to Mahadji Sindhia). He returned with the Jaipur envoys, Balaji Mahant (the spiritual guide of the late Rajah Madho Singh) and the Bohra minister on 6th March (1786). Mahadji himself paid the first visit to Balaji and prostrated himself before him. The Brahman in pontifical pride did not rise to welcome him, but graciously stretched his leg forward and the supreme lord of legions rubbed his forehead on the monk's holy toes (8th March)."[62]

According to the traditions maintained in the *Balanandi* temple in Jaipur, Balananda was a Rajput, while Sarkar describes him to be a Brahman. Also if Balananda was old enough to organize the Bairagis into a militant body as early as 1713, it is surprising that he was fit enough to be Jaipur's envoy in 1786, 73 years later. Ghurye does not mention the name of the *Tawarikh*. The date 1713 given by him may be wrong. There is a remote possibility, however, that there were more than one Balanandas', one being the disciple of the other. The tradition in the *Balanandi* temple on the other hand is that Balananda died in 1795 at the age of 140 years.[63]

Mahants of the *Balanandi* temple do not marry. Their succession runs from *Guru* to *Chela*. The succession list of the Mahants is as follows:

61. *Dastur Komwar*, Vol. XXXI, p. 669.
62. Sarkar, *op. cit.*, Vol. III, p. 234.
63. Information given by the present *Mahant*.

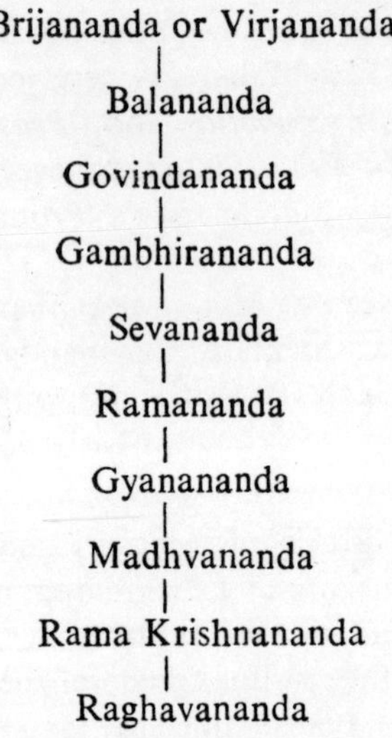

Raghavananda died on 14 August 1948. According to the *Diwan-i-Hazuri*[64] files, the next *Mahant* was Ladli Mohan Das. But according to the present *Mahant* Ramcharanananda, the '*gaddi*' was vacant for 15 years until he won a case in a court of Law and succeeded to the *gaddi* in 1963.

64. *Diwan-i-Hazuri*, p. 1658 in the file in the Rajasthan State Archives. Bikaner.

APPENDIX—I

JAI SINGH'S CONTACT WITH EUROPEAN ASTRONOMERS

The information that is available on the subject is all from the Jesuit letters. These have been summarised by Maclagan in his book *The Jesuits and the Great Mogul.*[1] In 1727 or near about that year one Father Emmanuel de Figueredo was the superior of the Jesuit Mission in the Mughal court in Delhi. Figueredo mentioned to Jai Singh that astronomy was making great progress in Europe and perhaps also suggested to him that he should obtain experts from Europe. Jai Singh requested Figueredo himself to proceed to Europe and obtain the service of experts from there. Figueredo went to Portugal and brought back by the end of 1728 (Maclagan) or end of 1730 (Moraes) two things. The first was a copy of the *Tabulae Astronomicae* by De La Hire published in 1702. De La Hire (1640-1718) was an astronomer of repute in those days. The first part of his table had an error of half a degree in the position of the moon. Maclagan suggests that "this was possibly due to a misprint." The name of the expert brought from Portugal by Figueredo, according to Maclagan, was Don Zavier or Pedro de Silva.[2] He is said to have been a medical man well versed in astronomy. It is quite likely that this gentleman did not know much of astronomy, and Joao V, the king of Portugal had not been able to send the kind of expert Jai Singh desired. We need not blame the King of Portugal too much for this.

After all, very few people specialise in such a difficult subject as astronomy even today. In those days their number specially in a small country like Portugal, must have been still fewer. In any case in such a Catholic country it would have been difficult for anybody to learn the latest theories on the subject.

1. Maclagan, *The Jesuits and the Great Mogul*, London, 1930.
2. *Ibid.*, p. 134

Even if such an expert were available it was unlikely that he would agree to leave his country and to undertake a dangerous journey to India, thousands of miles away, perhaps never to return home. Secondly, there was no knowing when the patron ruler in India would suddenly give up his hobby or die, in which case the expert would be left without any means of subsistence in a foreign country far away from home. Only a medical man who could make an independent living even without a patron ruler could take such a risk. The king of Portugal therefore sent a medical man who had a smattering of astronomy.

What exactly was the name of this gentleman is not clear. Maclagan, as mentioned above, gives two names, Don Zavier or Pedro de Silva. G.M. Moraes in his essay "Astronomical Mission to the Court of Jaipur (1730-1743),"[3] calls him Xavier de Silva. Tod also gives him this name. De Silva appears to have settled down in India. His descendants still live in Jaipur. Some of them live in houses built on the land given to their ancestors near Subhash Chowk. In an interview Martin de Silva who practises as Hakim, said that some years ago he had obtained the family tree from the Jaipur Palace records. According to this tree, two persons one of them Pedro de Silva or Don Pedro and the other his son Xavier de Silva had come to the Court of Jai Singh as astronomers and Hakims. Thereafter the family adopted medicine as their profession. Xavier's son was Gasper. He was also called Achchhe Mian. Gasper's son Martin, better known as Hakim Martin, was a well known physician of his time. A street in Jaipur was named after him. Martin's son Xavier, grandson Gustin and great grandson Martin (the informant) were all Hakims. The full family tree is as shown opposite.

Martin de Silva has in his possession as a family heirloom a celestial sphere about 15 cms. in diameter inscribed in Arabic. The sphere is for a latitude of about 20°. Nothing else in the family gives it any astronomical connection.

Coming back to Jai Singh, we find that in 1733 he was again in search of European astronomers. In 1733 he invited

3. *Journal of the Bombay Branch of the Royal Asiatic Society*, 27 (1951), pp. 61-65, 85.

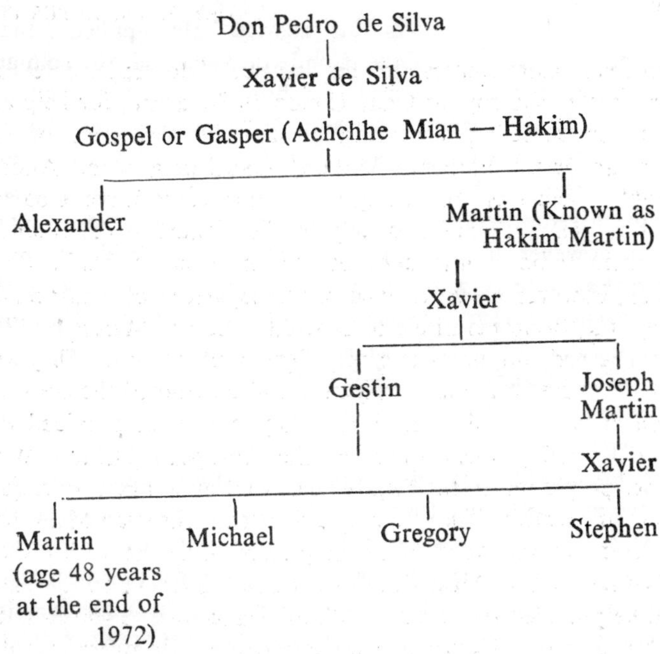

two Jesuits from Chandernagore in Bengal to assist him in his observations of a coming eclipse. Accordingly, on January 6, 1734, two Fathers, Pons and Claude Boudier were sent from there. "It happened that these missionaries were in difficulties with the Chandernagore authorities and a new mission at Jaipur was looked as a means of completing the religious "blockade" of the Mughal dominions. The Raja moreover had shown himself most friendly to the Christians in his State, had commenced building a church for them and himself presented offerings at Mass, so that his wishes could not lightly be refused. On their arrival they seem unfortunately to have wasted much time in disputing with the local Brahmans as to the extent to which Indian astronomy was indebted to the ancient Greeks, and we have no knowledge of the scientific results of their visits. They set out in due time to see the observatory at Delhi and from that place they returned, probably owing to continued ill-health to Chandernagore.[4]

Jai Singh, however, did not give up his attempt to enlist

4. Maclagan, *op. cit.*, p. 134.

European astronomers in his service. "He applied to the Portuguese Viceroy at Goa, Conde de Sandomil, for help and the latter succeeded in securing for him the assistance of two Bavarian Jesuit Fathers: Anthony Gabelsperger and Andrew Strobl. There was some delay before they could leave Goa and further delay at Surat owing to the disturbed conditions in Northern India, consequent on the invasion of Nadir Shah. When, however, news arrived of the departure of Nadir Shah's army, they were permitted to proceed, and on March 4, 1740, they reached Jaipur. There they were well received. They were given a house for their residence and they noted the consideration of the Raja in ordering that they should be provided with chairs to enable them to sit in the European fashion. When Gabelsperger fell ill the Raja would send messengers to enquire after his health. The Raja would attend Christian Mass with all reverence and would treat the picture of Christ with respect. When he came to Mass he left substantial gifts upon the altar and he provided the Fathers with allowance of five rupees a day with five rupees weekly for Church expenses. In order that they should not be without meat, he allowed them the use of goat flesh and sent them meat of this description from his own kitchen. When the Mogul Emperor sent for Father Strobl to come to Delhi, the Raja more than once found excuses for delay, and indeed appears to have intended to send Strobl as a delegate to the Pope and to the Kaiser. This was prevented by the occurrence of local disturbances in Jaipur; and in 1741, Father Gabelsperger died. Two, years later, the Raja himself passed away.

For a short time after Jai Singh's decease, Father Strobl still had good hopes of his successor, and continued to receive support for himself and for his church. The Christian doctor at the court (doubtless de Silva mentioned earlier) who had been a great protector of the Jesuits was, however, shortly afterwards degraded and Strobl's position became less easy. Within three years of Jai Singh's death, he had obtained leave to proceed to Delhi, and there he remained for three years..."[5]

Father Joseph Tieffenthaler was another missionary who passed through Jaipur shortly after Jai Singh's death. He

5. Maclagan, *op. cit.*, pp. 134-35.

arrived in India in 1743 or 1744, at the age of 29 and spent the rest of his long life in India. He died at Lucknow in 1785. "He was apparently intended originally for the Jaipur observatory, but the death of Raja Jai Singh in 1743 and the cessation of work at the observatory rendered this form of employment impossible. He was accordingly sent from Goa to Agra to work in the college and shortly afterwards he began his wanderings to Muttra, Delhi, Marwar, Goa, Surat, Jodhpur, Ajmer, Sambhar, Jaipur, Gwalior and innumerable other places."[6]

Father Joseph Tieffenthaler was an Austrian. He was an astronomer, a mathematician, a geographer and a historian. Thus he was one of the few learned Europeans who came to this country, and it is unfortunate that he arrived here too late to be of any assistance to Jai Singh. Tieffenthaler had sent to Europe three volumes of his writings. These were (i) a long geographical account of India in Latin, entitled "*Descriptio Indiae*", (ii) a treatise on the *Brahmanical religion* and (iii) a *Natural History of India.* Only the first has survived This geography of Tieffenthaler contains a description of Jaipur and its observatory also. He was very much impressed with the size of the *Samrat Yantra* but commented adversely on the situation of the observatory. Being "in a low situation surrounded by walls, the observer cannot see the rising and setting of the stars. Also the dial gnomon and other parts being in lime plaster prevent one from making very exact observations."[7]

6. Maclagan, *op. cit.*, p. 137.
7. Kaye, *A guide to the Old Observatories of Delhi, Jaipur, etc.*, Ch. III.

APPENDIX II

A NOTE ON THE POSTAL HISTORY OF THE JAIPUR STATE

We do not know whether the public of Jaipur had any facility for transmission of letters within the State prior to 1861. In or about that year a postal department was started in this State. The primary object of the department was to transmit the official orders and reports, but the department also served the public. The postal department was called *Mahakma Khabar* and the work was done by *Khabar Nawises* (news-writers) and *Harkaras* (Couriers). In the beginning the mail was carried by camels and runners but later on, in 1930s the motor buses also came into use. The total number of State or Raj Post Offices in 1935 was 103.

British India post offices, called Imperial post offices, were also allowed within the State. As early as 1876, there were 38 such post offices in the State. Their number rose to 86 in 1901. In 1926-27 their number was 54 and this increased to 63 in 1927-28. The administration report of the Jaipur State for these two years states,

> "The lack of facilities for communicating with places outside the State territory is felt in the district not served by the Imperial Postal system, but . . . it has not been thought advisable to replace the *Raj* by the Imperial Post Offices during the minority administration. The demand for Imperial offices has been on the increase and applications are sanctioned by the Council (of State) in the interests of the public though the income of the *Raj* Postal Department is thereby adversely affected."

In 1935 the number of Imperial post offices were 75 of which there was one Head Office at Jaipur and there were 33 sub-offices (including 4 in Jaipur city namely, 1. Jaipur city,

2. Johri Bazar, 3. Kotwali and 4. Ramganj) and 41 branch offices. Twenty-three of the sub-offices also had telegraph offices connected with them.[1]

Stamps

Though the State had its own postal system from 1861, it did not issue any stamps[2] until 1904. Until then postage had to be prepaid in cash. The rates of postage were the same as in the British India. People wishing to send letters to places within the State had to bring their letters to the post office (*Chabutra*) where the receipt of the postage paid in cash was acknowledged by putting a rubber stamp impression on the letter. No postage was necessary on the letters and parcels on *Darbar* service. These were carried free until 1929. From 1929 official letters also carried stamps. The word "Service" was over-printed on stamps meant for official use. It is not quite clear why Jaipur waited so long before deciding to charge postage on official letters. Many other States such as Indore (1904), Hyderabad (1873), Cochin (1913) etc., had introduced official stamps much earlier.

The stamps issued from 1904 to 1930 had the picture of the chariot of the Sun god *Surya* on its face. The first stamp issued was a crude lithograph locally printed. Later, these chariot stamps, except for one set in 1941 printed locally in the Jail press, were printed in London. One peculiarity of all these chariot stamps except the lithograph ones, is that they show the flag on the chariot flying against the wind. Why this was not corrected is not clear.

The State issued two sets of commemorative stamps, once in 1934 on the occasion of the investiture of the Maharaja Man Singh, and again in 1947-48 on the occasion of the Silver Jubilee of Maharaja's accession to the throne. In between these two periods the definitive stamps of the State bore the picture of the bust of the Maharaja in regal dress. Stamps from 1931 onwards were printed in Nasik.

The Jaipur postal system was merged with the Indian postal

1. *Jaipur Album*, Appendix II, p. 3.
2. Compiled from the information available in the Stanley Gibbon's *Catalogue of Postage Stamps for the Commonwealth*, London, 1962.

system in April 1950, a year after the State merged in Rajasthan. During this year the stamps of Jaipur along with the stamps of Bundi and Kishangarh were over-printed Rajasthan. These over-printed stamps could be used for sending mail throughout the country.

APPENDIX III

COINS AND METROLOGY

A Mughal mint was established in Jaipur near about 1740. The earliest coin from the mint in the collection of the Indian Museum Calcutta[1]—No. 1926 (a) bears the date 1153 H. (corresponding to March 1740 to March 1741) in the 23rd year of the reign of Muhammad Shah. The earliest coin from this mint in Jaipur Museum also bears the same date.[2] The Calcutta Museum coin is a silver rupee with the following inscription in the Persian script:

Obverse—Sikka Mubarak Badshah Gazi 1153 Muhammad Shah
Reverse—*Zarb-i-Sawai Jaipur*—San 23 julus-i-maimanati-manus.

The weight of the coin is 174.5 grains. (Since the time of Akbar, Mughal silver rupee weighed between 170 and 175 grains=11½ mashas as per *Ain-i-Akbari*. The tola equal to 12 mashas during the British days, weighed 179.4 grains).

The illustration of this coin (No. 1926(a)) given in the catalogue shows that it is the usual Mughal rupee nearly standardized during the reign of Aurangzeb and it does not bear any mint mark. Later, the characteristic mint mark of Jaipur was a 'Jhar' or a spray of six branches, from which the coins were named *Jharshahi* coins. This mint mark started appearing from the time of Madho Singh (1750-1778).[3] From

1. *Catalogue of the Coin in the Indian Museum*, Calcutta, Vol. III, Pt. I, Oxford, 1908.
2. "*Coin Collection of the Jaipur Museum*", an article by Satya Prakash in the *Journal of the Numismatic Society of India*, Vol. XXIII (1961), p. 470.
3. *Catalogue of the coins in the Indian Museum*, Calcutta, Vol. IV, Oxford, 1928, pl. XV, 5.

this time it may be said that the coins were no longer Mughal coins but Jaipur coins. However except for this mint mark, there was no other change, and coins continued to be struck in the name of the Delhi Emperor contemporary with those of the rulers of Jaipur. This continued even up to the last Emperor of Delhi—Bahadur Shah II who was deposed in 1857. It was only in 1860s that the name of the ruler of Jaipur started appearing on the coins. The coins of Ram Singh (1835-1880), the ruler at that time bear the following inscriptions:[4]

Obverse—"Zarab-i-Sawai Jaipur 186—Bahad Malika—Mahajwa—Saltanat—Inglistan—Victoria"—Struck at Jaipur in the year 186—by permission of the Great Queen of the Empire of Inglistan.

Reverse— San Jalus Manus—Maimanat 31—*Maharajadhiraj Sawai Ram Singhji*—In the 31st year of the fortunate reign of Maharajadhiraj—Sawai Ram Singhji.

All the specimens of this rupee in the Indian Museum in Calcutta weigh 175 or 176 grains.

We may, therefore, assume that the weight of the rupee in Jaipur was 175 grains though in some cases it went up to 176 grains.

Copper Coins

The large copper coins issued from the mint according to the Calcutta catalogue, weighed between 281 and 288 grains (There are some coins of lesser weight up to 245 grains but perhaps these are worn out specimens).

There are some smaller copper coins weighing 96 grains approximately. Since the name of the coin is not mentioned anywhere, we may assume that the larger copper coins were called paisa and the smaller coins were fractions of paisa.

Gold Coins

The Calcutta Museum catalogue mentions only two gold

4. *Ibid.*, Vol. IV, pp. 238-239; G.N. Sharma, *Rajasthan ke Etihas ke Srota*, pp. 33-35.

coins (*Muhar*)—one struck during the rule of Jagat Singh (1803-1818), and the other during the reign of Ram Singh (1835-1880). Both the coins weigh 167 grains. Both these coins were perhaps *nazri* coins.

The right to issue coins had been restricted by the British government sometimes before 1913. In fact by that year very few native States were allowed to issue their own coins in any metal whatsoever. By 1913 the privilege of coining their own money was allowed only to the following States:[5]

> Hyderabad, Udaipur, Jaipur, Tonk, Orchha and Travancore in silver and copper.
>
> Kutch, Jaisalmer and Kishangarh in silver only. Gwalior, Ratlam and Baroda in copper only.

The Jaipur mint issued a large number of *Nazri* gold coins in 1922[6] on the occasion of the accession to the Gaddi of Man Singh, the last ruler of the Jaipur State. This was the last time when such *nazri* gold coins were minted.

All the gold coins in the Jaipur Museum issued since the time of Pratap Singh (1779-1803) are *nazri* coins.[7] Perhaps gold coins for market transactions were not issued at all since then; and we may assume that such coins were not used for ordinary purposes. As it is, a trimetallic system (gold, silver and copper) is very cumbersome for market transactions.

Relative Values of Silver and Copper

It would be interesting to speculate about the relative values of these two metals, copper and silver, during these years. The only important copper mines worked in those days in northern India were situated within the area of the Jaipur State. These were in Bairat,[8] about 70 km. north-west of Jaipur city, and

5. *Catalogue of the coins in the Indian Museum*, Calcutta, Vol. IV, p. 155.
6. *Manuscript catalogue of gold coins in the Jaipur Museum* in the possession of the present author.
7. *Ibid.*
8. In fact there was a mint for copper coins in Bairat from the time of Akbar, Calcutta Catalogue, Vol. III, part I, p. 44.

Khetri about 150 km. north of the city. On the other hand there were no silver mines known in India till about 30 years ago. (The lead, zinc and silver mines of Zawar near Udaipur have started producing silver only recently). All the silver required therefore was imported from abroad. The value of silver relative to copper increased as one moved away from the sea coast towards Jaipur.

In Akbar's time a *dam*, which was a copper coin, weighed about 325 grains and a silver rupee about 175 grains. According to the *Ain-i-Akbari*,[9] there were 40 *dams* for a rupee which meant that weight for weight silver was 74 times the value of the copper.

In Jaipui in 1751, there were 28 paisas in the rupee.[10] This would give a ratio of 1 to 45 between silver and copper in value, if we take a rupee to weigh about 175 grains and paisa about 285 grains.

The rise in the value of copper in relation to silver since Akbar's time might mean either that with the increase in trade with Europe silver prices were going down or perhaps that the copper mines of northern Jaipur were getting exhausted and so the price of copper was rising.

In 18. 9 there were 30 paisas for a rupee in Jaipur.[11] This would give a ratio of silver to copper as 175 to 30 × 285 or 1 to 49. In other words silver at that time had become slightly costlier in terms of copper.

Metrology

Hanuman Sharma mentions[12] that in 1839 a seer weighed 84 tolas. This remained the ratio until the merger of the Jaipur State in Rajasthan in 1949. The administration report of the Jaipur State for S. 2003 or 1946-47[13] mentions that the State rupee known as *Jharshahi* rupee weighed 174.73 grains and that the Jaipur seer weighed 88 *Jharshahi*, 84 *Kaldar* (British

9. *Ain-i-Akbari*, Vol. I, p. 32.
10. Hanuman Sharma gives this value quoting *Purana Kagaz* No. 62, in his *Nathawaton ka Itihas*, p. 285.
11. Hanuman Sharma, *op. cit.*, p. 267.
12. *Ibid.*
13. *Op. cit.*, p. 13.

Indian rupee). In other words, Jaipur maintained the weight of a seer at 84 tolas (about 978 grams) from at least the beginning of the nineteenth century. We may assume that the weight of the official Jaipur *seer* was the same i.e. 84 *tolas* in the eighteenth century also.

It is necessary to call this *seer* the official *seer* because in the first half of the eighteenth century we have the evidence of Girdhari[14] that 32 kinds of weight systems were prevalent in the city.

In other words the trader gained both ways. While buying grain from a farmer he would use a seer of a heavy weight, and while selling the same grain to a consumer he would use the seer of a lighter weight.

Land Measure

The type of confusion which is found in the weight system prevailed in the case of the land measure also. Thus nobody knew the exact area of a *bigha*. *Bigha*, it may be mentioned, is also a linear measure. and a piece of land one *bigha* long and one *bigha* wide is said to have an area of one *bigha*. E.R.K. Blenkinshop, I.C.S., who was appointed as Settlement Commissioner by the Jaipur State in 1924, found it almost impossible to determine the size of a bigha.[15]

> "I can offer no revenue statistics of any value. There are some 40 different bighas in use in different parts of the State, based on chains or rather ropes varying from 100 feet to 185 feet. The cultivator claimed that the cash rents were not liable to enhancement, and so instead of raising the rate per *bigha*, the size of the *bigha* was reduced by taking 17 gathas to the chain in place of 20 and of course, when the sanctity of the chain is tampered with, any result may be arrived at."

14. Girdhari's *Bhojanasara*, Couplet No. 201, Appendix VII.
15. Blenkinsop, *Note on Settlement Programme*, Jaipur, 1924, p. 11.

APPENDIX IV

PRICES OF FOODGRAINS

The Jaipur Government used to get a daily report of the market prices from all the principal markets in the State. The market prices of the important commodities were sent to the capital and these were preserved as permanent records. These reports were called Nirakh Bazars.

The records have now been transferred to the Rajasthan State Archives at Bikaner. The earliest of these daily market reports available in Bikaner are dated 1722 V.S. (1665 A.D.), and the last of them are dated 1884 V.S. (1827 A.D.). Most of the reports for the intervening period and for the period after 1827 A.D. are now lost or have been destroyed. So far as the Jaipur city was concerned the reports for only the following years are available:

1. Manak Chowk Bazar—VS 1784 (1727 A.D.)
   VS 1785 (1728 A.D.)
   VS 1790-95 (1733-38 A.D.)
   VS 1879-84 (1822-27 A.D.)
2. Sire Deorhi Bazar— VS 1836 (1779 A.D.)

Some of the reports from markets outside the city available in the Archives are as follows:*

Market	*Year (V.S.)*
1. Pargana Malarna	1779, 1802, 1809-11
2. Pargana Liwali	1722
3. Punkhar	1722
4. Chatsu	1781, 1789, 1794, 1808, 1812

* Information obtained through the courtesy of Shri J.K. Jain, Director of Archives, Rajasthan, Bikaner.

5. Toda Raisingh	1817, 1824, 1837
6. Baswa	1778, 1785, 1819, 1831
7. Maujmabad	1771
8. Sanganer	1782, 1784
9. Hindaun	1786, 1815
10. Gazi-ka-Thana	1784, 1785, 1786, 1787, 1812, 1813, 1817.

What use was made of these daily market reports is not clear. In a region like Jaipur, where the rainfall is erratic, the market prices would fluctuate from year to year and sometimes from month to month, and since transportation was difficult they would differ from place to place. The reports of the food-grain prices would thus give an idea of the general well-being of the people in the different parts of the State. We do not know whether the department concerned with these market reports also kept the ruler informed about them or quietly filed them in their *tankihs*. At best we can imagine that ruler would call for them if he received complaints of scarcity from some part of his state.

Manner of Reporting

The market report would first give the price of a gold *mohur* in terms of the silver rupee. After this the prices of food articles in seers per rupee were given. These articles were generally rice, wheat, barley, wheat, flour, *ghee*, oil, *til*, *jawar*, *moth*, *bajra*, *moong urad*, *khand*, *sugar*, *shakar*, *gur*, salt, *maize*, *moong dal*, *urad dal*, gram, *besan* (gram flour), *arhar*, etc.

A typical Nirakh Bazar, say of Thursday, Phagun Badi 9, V.S. 1884 of the Manak Chowk Bazar mentions that the price of a gold *mohur Taksal* was 15/16 silver rupees. For other articles, it mentions "*Jinsi* tol 35 Ko". This could, of course, mean that the seers in which the other articles were measured weighed 35 silver rupees or 35 tolas. On the other hand it is generally assumed that the Jaipur seer weighed 84 tolas. It is thus quite difficult to get the absolute values of the commodities from these Nirakh Bazars, unless we know the system of weights and measure used at that time. But the relative values of the various commodities are easily found. For instance, on this day wheat was selling at 29½ seers per rupee and ghee at 4¼ seers per rupee in the Manak Chowk Bazar. Prices in some cases were given for different qualities of foodgrains. For instance, prices of four qualities of rice and two qualities of wheat were reported in the case of this Nirakh Bazar.

Dr. Hendley's Tables of Prices for 1761 to 1897

Records of the *Nirakh Bazars* for the city markets are available from 1761 A.D. to 1897. The average prices of the three principal foodgrains, viz., wheat, barley and bajra, for each rabi and kharif season were calculated under the orders of the then Prime Minister of the State Kanti Chandra Mukherji and supplied to Dr. T. Holbein Hendley Dr. Hendley published these prices for the years 1761 to 1893 in his *A Medico-Topographical account of Jeypore* (Calcutta 1895). In Dr. Hendley's *A General Medical History of Rajputana* (Calcutta 1900) the price list was continued to 1897. He also noted whether a particular year was a year of famine or scarcity.

Dr. Hendley's tables of prices are important, but the main difficulty of finding the absolute value of a commodity remains, for we do not know either the weight of a seer or the value of the silver content of a rupee. These points have been discussed in the section on coins and metrology; and we may assume that the seer in Dr. Hendley's table weighed 975 grams (the seer used during the British period in India weighed 933.1 grams). We may also assume that throughout this period the rupee was made of almost pure silver and weighed 174.73 grains i.e. less than a British period tola which weighed 179.4 grains or 11.6638 grams.

Price List of Foodgrains given in the Annual Reports

Lists of annual average prices of foodgrains were also published in the Annual Reports of the Jaipur Medical and Meteorological Institutions until 1925. (These annual reports had been started by Dr. Hendley in 1874 and they were continued up to 1930 but the foodgrain prices were not printed in the last five reports). Here also we have the same difficulty about the weight system and the value of the rupee. We do not know whether the seer and the rupee mentioned in these tables of prices were Jaipuri (*Jharshahi*) or Bri'ish Indian. At the end of the period, that is near about 1930, the *Jharshahi* standards had almost disappeared from the market transactions, but this was not so in the earlier period when *Jharshahi* standards were commoly used in Jaipur. However, since the publications of these price lists were started by a British Officer in the services of the Jaipur State, we may assume that he was using the British Indian seers and rupees.

DR. HENDLEY'S TABLES

Table I: Prices of Foodgrains—1761-1897

"Through the courtesy of Rao Bahadur Kantee Chandra Mookerjee, C.I.E., the Chief Member of Council at Jeypore, I am able to give a price list of the principal foodgrains for both the spring and autumn crops from the year 1761 A.D. to 1897. I have added notes wherever it has seemed desirable.

Average price of foodgrains sold at Jeypore in seers per rupee. B. Blair's Indian Famines. D. Delhi Gazetteer. K. Karnal Gazetteer. H. Hissar Gazettcer. G. Gazetteer of Agra and neighbouring district, N.W.P. For East Jeypore records at a temple near Hindaun

YEAR A. D.	Rabee (Spring) Wheet Seers	Barley Seers	Bajra Seers	Kharif (Autumn) Wheat Seers	Barley Seers	Bajra Seers	Remarks
1	2	3	4	5	6	7	8
1761	18	23	18¼	18¼	24¾	19¼	
1762	22¾	31	22¾	21¾	36½	27	
1763	20	27	22¾	16¾	21¼	18¾	
1765	—	—	Not available		—	—	
1766				-do-			
1767				-do-			
1768	30	40	38	30¾	50	47¼	
1769	36	54¾	45¼	28	50	54¾	

1	2	3	4	5	6	7	8

From the end of 1768 to Dec. 1770, 10,000,000 human beings died of famine in Bengal. B. Scarcity less in Upper Provinces. D.

1	2	3	4	5	6	7	8
1770	24¼	30¾	43¼	17¾	28	31¾	
1771	18¾	25	27¼	17¾	24¾	29¼	
1772	22¼	13¼	28	23¼	30¾	26	
1773	21¾	27½	22	22¾	33¼	32	
1774	22¼	30¾	28	15¼	25¾	26	
1775	—	—	Not available		—	—	
1776			-do-				
1777	25¼	36¼	28¾	17¼	21	21	
1778	21¼	27¼	24	17½	23	18¾	
1779	19¼	24	22	24	18¾	18	
1780	21	29¼	17¾	19½	30¾	29	
1781	24	38	31	23¼	46¾	41¼	
1782	23	30¾	7¼	24¾	36	31	

Drought in Northern India. B. Season dry. Harvest poor in Hisar. The whole country depopulated in the great famine of 1783 (*chalisa*). Thousands of fugitives also came from Bikaner. The great famine in Agra known as the *chalisa*. G. Famine raged in the Punjab and the N.W.P. Provinces. Girdlestone believes it extended into Rajputana. The increased price show that it did. B. Said to be most severe. Known in the N.W.P. G. Copius rains fell in Sept., Oct. 1783 in Hissar, and harvest of the spring of 1784 was abundant but the good effects of improved prices do not seem to have reached Jeypore until 1785. H.

The terrible *chalisa* Sambat 1840---Grain 4 seers for rupee one in Kurnal. K.

1	2	3	4	5	6	7	8
	1783	23	28¾	28¾	15	17	15¼
	1784	11¾	14	12	11¼	17	16¾
	1785	26	37¼	34¾	26¾	47	42
	1786	37	58	50¾	26	46¾	46¾

1	2	3	4	5	6	7	8
1787	25¾	36¾	38	22¾	36	40¾	
1788	29¼	28¼	36	27	28¾	40	
1789	34¾	45½	42	29	40	38	
1790	22¼	28¼	25	17	20	18	
	In 1790, the Delhi district was visited by scarcity. B.						
1791	15¾	18¾	16¾	15½	20¾	19¾	
1792	17¼	22¼	19¾	12	17	15¼	
1793	15¼	20	47¾	21¾	34¾	37	
1794	22¾	32	32	24	35½	34	
1795	27½	36¾	41¼	26¾	41¼	49¾	
1796	30	45½	48¾	28	48¾	46¼	
1797	33½	51¼	60	33	57½	64	
1798	40	60	63½	31	56	63½	
1799	40	60	56	35	55¼	54¾	
1800	36	49½	40	18	22	22¾	
1801	35¼	38	24¾	31¾	40	34	
1802	32¾	39½	29	30	41¼	37½	
1803	22¾	32¾	30¾	14¾	18	15	
	A severe famine in the N.W.P. but limited in area. It lasted until the autumn of 1804 and clearly reached Jeypore. B. Total failure of crops. Little mortality in Kurnal. K.						
1804	13¼	18¼	15¼	12¼	23¾	28¾	
1805	16¼	25¼	23¾	16½	25	25¾	
1806	24	34	30	19¾	29¾	30¼	
1807	22½	29	26¾	20¾	26¾	21¼	
1808	18	23¾	18	11	12¼	12	
1809	16¼	21½	17¼	14¾	22¾	24¾	
1810	23¼	33¼	29¼	26¾	39¼	35¾	
1811	—	—	Records destroyed by white ants.				
1812	—	—		-do-			
1813	7½	8¾	8	13¾	18	25	
	Round Agra crops indifferent in this year. B. Rains failed in Mathura. No autumn harvest, spring crops 1813 failed. G. Famine prevailed in and around Agra in 1813 and clearly about Jaypore. Rains late						

1	2	3	4	5	6	7	8
	in 1813. B. Half the landed property in Agra Zila changed hands. G. Grain 10 seers per rupee in Karnal. K.						
1814	16¾	22	21	22	29¼	29¼	
1815	20¾	27¼	25¼	19	30¾	30¾	
1816	19½	26	25¾	18¾	25¼	25¼	
1817	16¾	21¾	19¾	14¼	17	16	
1818	15	21½	14¾	12	18¼	20¼	
1819	17¼	25¼	21¼	15	22¾	21¼	
	Famine attacked the N.W.P. and Bundelkhand.						
1820	14	18¼	18¼	11¼	16¾	20¼	
1821	16	20	20¼	19	26¾	26¾	
1822	20	26¼	26¾	19¼	34	31¼	
1823	24	36	30	24½	49¼	50¾	
1824	26¼	43¼	45¼	18¼	28¼	24	
	Karnal in 1825. None sown. Distress still more severe to the South. K.						
1825	18¼	25	23¼	19¼	26	26¾	
	Famine or scarcity recurred in the N.W.P. and adjacent countries in 1825, 1826, 1827 B.G. Great drought in Delhi.						
1826	21	29	26¼	21	37¼	39¼	
1827	23¼	38	33	19¾	45¼	48	
1828	26¾	50	47½	18¾	38¼	45½	
1829	23	35	41¼	21	28¾	29¼	
1830	25¼	36¾	26¾	22	33¼	30	
1831	25¼	36¾	30¾	25¾	45¼	51½	
1832	29	60	57½	26	42	38¾	
	Famine or scarcity received in 1832 in the N.W.P. and adjacent countries. Was this 1833?. B. Most terrible famine known in Karnal. K.						
1833	21¼	26¾	28¾	14¼	16¾	14	
1834	16¾	25¾	15	14¼	25¾	31¼	

1	2	3	4	5	6	7	8
	Rains failed in Karnal. 1834. Great distress. K. Jeypore (East). Famine and locust.						
1835	20	28¾	30¼	19¼	30¼	33¾	
	Spring rains abundant in Karnal K.						
1836	25	36¾	37	23	34¼	35¾	
1837	20	2.¼	23¼	16¾	20¾	19¼	
	8,00,000 deaths in the N.W.P. Harvest indifferent from 1832. Prevailed to the autumn harvest of 1838. Rains failed in Mathura. S.						
1838	14¼	21	18	14	22¼	27¾	
	The 1838 famine known as the Chauranwe 1894 Samvat G. Drought in Karnal 1837 K. Jeypore, East. Famine and scarcity of rain.						
1839	16¼	24¾	25¾	14¼	23¼	25	
1840	13	17¾	17¾	14¾	22¾	25	
1841	18¾	26¼	26¾	20¼	28¼	29¼	
	Great Mortality from fever in Delhi district. Crops died for want of labour. K.						
1842	20	26¾	27	20¼	30	32¾	
	Rains failed in 1842 in Karnal. K.						
1843	20	28	28¼	17¼	27¾	28	
1844	20	26	24	20	27¾	24¾	
1845	22	31¼	23¼	18	28	29¼	
1846	22¼	30	36¼	19¾	28	26¼	
1847	20¼	28	22¾	15¾	22¼	21¾	
	East Jeypore, famine.						
1848	18¼	22¼	19¾	17	19¼	19¼	
1849	17¾	25	22	17¾	31	32	
1850	24	34¼	31¾	23¾	35¼	36¼	
1851	25½	35	32	18½	28	29	
	Drought which extended into 1852 in Karnal. K.						

1	2	3	4	5	6	7	8
1852	22½	34	30½	17	31	33½	
1853	24	33½	32	22	28½	24½	
1854	24	32	27½	25	37	37	
1855	23½	32	31	22½	32½	28	
1856	23	30½	24	19½	29	30	
1857	25	36	30	24½	32¼	27	
1858	25	34½	24	23	34	30	
	Rain fall scanty in Karnal. K.						
1859	23½	33½	32	19	34	33½	
	Only showers in Karnal. K.						
1860	19	33	30	12½	17	14½	
	Famine in 1860-61 in the N.W.P. and Punjab deaths 2,000,000 (thought to be over-rated) B.D.						
1861	15¾	29½	19	12	25¾	25¾	
	Bad famine also in Karnal. K. and Hisar H.						
1862	18	26	22½	17½	24	22	
1863	18	22¼	15	17½	24	17½	
1864	17½	23½	17	13½	22½	19½	
1865	12½	20	17½	10	15½	15¾	
	In Allahabad supposed to be on the verge of a famine. S.D.						
1866	15	22	17½	14½	20	20½	
1867	16½	24	21½	14	23½	24	
1868	15	20	18½	9¼	11	9½	
	The great Rajputana famine of 1868 and 1869 felt most severely in Marwar and Ajmer. B.D.						
1869	6	8	6	7½	14	16	
	Both crops failed in Karnal in 1868. Scanty harvest in 1869. No rain until Aug.; more severe famine than in any other Punjab district. K. Severe in Hissar. H. The starving population from Bikaner, Jeypore and C. poured first into Hissar H.						

1	2	3	4	5	6	7	8
1870	11	17	17	14½	20½	20½	
1871	19	28	22	14	25½	22¼	
1872	17	26	21	14½	24	24½	
1173	13½	20½	19½	12¼	17	16	
1874	17	26	21	14½	24	24½	
1875	18	25¼	18½	16½	25½	24½	
1876	16½	23½	21¼	17	29	26½	
1877	19½	26	25	19¼	29	29	
	Autumn rains failed in Hissar. H., and scarcity prevailed in 1877-78. H.						
1878	12¾	15½	14	10¾	12¾	12	
	Famine in Mathura and scarcity in other districts. S. Delhi also.						
1879	13¼	19	16½	9½	13	13¼	-
	Mortality very high in Mathura. Poor house open in Mathura to June 1879/S in East Jeypore; much loss by locusts. Rains failed in Mathura. G. Rains also slight.						
1880	13	19¾	17¼	13	24½	23	
1881	15¼	22¼	21	15	24	22	
1882	16½	24	21½	16½	23	22¾	
1883	17¼	23½	20	15¼	24½	22½	
1884	15	22	20	16	23	21	
	Summer and winter rains of 1883-84 failed in Karnal. Grass famine intense. K.						
1885	18¼	24	20½	19	29	28	
1886	21½	32½	28½	16½	28½	23½	
1887	19	33	25	12	25½	22½	
1888	12	21	17½	11½	15	14¼	
1889	15½	21½	15½	16¼	22¾	19½	
1890	16	23½	21¾	14½	21	18¾	
1891	14½	19	16½	13½	20	17½	
1892	11¾	15	12¾	13½	20	19	
	1891-92 Scarcity in Rajputana, most pronounced in Ajmer and neighbouring districts.						

1	2	3	4	5	6	7	8
1893	14	18½	17	12	20½	19½	
1894	16	32½	20¼	17	31½	22½	
1895	11¾	18¼	18½	15¼	28½	15½	
	1895-96 Famine in North Western Provinces (U.P.), Parts of Bengal and Central Provinces.						
1896	12½	17½	10¾	7½	11	13	
1897	8½	10¼	12	9½	13¼	9½	
	1896-97 continued to the Summer, not much felt in Rajputana. Prices were high chiefly on account of export of grains.*						

* From *A Medico-Topographical Account of Jaipur* (Calcutta, 1895) and *A General Medical History of Rajputana* (Calcutta, 1900) by Dr. T. Holbein Hendley.

PRICES OF GRAINS

Table II—Statement showing the Prices of Foodgrains in Jaipur City from 1874 to 1930

Year	Wheat (Seers per rupee)	Barley (Seers per rupee)	Bajra or Millet (Seers per rupee)	Remarks
1	2	3	4	5
1874	14.79	20.67	17.06	
1875	16.95	24.09	22.07	
1876	19.83	28.01	26.17	
1877	16.44	22.00	21.22	
1878	11.00	14.52	13.22	
1879	11.01	16.92	15.31	
1880	13.92	22.58	20.69	
1881	15.24	22.00	20.36	
1882	16.43	25.36	20.28	
1883	16.35	23.54	20.93	
1884	17.19	14.17	20.61	
1885	18.81	27.83	24.52	
1886	17.70	22.00	23.47	
1887	12.28	22.00	18.39	
1888	14.16	19.72	14.71	
1889	15.46	22.31	19.58	
1890	15.09	21.38	18.20	
1891	13.15	18.11	15.13	
1892	13.14	19.40	16.14	
1893	14.54	25.31	22.25	
1894	16.33	29.75	21.50	
1895	13.92	23.66	18.48	
1896	11.07	15.38	12.42	
1897	9.03	12.68	11.26	
1898	12.61	19.16	18.53	

1	2	3	4	5
1899	11.00	15.51	13.68	
1900	9.73	13.76	12.67	
1901	11.75	19.64	21.72	
1902	12.12	16.21	16.21	
1903	12.83	19.90	20.39	
1904	14.60	22.14	20.95	
1905	12.77	29.23	16.90	
1906	10.95	15.33	13.72	
1907	10.87	15.77	17.92	
1908	8.41	12.63	11.52	
1909	9.94	16.12	14.65	
1910	11.72	17.92	15.45	
1911	13.51	17.84	16.61	
1912	11.43	14.40	13.10	
1913	10.86	14.04	13.28	
1914	9.29	12.25	10.69	
1915	8.50	13.06	11.34	
1916	9.32	12.02	12.10	
1917	9.50	13.25	13.75	
1918	7.62	10.56	7.06	
1919	6.19	8.62	6.31	
1920	6.34	8.37	7.56	
1921	6.10	8.00	5.95	
1922	6.44	9.00	8.22	
1923	9.31	13.44	12.62	
1924	9.75	13.75	11.25	
1925	7.12	11.75	8.69*	

* From the *Report on the Jaipur Medical and Meteorological Institution* for the year 1925.

APPENDIX V

PROFESSIONS AND CASTES OF THE POPULATION OF JAIPUR ACCORDING TO BOILEAU (1835 A.D.)

Name of Castes	Profession or trade	Houses		Population	
		Moosulman	Hindu	Moosulman	Hindu
1	2	3	4	5	6
Aheree	Watchmen	—	600	—	3000
Bed or Baid	Physician	—	250	—	1250
Bhet	Poets	—	200	—	1000
Bheel	Bowmen	—	80	—	400
Bhungee	Sweepers	—	700	—	3500
Bhura	Pimps	—	250	—	1250
Bhutiara	Cooks	—	600	—	3000
Biloch	Camel-men	150	—	750	—
Brahmun	Priests	—	—	—	—
,, Boora	Undertakers	—	80	—	400
,, Bora or Puleewal	Merchants	—	500	—	2500
,, Dakot	Sextons	—	1100	—	5500
,, Gor	—	—	17000	—	85000

1		2	3	4	5	6
,,	Kapree	Who beg from Bunya	—	500	—	2500
,,	Keertunia	Musicians and Dancers	—	40	—	200
,,	Khundelwal	—	—	300	—	1500
,,	Pohkurna	—	—	300	—	1500
,,	Purohit	Family Priests	—	—	—	—
Brahmun	Purohit	Chaplains of State	—	200	—	1000
Khutria	Pareek	Private Chaplains	—	350	—	1750
,,	Sreewunt	—	—	250	—	1250
,,	Sonawud	—	—	1100	—	5500
Bunya		Merchants and Shopkeepers	—	—	—	—
,,	Beejaburgee	—	—	1100	—	5500
,,	Dusan	Servants of Ugurwalas	—	100	—	500
,,	Muhesree	—	—	4000	—	20000
,,	Oswal	—	—	900	—	4500
,,	Siraogee	—	—	5500	—	27500
,,	Ugurwal	—	—	5000	—	25000
Burhaee		See Kathee	—	—	—	—
Burwa		Geneologists	—	100	—	500
Chakur		Servants of Thakoors	—	450	—	2250
Cheepee		Calico-printers	—	3000	—	15000
Chejara		Masons	1100	—	5500	—

Chitramee	House-painters	—	200	—	1000
Choonput	Lime-burners	—	450	—	2250
Chooreegur	Danta-ka-Bracelet makers of Ivory	100	—	500	—
,, Lakh ka	See Muneehar	—	—	—	—
Chumar	Cobblers and Porters	—	500	—	2500
,, Megwal	—	—	—	—	—
Dhoondee	Religious Devotees	—	125	—	625
Dom	Horn-blowers and Drummers	—	200	—	1000
Durzee	Tailors	—	1200	—	6000
Fukeer	Mendicants	500	—	2500	—
Ghiṣiara	Grass-cutters	—	350	—	1750
Goojur	Cow-herds	—	500	—	2500
Bijra	Eunuchs	—	80	—	400
Hukeem	Physicians	900	—	4500	—
Jat	Cultivators	—	1000	—	5000
Jogee	Religious Devotees	—	250	—	1250
,, Kumphuta	with split ears	—	100	—	500
Jolaha	Weavers	700	—	3500	—
Joshee Punchrungs	Religious Devotees	—	100	—	500
Jureea	Lapidaries	—	125	—	625

1	2	3	4	5	6
Jutia	Tanners	—	300	—	1500
Kaith	Writers	—	2500	—	12500
Kahar	Bearers of Bghees	—	250	—	1250
,, Muhra	,, of Palkees	—	550	—	2750
Kathee	Carpenters	—	300	—	1500
Keer	Basket-makers and growers of Singhara	—	200	—	1000
Khalpeea	Tanners of Goat-skins	—	125	—	625
Khuteek	Parchment-makers	—	250	—	1250
Koomhar	Potters	—	500	—	2500
Koonjura	Green-grocers	550	—	2750	—
Kuleegur	White-washers	200	—	1000	—
Kulwara	Distillers	—	1100	—	5500
Kusbee	Prostitutes	—	—	—	—
,, Pathur	,, who eat meat	—	1300	—	6500
Kusara, See also Thuthera	Braziers	—	1000	—	5000
Kusaee	Butchers	250	—	1250	—
Kuthawa	Wood-men	—	225	—	1125
Lohar	Iron-smiths	—	200	—	1000
Malee	Gardeners	—	2000	—	10000
Meena	Thieves	—	200	—	1000

Meerasee	Mendicants	—	150	—	750
Moosulman	Mohumadans	3000	—	15000	—
Mochee	Shoe-makers	150	300	750	1500
Muhawut	Elephant-drivers	125	—	625	—
Muneehar	Lac-workers	200	—	1000	—
Muhra	See Kuhar	—	—	—	—
Naee	Barbers	—	500	—	2500
Naichagar	Makers of Pipe-snakes	50	—	250	—
Balbund	Farriers	200	—	1000	—
Niaria	Refiners and Assayers	—	350	—	1750
Numdia	Felt-ajers	200	—	1000	—
Ogur	Devotees who eat in any company	—	140	—	700
Pewundee	Frauiterers	—	900	—	4500
Puthurphor	Stone-cutters or Quarriers	600	—	3000	—
Raegur, See also Jutia	Tanners of Sheep	—	200	—	1000
Ranbaree	Camel-men	—	103	—	515
Rajpoot	(Thakoors)	—	2000	—	10000
Runa	Musicians of State	—	125	—	625
Rungrez	Dyers	250	—	1250	—
Salotree	Horse-doctors	350	—	1750	—

1		2	3	4	5	6
Shamee		Religious Devotees	—	—	—	—
,,	Sunjogee	,, who marry	—	1500	—	7500
Sonar		Goldsmiths	—	900	—	4500
Suka		Water-carriers	400	—	2000	—
Tutgur		Canvas-makers	100	—	500	—
Topchee		Game-killers	—	200	—	1000
Tumolee		Pan-sellers	—	300	—	1500
Tuthera		Brass-smiths	—	500	—	2500
		GRAND TOTAL	10075	68798	50375	345990
Indur ban or Elephant Cars			4			
Pukka Mundurs with spires			1400			
Shops in the Market about			21000			

(From—Boileau, *Personal Narrative of a Tour through the Western States of Rajwara in 1835*, pp. 232-235).

APPENDIX VI

LIST OF FAMOUS TEMPLES AND BUILDINGS ETC. CONSTRUCTED BY THE MAHARAJAS AND MAHARANIS OF JAIPUR

(This list was compiled by the staff of the City Palace, Jaipur sometimes after the integration of the State, in 1949)

S. No.	Description	Where situated	By whom constructed	Construction year (A.D.)
1	2	3	4	5
1.	Temple of Shri Jamwa Mataji	Jamwa Ramgarh	Maharaja Duleh Rajji	1007-37
2.	Old Palaces below hill	Amber	Maharaja Raj Deoji	1180-1217
3.	10 Pillared Palace	Vishram Ghat, Mathura	Maharaja Ratan Singhji	1537-1548
4.	Jama Masjid	Amber	Maharaja Bharmalji	1569
5.	Old Amber Palace on the hill	Amber	Maharaja Man Singhji I	1590-1615
6.	Shri Shilla Deviji's Temple	Amber	-do-	1604, 1942

1	2	3	4	5
7.	Jagat Shiromaniji's Temple	Amber	Shri Kankawatiji, Maharani of Maharaja Man Singhji I, built this temple in commemoration of her beloved son Maharajkumar Jagat Singhji	1601
8.	Man Mandir	Pushkar	Maharaja Man Singhji	1590-1614
9.	Man Mandir	Benaras	-do-	1590-1614
10.	Govind Deva Temple	Brindaban	-do-	1592
11.	Canotaph of Maharaja Man Singhji	Ellichpur (Berar)	Maharaja Bhao Singhji	1615-1622
12.	Dewan Khana and Ganesh Pole	Amber Palace	Mirza Raja Jai Singhji	1639
13.	Jai Niwas Garden	Jaipur	Maharaja Sawai Jai Singhji	1726
14.	Observatories	Delhi, Banaras, Ujjain, Muttra and Jaipur	-do-	1724-34
15.	Shri Sitaramji's Temple	Vishram Ghat Mathura	-do-	1732
16,	Shri Surajji's Temple	on Galta Hills	Rao Jagram under the patronage of Maharaja Sawai Jai Singhji	1734

17.	Sudarshangarh Fort	Jaipur	Maharaja Sawai Jai Singhji	1734
18.	Jal Mahal	Amber road	-do-	1734
19.	Chandra Mahal	City Palace	-do-	1734
20.	Badal Mahal	Jaipur	-do-	1734
21.	Dewan Khana Am.	City Palace	-do-	1734
22.	Sharbata (Darbar Hall)	City Palace	-do-	1734
23.	Shri Govind Deoji's Temple	Jaipur	-do-	1735
24.	Shri Gowardhan Nathji's Temple	Gowardhan Parwat	-do-	1736
25.	Ranawatji's Garden (later on called Majika Bagh or Residency)	Jaipur	Shri Ranawatji Maharani of Maharaja Sawai Jai Singhji	1739
26.	Shri Kalkiji's Temple	Jaipur (Sireh Deorhi Bazar)	Maharaja Sawai Jai Singhji	1740
27.	Ishwar Lat	Jaipur	Maharaja Sawai Ishwari Singhji	1749
28.	Shri Govind Deoji's Temple	Udaipur (Near the temple of Shri Iklingji)	Maj Sahiba Shri Ranawatji w/o Maharaja Sawai Jai Singhji	1764
29.	Shri Niritya Gopalji's Temple	Brindaban	Maji Sahiba Shri Dhundawatji w/o Maharaja Sawai Madho Singhji	1779

1	2	3	4	5
30.	Shri Brijnandji's Temple	Jaipur	Maharaja Sawai Pratap Singhji	1792
31.	Hawa Mahal (Wind Palace)	Jaipur	-do-	1799
32.	Chatar Shiromaniji's Temple	Brindaban	Maji Sahiba Shri Ranawatji w/o Maharaja Sawai Pratap Singhji	1810
33.	Shri Brijraj Behariji's Temple	Tripolia Bazar, Jaipur	Maharaja Sawai Jagat Singhji	1813
34.	Radha Agar Shiromaji's Temple	Brindaban	Maji Sahiba Shri Rathori Udaibhanotji w/o Mahraja Swai Jagat Singhji	1819
35.	Chand Behariji's Temple	-do-	Maji Sahiba Shri Champawatji w/o Maharaja Sawai Jagat Singhji	1820
36.	Sareh Behariji's Temple	Pushkar Ajmer	Maji Sahiba Shri Rathoreji w/o Maharaja Sawai Jagat Singhji	1820
37.	Gokulnandji's Temple	Brindaban	Maji Sahiba Shri Bhatiyaniji w/o Maharaja Sawai Jagat Singhji	1820

1	2	3	4	5
38.	Mohallalji's Temple	-do-	Maji Sahiba Shri Jhaliji w/o Maharaja Sawai Pratap Singhji	1822
39.	Krishna Chandra Temple	Brindaban	Maji Sahiba Shri Bhatiyaniji II w/o Maharaja Sawai Jagat Singhji	1836
40.	Shri Anand Manoharji's Temple	-do-	Maji Sahiba Shri Bara Bhatiyaniji w/o Maharaja Sawai Jagat Singhji	1827
41.	Naya Mahal Defunct Council Building	Sireh Deorhi Bajar, Jaipur	Maharaja Sawai Ram Singhji II	1853
42.	Shri Ramchandraji's Temple	-do-	Maji Sahiba Shri Chandrawatji, mother of Maharaja Sawai Ram Singhji II	1854
43.	Shri Ratneshwarji's temple known as Deoriji's temple	Johri Bazar	Maji Sahiba Shri Deoriji w/o Maharaja Sawai Jai Singhji III	1865
44.	Mayo Hospital	Jaipur	Maharaja Sawai Ram Singhji II	1870
45.	Museum	Ramniwas Garden, Jaipur	-do-	1869
46.	Ram Prakash Theatre Hall	Jaipur city	-do-	1879

1	2	3	4	5
47.	Extension to the Sudershangarh Fort	Jaipur	Maharaja Sawai Madho Singhji II	1887
48.	Shri Ramchandraji's Temple	Chandpole Bazar, Jaipur	Maji Sahiba Shri Dhirawatji w/o Maharaja Sawai Ram Singhji II	1894
49.	Gangaji's Temple	Gangotri	Maharaja Sawai Madho Singhji II	1915
50.	Mubarak Mahal	City Palace	-do-	1900
51.	Radha Madhoji's Temple	Brindaban	-do-	1915
52.	Kushal Behariji's Temple	Barsana	Maharaja Sawai Madho Singhji II	1916
53.	Madho Behariji's Temple	Station Road, Jaipur	Maji Sahiba Shri Tanwarji w/o Maharaja Sawai Madho Singhji	1926
54.	Ram Bagh Palace (Remodelled)	Jaipur	Maharaja Sawai Man Singhji II	1926-42
55.	Zanana Hospital	-do-	-do-	1932
56.	Maharaja's College	-do-	-do-	1934
57.	Bhagwantdas Barracks	-do-	-do-	1936
58.	Infantry Barracks	-do-	-do-	1936
59.	Kachhawa Horse Barracks	-do-	-do-	1936
60.	Lady Willingdon Hospital	-do-	-do-	1936
61.	King George V Solorium	-do-	-do-	1939
62.	Jaipur House	Delhi	-do-	1940

APPENDIX VII

VERSES ON JAIPUR IN GIRDHARI'S BHOJANASARA (1739 A.D.)

This extract from Girdhari's *Bhojanasara* was published by P.K. Gode in his article "Two Contemporary Tributes to Minister Vidyadhara, the Bengali Architect of Jaipur at the Court of Sawai Jai Singh of Amber (A.D. 1699-1743)" in *Dr. C. Kunhan Raja Presentation Volume*, pp. 285-294 (Madras, 1946):

अथ सवाई जैपुर बसायो ताकौ वर्णन ।। दोहा ।।
पुराकरे बहु हरष करि मनमहिमोद बढ़ाय
विद्याधर सौ बोलि कहि सहरसु एक बसाय ।।१८२।।
जैंनिवास या सहरमधि आवै यहै विचारि
चौपरि केरु बजार बहु घरि पिछवारै सारि ।।१८३।।
अथ जैंनिवास वर्णण ।। दोहा ।।
मुकत महल राजहि महल बादल महल सुजानि
सिदरा और हमाम सुनि बुरजि रसोई ठानि ।।१८४।।
बड़ी बड़ी नहरै जहां हौद तडागहि देषि
भर फंहरि नलिन तौ कुंडा चादरि पेषि ।।१८५।।

।। **कविता** ।।

देषौ नये तरु नये पातनि केनी केन
येन ईन ईसाषा नये फलफूल नये हैं
नये नये सौरभ सुवात निमैं आवैं
नये नये अलि गुंजे पुंजे बौले बोल नये हैं
नये नये कैकी कीर चातक चकोर नये
नये नये कोकिल कुहुकै बांनी नये हैं
सवाई असाह रहाराजनि मुकुटमनि
जै निवास बाग में बसंत नित नये हैं ।।१८६।।

।। दौहा ।।

बेग बसै यक वर्ष मै बारहै कोस ही फेर।
देस देस के बौलियौ व्योपारी सुनिहैरी ।।१८७।।
कूचे टीवे रेत नले बहुत हैपुर।
तिनकौ दुरिकराय कै करो हवेली सूर ।।१८८।।
लेहु षजानौ बहुत है लागै सोही लगाय।
सवाई जैपुर सुनौं सहरसु येक बसाय ।।१८९।।
करि असीस बिनती करी देहो बेग बसाय।
संबत सतरेसे सुनीं चौरासी मनुलाय ।।१९०।।
पौसहि सुदि परिवाजहा बारसनी सरवरा।
गिरधारी या सहरको जनम महासुभवार ।।१९१।।
या कौडर सबुजगत है व्हैं यदै विचारि।
या कौडरना हि न कहु गिरधारी यह धारी ।।१९२।।
बहु द्विजकौ भोजन दये दक्षिना दई बुलाय।
दे असीस यह उच्चरं बसहु सहर वहं माय ।।१९४।।

।। कविता ।।

मंदिर अनेक जहां गौव्यं देव गोपीनाथ
शिवरु गनेशरु दिनेस के दिवाले है।
देवी दव षियत गेंह गेह झालरिसु घंटा
झाझिदुंदभि के नादनी के चाले है
बापी कूप बाग मानसागर सुपूर भरे नदी
चली आवै नावें चढै नर नाले हैं।। १९५ ।।

।। दोहा ।।

चौपर केरु बजार है हाटैंक ई हजार
देस देस के करते हैं व्योपारी व्यौहार-।। १९६ ।।

।। कविता ।।

गजबाजी बिकैदरी यावनिकै अरु कछकै उंट अनेकही आवै
बैलबिकेक करे जी घनें अरु में सिवतीसी कीलाषनुयावै
जरीजरवाव पटंबर अंबर-जरायकै भूषन जग बिसाहै
राजाधिराज बसायोसु जैपुर कतं तहां तेषरीदिकैं ल्यावे ।। १९७ ।।

॥ दोहा ॥

बसत फिरंगी हून हांसागर तजिकै आय ।।
जिनकै बुधि बबैक बहुकहिये कहा बनाय ॥ १९८ ॥
जैसें देस देस के आय हैं बहु साह ।
लाष करोरि नकीसुनौ हूंडी चलत सुताह ॥ १९९ ॥
जिनके लछि अयार है करत रहत व्यापार ।
गिरधारी सुषते रहैतत सकर नहीं निहारि ॥ २०० ॥
कौऊं कांहते कछु हन नाहक नहीं बोल ।
गिरधारी या सहर मै कस्यो बतीसहितोल ॥ २०१ ॥

॥ कविता ॥

यज्ञ करें द्विज प्रातहितै फुनि बैद पढ़ें अरु औरें पढ़ावै ।
सुभ्रत साधिक है सब धर्म्म अधर्म्म की बात ही दूरि नसावै ।
घरही घरमांड कथा डुनियेरपुरान अठारहरुं सबगावें ।
राजाधिराज बसायौ सुजैपुर जै जै करे हरिनांव सुनावै ॥ २०२ ॥

The Hindi rendering (done by Prof. B.D. Verma) was published by Gode along with the original. This was:

"Sawai laid the foundation of Jaipur, the description of which is as follows:

Doha

He laid out many streets, and thus enhanced the joy of heart. He said to Vidyadhara that a city should be founded here. (182).

Jainivas should come within this city, this is my wish. There should be many cross-roads with shops on them. The back-yards of the houses should meet together. (183).

Description of Jainivas

There were Mukatmahal, Rajamahal, Badalmahal, three-doored Verandahs, bath-rooms and Kitchens in that palace. (184).

Big canals were running. There were many reservoirs of

water and tanks and the water falling from the fountains spread like sheets. (185).

Kavita

Behold! Here are new trees, new leaves, new branches, new flowers and fruits, new beautiful parrots sit on them. New bees are humming and birds are singing new tunes. There are new peacocks, parrots, chatakas, chakoras. New koel is cooing and producing new notes. Sawai Jaisaha Maharaj Mukatmani has his Jainivas Garden with a perennial spring reigning therein. (186).

Doha

It (Jaipur) should be populated in one year and should be twelve Kosas in extent. Merchants from different places should be called to stay here (i.e. to make it their home). (187).

There are shrubs, sand-dunes, gullies all over. These should be levelled up and then the Havelis should be constructed. (188).

I have got immense treasure. Take what you want and use it. Sawai Jaipur should be made a unique city. (189). He blessed him and said, "It will be done soon (i e. the city will soon be populated). It was the year 1784. Listen to this attentively. (190).

It was Poos Sudi 1 and the day was Saturday, when the foundation of this city was laid at a very auspicious moment. (191).

The whole world will be afraid of this but this will not be afraid of anything. This is the firm belief of Girdhari. (192).

Many Brahmins were feasted and were given Dakshina. They are blessed, "May this city be beautiful and immortal". (194).

Kavita

There are many temples here such as those of Govindadeva, Gopinath, Siva, Ganesha and the Sun. Their worship is performed to the accompaniment of bells, cymbals and trumpets.

There are wells, step-wells in gardens. The Manasagar is overflowing and the river is flowing swiftly. (195).

Doha

There are many cross-roads with shops on them and thousands of markets (*hats*) where merchants of different countries are plying their trades. (196).

Kavita

Many elephants, Arab horses and camels from Kutch come here. Embroidered cloth and plain cloth and jewelled ornaments are brought to Jaipur for sale from different parts of the World as Jaipur is founded by Rajadhiraja. (197).

Doha

The Europeans also live here. They have come here after crossing the oceans. They are very wise and intelligent. (198). In this way the merchants of many places have come there. Hundis of lacs and crores are current here. They are all happy and do their business peacefully. O! Girdhari, none look at them with any spirit of envy. (200).

No body speaks improperly with any person. O! Girdhari in this city all the 32 weights are quite correct and precise. (201).

Kavita

The Brahmans engage themselves in Yajnas from early dawn. They study the Vedas and teach them to others. Everybody looks to his own religion and all evil deeds are set aside. In every house Katha is being performed. They all sing the 18 Puranas. Rajadhiraja founded this city of Jaipur, where all the people are praising God and sing His greatness. (202).

APPENDIX VIII

SALE DEED OF CHILDREN

(The original documents, one dated 1803 A.D. and the other dated 1811 A.D. are preserved in the Lunkaranji Pandya's temple, Jaipur) (See page 71).

।। श्रीरामजी ।।

लिखतं आरतराम पापडवाल वासी दूबली का हाल वासी स्वाई जैंपुर का की बहू अत्र में पंडित जी सरुप चंदजी वा सदासूखजी का रुपया ७१ अंके रुपया इकैतरि लीया तीमें म्हारो बैंटो चूनीलाल बरस ६ को थाने दीयौ सौ थे राखौ पालौ पढावौ गुणावैं फिर म्हारो ई डावडा सू दावौ नहीं अर ई रुपया कै पेटै रुपया २१ हाल रोक लैर म्हारौ बडौ बेंटौ स्योजी राजारामजी सौगांणी कै गहणी छौ रुपया १३ में यौ तो बैंने देर छुडायो बाकी रुपया मैं रोक लीया सौ अब घटता रुपया ५० ई डावडा को बाप आसी जिद म्हीना दोय मैं लैसी अर डावडा को बाप मोडो वैगो आवै तो हूं खावानै लेस्यूं बाकी रुपया पचास में सौ भर देमी अर म्हारौ घणी आय डावडा कौ झगडौ नहीं देवा कौ करे तो घणी सू म्हारी मन हूं मनास्यौ में म्हारी राजीबाजी बैंच्या फेरि फिराउ तो राज़ दरबार पंचा मैं झूंठी मिति मांगाश्र सुदि १३ संवत १८६०

मसू आंकड़ी आरतराम पापडीवाल दूबली का की मूव की बपूरलो लिख्यौ सही दसकत चौधरी निरमेराम का कहे घिराणी के लिखी ।

द: सवाई राम सौगाणी चंदाणी का
भुवा को बेंटो भाई दौम्य घण्या क कहया

दसकत बखतरामजी	लीखी डावडा को बाप झगडो कर
कनरी कदस्द	माहान आग हौरी म्हें पंच डावडा
राजबलब	को बाप झगडो पाडं जीसु कर तो
	लागती का वा वाई बुरदिया रुपया
लिखत्यु चुन्नीलाल की ।।	मांगे हीरी गुर्वण डावडो ले लेगौ ।

।। श्री रामजी ।।

लिखतं कुस्याल सुरतराम डोल्या वासी कुली पवरिका अत्र म्हारो डावडो सुखलाल पंडित जी श्री सरुपचन्दजी वा सदासुखजी घनराजजी कै बेच्यो रुपया ३७ अंके सैंतीस लाया डावडो थाने दियो अर इ डावडा की बैई कोई थासु म्हारो भाई सगो झगडो करे करावै अर हु फेरी फिरु फिराऊ तो राज पंचा में तकसीर-वार म्हारा राजा बाजी सु डावडो दायो यो डावडो थांको अर रुपया म्हारा कोइ बात को झगडो झांठो होय सौ म्हारी हु नमैंडस्युं मीती माह सुदी १२ संवत १८६८ का दसकत कुसाल सुरतराम डोल्या बुपर को लीखे सही मैं माकी राजी बाजी दीनु रुपया लीना।

मूल पत्र श्री दि० जैन मंदिर, लूणकरणजी पांड्या जयपुर में सुरक्षित है :

APPENDIX IX

INFORMATION ABOUT VIDYADHAR IN THE STATE RECORDS OF JAIPUR

Information about Vidyadhar contained in the State records were supplied to Jadu Nath Sarkar by the Mahakma Khas Jaipur in 1939. These were compiled from the *Dastur Komwar* and perhaps from some other records also. Portions relating to Vidyadhar are reproduced below. It will be seen that Vidyadhar became a Minister (*Desh ko Diwan*) in 1729, more than a year after the foundation of Jaipur. He was rewarded for three engineering works. In 1734, he was given *Siropao* for the speedy construction of the seven storeyed City Palace, and in 1735 he was rewarded again for bringing the Darbhavati river to Sawai Jaipur. Earlier in 1726 he had been given *Siropao* for constructing the Jaigarh fort. This is according to the *Dastur Komwar* records which are also reproduced:

MAHAKMA KHAS,
JAIPUR
Dated the 21st August, 1939.

My dear Sir,

XX XX XX XX

10. The account of Vidyadhar's family is available from Samvat 1775 (1718 A.D.) to Samvat 1841 (1784 A.D.). Viddyadhar was a Bengali Brahman or Brahman Panda. He was the son of Santosh Ram. In Samvat 1775 (1718 A.D.) he was Naib Darogha of Mustofi Kacheri (a branch of Accounts Department). In Samvat 1785 (1729 A.D.) he was appointed 'Desh Diwan'.* In Samvat 1791 (1734 A.D.) he got *Siropao* of *Ashvamedha*. In the same year he got *Siropao* for speedy construction of a seven storied palace.**

*Revenue Officer=Judicial Officer.

**Jaipur City Palace.

In Samvat 1792 (1735 A.D.) he was granted *Siropao* for bringing the Dravayawati river to Sawai Jaipur. It flows below Nahargarh. In Samvats 1801, 1803 and 1805, he was granted special *Siropaos.* On *Phalgun Bud* 8th Samvat 1807 (after the demise of Sawai Ishwari Singhji and succession of Swai Madho Singhji), he was granted *Siropao* for Desh Dewanship and on Phalgun Sud 9th he was granted an elephant named 'Hiragaj'.

11. He died between *Phalgun Sud* 9th and *Jeth Bud* 3rd Samvat 1807.

12. On *Jeth Bud* 11th Samvat 1807 Viddyadhar's son Murli Dhar was appointed Desh Dewan in place of his father. On *Sawan Bud* 5th Samvat 1835 (after the demise of Maharaja Sawai Prithvi Singhji and succession of Maharaja Pratap Singhji) he was reconfirmed as Desh Dewan.

13. The geneological table of the family is as under:—

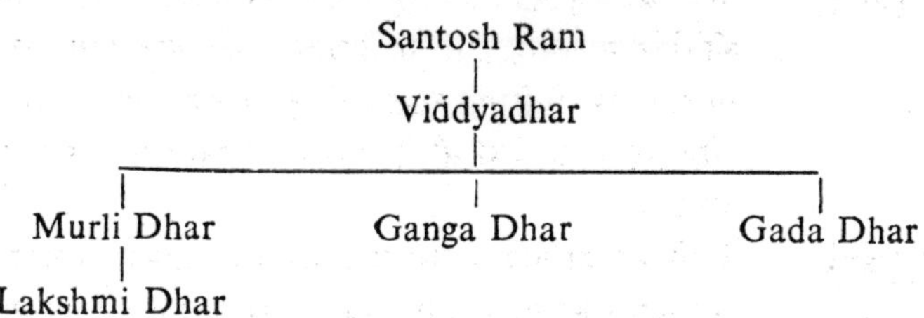

Murlidhar held a grant of Rs. 5,000/- p.a., Ganga Dhar of Rs. 1,000/- p.a. and Gada Dhar of Rs. 500/- p.m. Lakshmi Dhar was granted Rs. 800/- annually.

14. A street in the middle of the Jaipur city is called 'Viddyadhar ka Rasta' and a garden in Ghat* is called by the name of 'Viddyadhar ka bagh'. All the said estate is at present under Khalsa and none of the descendants of the family is traceable.

Hope this finds you in the enjoyment of excellent health.

Yours sincerely,
Sd/-
B.N. Temani.

*Two miles to the South-East of Jaipur.

To
Sir Jadunathji Sarkar, Kt., C.I.E.,
169, Southern Avenue,
Kalighat, P.O.
Calcutta

It appears that Vidyadhar was never separately rewarded in cash for his contribution in the planning (1727 A.D.) or in the construction of the Jaipur City. Perhaps the reward came in the shape of his promotion (1729 A.D.) to the post of *Desh Diwan* from the post of a Clerk in the Accounts department. The foundation stone of the city was laid in November 1727. In 1729 the construction of the city was in progress.

दिवान—विद्याधर ब्राह्मण बंगाली

संवत १७७५ से १८०७ तक

संवत् १७७५	विद्याधर-नायब दरोगा कचहैड़ी मसतौफी देस कनै
संवत् १७८१	मिती आसोज सुदी ७ ने मुबाफिक फरद ज्यौ किशन राम की बैटी को व्याह हुवो वा विद्याधर को व्याह् आगे हुवो वा अबे फैर होसी सो वास्ते यांके हुकम हुवौ रुपया ५००० सीगें इनाम के देवौ सौ ये रुपया किशन राम के खताया येकठा।
संवत् १७८३	मिती भादवा वदि ५ मुकाम आमेर का वहस्म विद्याधर संतोषराम का पंडा ज्यो सवाई जैगढ़ सिताब आछयौ बणायो सो अजरुप महरबानगी बखस्या सिरौपाव
संवत् १७८५	मिती असाढ़ वदि १४ मु० विद्याधर पंडा ने देस दीवाण किया तीका अजरुप महरबानगी सिरौपाव कीमती साबिक रुपया १०७-४। हुक्म हुवा विद्याधर ने देस को दीवान लिखो प्रगना कौ न्याय करें अदालत करें। दीवान गीरी देस कौ सिरौपाव बख्शी।
संवत् १७९१	मिती जेंठ सुदि ५ ने अजरुप महरबानगी बावह महैल सत खण को ज्यो सिताब बणायो तीका सिरौपाव कीमती साबिक ८५-३।
संवत् १७९२	मिती काती सुदि ४ ने बाबत अजरुप महरबानगी द्रव्यवती नदी सवाई जयपुर में लाया तीका बख्शा थान ३ जोडी १।
संवत् १८०७	फागुन वदि ८ ने बाबत देस दिवानगीरी को सिरौपाव बख्शो।

"	"	मिती फाल्गुन सुदी ६ अजरुप मेहरबानगी हाती हीरागज बख्शा ।
"	"	फाल्गुन वदि १३ दक्षिण का लश्कर में सूं आयो तीका सिरौपाव ।
"	"	मुरलीधर ढोटा विद्याधर का ने जो बाप मु० अल्हे को कालबसि हैवो तीकी मातमी को सिरौपाव जेठ वदि ३ ने दिया ।

APPENDIX X

RULERS OF THE JAIPUR STATE

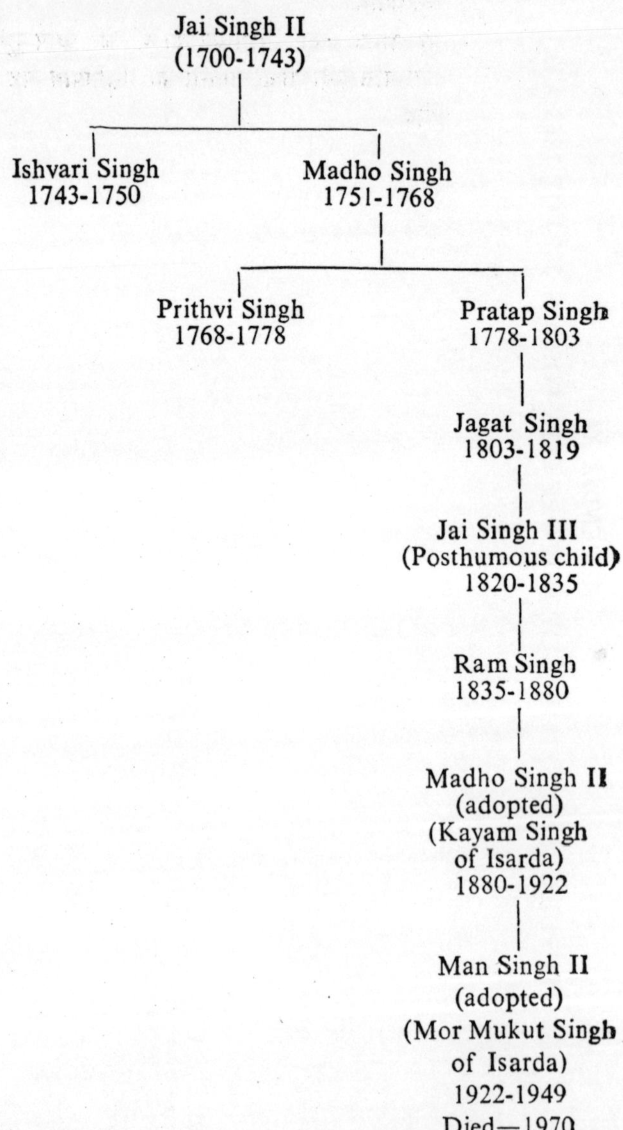

In 1949, the Jaipur State was integrated in Rajasthan.

APPENDIX XI

IMPORTS AND EXPORTS OF JEYPORE CITY FOR V.S. 1924 OR 1868 A.D.

S. No.	Name	East, Agra etc.		North, Rewaree, Bhewanee, Delhi etc.		West, Pali, Marwar, Naseerabad etc.		South, Tonk, Haraotee, etc.		Total	
		Mds.	Price	Mds.	Price	Mds.	Price	Mds.	Price	Mds.	Price
1	2	3	4	5	6	7	8	9	10	11	12
1.	Sugar										
	Import	26000	455000	6000	105000	—	—	—	—	32000	560000
	Exports	—	—	—	—	—	—	—	—	—	—
2.	Gur, Coarse, Sugar, Til, Rice, Singara										
	Import	22000	165000	23000	172500	—	—	—	—	45000	337500
	Export	—	—	—	—	—	—	—	—	—	—
3.	Groceries, Kirana										
	Import	1200	9000	6000	45000	770	5775	175	1312	8145	61087
	Export	250	1875	—	—	—	—	130	975	380	2850
4.	Cloth										
	Import	600	100000	3400	590000	200	15000	27	4800	4227	609800
	Export	40	4000	260	2600	3150	15750	700	70000	4150	224100
5.	Metals										
	Import	40	1400	2220	77000	7	245	—	—	2247	78645
	Export	12	600	—	—	42	2100	17	8500	77	3350

1	2	3	4	5	6	7	8	9	10	11	12
6.	Peddlars wares										
	Import	600	30000	900	45000	150	7500	17	850	1167	83350
	Export	200	10000	470	2350	730	3650	330	1650	1730	8650
7.	Silk, Pushmeena & Gold clothes.										
	Import	17	800	67	3200	10	600	—	—	94	34600
	Export	4½ seers	450	9 seers	900	4m. 16 srs.	17600	25 srs.	2500	5m. 14½ srs.	21450
8.	Kusoma or Safflowers										
	Import	60	1200	3200	64000	—	—	—	—	3260	65200
9.	Tobacco, Palee	—	—	—	—	2000	50000	—	—	2000	50000
	Import Common	1520	11700	70	490	—	—	—	—	1630	12190
	Matunee.	2500	17500	—	—	—	—	—	—	2500	17500
	Export	—	—	—	—	55	385	23	161	78	546
10.	Opium Import	15	6400	—	—	5	3000	—	—	20	9400
11.	Indigo Import	40	4800	—	—	—	—	—	—	40	4800
12.	Potatoes Import	70	560	30	240	—	—	—	—	100	800
13.	Pan Import	—	—	—	—	—	757	757	19950	757	19950
14.	Iron Import	75000	75000	—	—	—	—	—	—	75000	75000
15.	Cotton Export	10500	130000	—	—	—	—	—	—	10500	130000
16.	Oil Seed Exp.	32000	32000	—	—	—	—	—	—	32000	32000
17.	Ghee Imports	900	27000	400	12000	—	—	500	15000	1800	54000
18.	Till Seeds Imp.	2200	13750	—	—	—	—	—	—	2200	13750
19.	Gram Imports	3700	7400	100000	200000	7000	140000	—	—	110700	221400
	Total Import	136567	927110	1265357	1151430	10142	98120	1526	42762	293587	2319762
	Total Exports	43000m. 4½ srs.	178925	730m. 9 srs.	5850	4091m. 16 srs.	26945	1256m. 25 srs.	84660	49080m. 14½ srs.	296386

(Reproduced from the *Report on the Political Administration of the Rajpootana States* for the year 1869-70).

Bibliography

I—PRIMARY SOURCE

A—Official Records (Archival)

The *Kapaddwara* Records are the records of the Household department. Most of these records have been handed over to the Rajasthan State Archives at Bikaner. Some of the documents are still preserved in the City Palace at Jaipur; but a descriptive catalogue of these documents has been given to the Rajasthan State Archives.

Dastur Komwar are the records of the *dastur* or protocol or usage observed in respect of persons of different castes, communities and social status who met the ruler or on whom the ruler paid a visit. The Government of Jaipur had got these records prepared from the *Tauji* records and had preserved them in 32 bound volumes. There are two index volumes also. The records have been arranged castewise in these volumes. The period covered is 1718 to 1918. All the volumes are now in the Rajasthan State Archives at Bikaner.

The *Siyaha Imarat* of the Bikaner Archives contain information on buildings and other constructions. These are available for the years 1789 to 1844 V.S.

The *Jamakharcha Taujis* of the *Parganas* and of the various *Karkhanas* (departments) are useful for the details regarding the economic condition of the period under review. These are available for the years 1721 to 1812 V.S.

The *Nuskha Punya* (*Devasthan*) records are highly informative regarding the religious condition of Jaipur. They give accounts of the temples, donations, priests attached to the temples, etc. Some of them have been copied in bound volumes.

B—Hindi, Rajasthani and Sanskrit Works

Bhojanasar by Girdhari

Girdhari was a poet and probably resided at the Court of Jai Singh. He wrote a book on dietetics called *Bhojanasara* in 1739. This was 12 years after the foundation of the Jaipur city. Fifty-four lines of this work beginning with verse number 182 which mentions Vidyadhar, describe the Jaipur city of that period. The manuscript, the only one known, is preserved in the Bhandarkar Oriental Research Institute, Poona. The relevant portions along with the translation were published by P.K. Gode in his essay "Two Contemporary Tributes to Minister Vidyadhara the Bengali Architect at the Court of Sawai Jaya Singh of Amber (1699-1744) A.D.)" in *Dr. C.K. Raja Presentation Volume*, Madras, 1946. The lines have been reproduced in the Appendix VII.

Buddhivilasa by Bakhat Ram Saha

This work mainly deals with Jaina rituals. It was written in 1770 in Jaipuri dialect. It contains a description of the contemporary Jaipur city. It also describes a conflict between Jainas and non-Jainas that took place at the time of writing of the book. It was published by the Rajasthan Oriental Research Institute, Jodhpur in 1964.

Ishvaravilasa Mahakavya by Sri Krishna Bhatta

This work in Sanskrit by the court Poet of Ishvari Singh (1743-1750) was written in about 1749. It describes Jaipur during the reign of Jai Singh and Ishvari Singh. The detailed description of the *Ashvamedha* performed by Jai Singh is an important feature of this work. The book has been published by the Rajasthan Oriental Research Institute, Jaipur in 1958.

Vamsha Bhaskar by Suraj Mal Mishran

This work written in 1841 deals mainly with the history of Bundi. It contains many adverse comments about the rulers of Jaipur, especially Jai Singh and Jagat Singh.

Vir Vinod by Kaviraj Shyamaldas

This is an important historical work completed about 1875. Shyamaldas started with a history of Mewar but ended up by writing the history of nearly all the states of Rajputana. Shyamaldas had the outlook of a modern historiographer and rarely makes a statement without citing some authentic documents. The book was printed by the Mewar State in 4 volumes in 1886 but for some unexplained reason was later suppressed. Most libraries in Rajasthan have, however, been able to obtain copies of the book.

Bhaktamal with Priyadasji's Tika, Lucknow, 1969.

Brajanidhi Granthavali, Benaras, 1933. This collection of the poems of Maharaja Pratap Singh was edited by Harinarain Purohit of Jaipur.

Chaitanya Charitamrita by Krishnadas Kaviraj.

Chaurasi Vaishnavon ki Katha, Bombay, 1958.

Banarasi Das Jaina, *Ardhakathanak*, 2nd ed., Bombay, 1957.

C—Persian Works

Ain-i-Akbari, Vol. I-III, Blochman, Jarret and Sarkar, 1873, 1894. 1943.

Muntakhab-ul-Lubab, Bibliotheca Series.

Muntakhab-ul-Tawarikh, Ranking and Love.

D—Travellers' Accounts

Bernier, F. *Travels in the Mogul Empire* (1656-1668), Oxford, 1914.

Boileau, A.H.E. *Personal Narrative of a Tour through the Western States of Rajwara in 1835.* The book deals mainly with Western Rajasthan. But Boileau also passed through Jaipur, and gives some interesting statistics about the city.

Heber, R. *Narrative of a Journey through the Upper Provinces of India (in 1824-25)*, Vol. II, London.

Kipling, R. *From Sea to Sea.* London, 1900.

Loti, Pierre *India.* 3rd Ed. London, 1913.

Rousselet, Louis *India and its Native Princes.* London, 1882.

2—SECONDARY SOURCES

A—English

A Descriptive List of the Vakil Reports (Rajasthan) addressed to the Ruler of Jaipur. Bikaner, 1974.

A History of the Sect of Maharajas or Vallabhacharyas of Western India. London, 1865. The name of the author is not mentioned.

Arthasastra, Kautilya. Ed. by Shamasastry. 5th Edn. Mysore, 1956.

Bahura, G.N. *Catalogue of Manuscrips in the Maharaja of Jaipur Museum.* Jaipur, 1971.

Batra, H.C. *The Relations of Jaipur State with the East India Company (1803-1858).* Delhi, 1958.

Bhatnagar, V.S. *Life and Times of Sawai Jai Singh (1618-1743).* Delhi, 1974.

Bretzler *Jaipur Studien Zur Stadt und sozial-geographic einer Indischan Gross Stadt.* Ruhr University, Bochum, 1970. A copy of this work is available in the Rajasthan University Library.

Brown, Percy *Indian Architecture,* Vol. I. Bombay, 1942.

Cambridge History of India, Vol. IV.

Catalogue of the coins in the Indian Museum, Calcutta, Vol. III, Part I. 1908; Vol. IV, Oxford, 1928.

Catalogue of Postage Stamps of the Commonwealth.—1963.

De, S.K. *Early History of Vaishnava Faith and Movement in Bengal.* Calcutta, 2nd Ed. 1961.

Dutt, B.B. *Town Planning in Ancient India.* Calcutta & Simla, 1925.

European Travellers in India. Ed. by Wheeler and Macmillan. Ist. Ed. Calcutta, 1956.

Francklin, W. *History of the Reign of Shah Alum.* London, 1798. Reprinted by the Panini Office, Allahabad, 1934.

Garret, A.H. *Assisted by Pandit Chandradhar Guleri. The Jaipur Observatory and its builder.* Allahabad, 1902.

Growse, F.S. *Mathura : A District Memoir.* 2nd. Ed. Allahabad, 1880. (3rd Ed. Allahabad, 1883.)

Ghurye, G.S. *Indian Sadhus.* Bombay, 1953.

Hamilton, W. *A Description of Hindustan.* Vol. I. London, 1820.

Havell, F.B. *Indian Architecture.* 2nd Ed. London, 1927.

Hendley, T.H. *A Medico-Topographical Account of Jaipur.* Calcutta, 1895.

The General Medical History af Rajputana. Calcutta, 1900.

Jaipur Album. This is a collection of a number of articles on Jaipur, by various authors. Jaipur, 1935. The pages in each chapter are separately numbered.

Jaipur through the Ages. A collection of articles published on the occasion of the Rajasthan History Congress in Jaipur in 1968.

Jeypoor Trials. This is a detailed account of the trial of Jhootaram and others. Calcutta, 1837.

Kasliwal, K.C. *Jaina Grantha Bhandars in Rajasthan.* Jaipur, 1967.

Kaye, G.R. *The Astronomical Observatories of Jai Singh.* Calcutta, 1918.

A Guide to the Old Observatories at Delhi, Ujjain, Benares, Muttra. Calcutta, 1920.

Maclagan. *The Jesuits and the Great Mogul.* London, 1930.

Manasara on Architecture and sculpture. The text was edited and published by Prasanna Kumar Acharya. Oxford, 1933. The description of the Prastara type of village or town is given in *Shlokas* 208 to 226.

Menon, V.P. *The Story of the Integration of Indian States.* Paper-back edn. 1961.

Notes on Jaipur. This is a guide to the Jaipur City. It was prepared by the Residency Staff. 2nd Ed. 1916.

Piggot. S. *Pre-Historic India.* London, 1950.

Ram Raz *Essay on the Architecture of the Hindus.* London, 1834. This is a short essay followed by a large number of sketches of the plans of temples, towns, etc. as described in the *Manasara.*

Rustam Ali *Tarikh-i-Hindi in Elliot and Dowson,* Vol. VIII.

Sarda, Harbilas *Ajmer, Historical and Descriptive.*

Sarda, Harbilas *Life of Dayananda Saraswati.* Ajmer, 2nd Ed. 1968.

Sarkar, J.N. *Fall of the Mughal Empire.* Vol. I 2nd Ed. Calcutta, 1971; Vol. III, 3rd Ed. Calcutta, 1964.

Saxena, K.S. *The Political Movement and Awakening in Rajasthan.* Delhi, 1971. Sharma, G.N. *A Bibliography of Medieval Rajasthan.* Agra, 1965.

Social Life in Medieval Rajasthan. Agra, 1968.

Sharma, M.L. *History of the Jaipur State*. Jaipur, 1969.

Fateh Singh. *A Brief History of Jaipur*.

Zabar Singh. *The East India Campany and Marwar*. Jaipur, 1973.

Sanskrit Kalpataru, a collection of essays by various authors. Jaipur, 1970.

Soonawala, M.F. *Maharaja Sawai Jai Singh II of Jaipur and his Observatories*. Jaipur, 1952.

Tod, James *Annals and Antiquities of Rajasthan*. First published in London in 1829. It has been reprinted many times. The one used here is the two-volume edition. London, 1957.

Wills, C.U. *Report on the Land Tenures and special powers of certain Thikanadars of the Jaipur State*. 1933.

B—Hindi, Sanskrit and Rajasthani

Charan, Ramnath Ratru *Itihas Rajasthan*.

This book in Hindi was published in Jaipur on February 12, 1892. It is a concise history of all the important States of Rajasthan. The author says that the section dealing with the history of the Jaipur State was mainly based on *Vamsavalis* obtained from Thakur Raghunath Singh of Achrol, Raja Narsinghdas, Palawat Charan Balabux, and others. The following anecedotes about Jai Singh are given in this book:

(1) In Samvat 1768 (A.D. 1711) Jai Singh had gone for pilgrimage to Triveni. He caught smallpox and had to stay on there for seven months. (p. 111).

(2) In Samvat 1783 (A.D. 1726), he returned to Jaipur, after taking leave of Muhammad Shah. On the way he conquered Manoharpur. The Rao of that place was killed in the battle. (p. 115).

(3) When Jai Singh performed the *Ashvamedha*, the horse of the *Yajna* was released near the city; but even then some relations of Jai Singh, belonging to the Kumbhani branch of the Kachhwahas captured and detained the horse. Many Kumbhanis were killed in the ensuing battle. (p. 117).

Gahlot, J.S. *Jaipur wa Alwar Rajya ka Itihas*.

Hindi Vishvakosh, Vol. XI.

Jai Singh, Sawai. *Yantra Raj Rachana.* Jaipur, 1953.
Kaul, Raj Kumari. *Rajasthan ke Rajgharano ki Hindi Seva.*
Manusmriti.
Munshi, Devi Prasad. *Swapna Rajasthan.* Muradabad, 1892.
Sarma, G.N. *Rajasthan ke Itihas ke Srota.* Jaipur, 1973.
Shukla, Ram Chandra. *Hindi Sahitya ka Itihas.*
Singh, Narendra. *Maharaja Shri Ishvari Singh ka Jivan Charitra.* Jaipur, 1917.

3—REPORTS

Annual Report on the Jaipur Medical and Meteorological Institutions. These reports were published every year from 1874 to 1930. The complete collection is available in the Public Library in Jaipur.

City Survey Report of Jaipur. Rajasthan University, 1969. (This is a cyclostyled publication).

Census Reports for the Jaipur State for the year 1881, 1891, 1901, 1911, 1931 and 1941.

Census Reports for Rajputana and Ajmer-Merwara. 1921.

Jaipur Gas Works. Annual Reports for the year 1881, 1918 and 1919.

Memoirs of the Geological Survey of India. Vol. 86. Calcutta, 1959.

Political History of the State, Jeypore. Selections from the records of the Government of India—Foreign Department No. LXV, 10th April 1825. Calcutta, 1868.

Public Works Reports of the Jaipur State for the year 1880-81, 1883, 1885, 1888, and 1897.

Report of the Administration of Jaipur State. These reports starting in 1926-27 were published every year up to 1947-48.

Reports on Public Instructions in the Jaipur State. The Annual reports were published until 1924.

Reports on the Ramgarh Irrigation Projects, (1) 1883, (2) 1888 and (3) 1892.

Reports of the Rajasthan Capital Enquiry Committee, 1958, Jaipur, 1958.

Report of a Tour in the Punjab and Rajputana, 1883-84. (Archaeological Survey of India).

Report of the Anthropological Survey of India on 'Peasant Life in India, 1959-61'. A Bengali translation was published in the Bangiya Sahitya Parishat Patrika, Calcutta, 1961.

White Paper on Indian States. Delhi, 1950.

4—GAZETTEERS

A Gazetteer of the Bikaner State by Captain P.W. Powlett. This Gazetteer was first published in 1874. It was reprinted by the Government Press, Bikaner in 1932.

East India Gazetteer (in two volumes). London, 1828.

Imperial Gazetteer of India (in 24 volumes) Oxford, 1908.

Jaipur, compiled by Major C.A. Baylay. Political Agent, 1876.

5—JOURNALS

Ancient India, A Journal of the Archaeological Department. No. 5 (1949) and No. 9 (1953).

Annals of the Bhandarkar Oriental Research Institute, Poona, Vol. 28, 1947.

Jaipur Hitaishi, special Jaipur Number. Jaipur, 1942.

Journal of the Bombay Branch of the Royal Asiatic Society. Vol, 27 (1951).

Veer Vani. March, 1967.

Glossary

Arati	Waving lights before an image.
Ashvamedha	"Horse Sacrifice".
Bhajan.	Devotional song.
Bhakti	Devotion.
Chaturvarna rules	The caste rituals to be observed by the four classes of Hindus.
Chatshala	A primary school for Hindu children.
Chela	A disciple.
Chhatri	A memorial dome, generally erected at the site of the cremation.
Chowkri	A city block.
Danda	A measure of length, about 6 feet or 1.8 metres.
Darbar	The Ruler or his court.
Deeksha	Initiation (of a pupil).
Dupatta	A piece of cloth for covering the upper part of the body.
Faujdar	Captain of the police.
Gaddi	The seat of an abbot or ruler.
Gaudiya	Pertaining to Bengal. Here used for the Chaitanya sect of a Vaishnavas.
Goswami	An epithet generally used for a Vaishnava saintly person.
Guru	A spiritual preceptor.
Ishta Devata	The favourite god of a devotee.
Jagir	Land granted generally in lieu of salary or maintenance.
Jagirdar	One who holds a Jagir.
Joshi	A teacher in a chatshala.
Kirtan	Devotional song.
Leela	Dalliance.
Mahant	Abbot.

Maktab	A primary school for Muslim children.
Maund	A measure of weight, equal in British days to 40 Seers or 37.3 Kgms.
Mohur	A gold coin.
Mulla	A teacher in a Maktab.
Nazri coin	A coin meant for presentation to a superior.
Nirakh Bazar	Market report.
Pandit	A learned man.
Prasad	Offering to a god.
Puja	Worship.
Pujari	A priest.
Sadhu	A saintly man.
Sammati patra	A letter conveying a decision on a matter of religious belief.
Sampradaya	Sect.
Sanyasi	A Shaivite ascetic.
Sebait	A priest, usually a hereditary priest of a temple.
Seer	A measure of weight about 933 grams during the British days.
Shaivite	Believer in Shiva as the supreme God.
Shakta	Believer in Shakti or God as mother.
Shastra	Science, I aw, etc.
Shivalinga	A symbol of Shiva.
Sloka	A couplet in Sanskrit.
Taksal	Mint.
Tankih	Bundle of office papers.
Tola	A measure of weight, about 11.7 grams.
Vairagi	A Vaishnavite ascetic.
Vaishnava	One who believes in the devotional method for approaching God. One who believes in Vishnu or one of his incarnations as supreme God.
Vajapeya	A sacrifice mentioned in the Vedic literature.
Yajna	A Vedic sacrifice.

Index